Big Bill Haywood and the Radical Union Movement

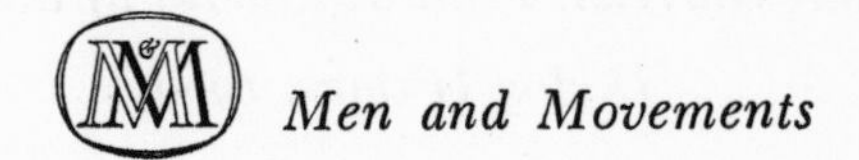

Men and Movements

The Technocrats, Prophets of Automation

Henry Elsner, Jr., 1967

Vito Marcantonio, Radical in Congress

Alan Schaffer, 1966

Father Coughlin and the New Deal

Charles J. Tull, 1965

Eugene V. Debs, Socialist for President

H. Wayne Morgan, 1962

Conscience in Politics: Adlai E. Stevenson in the 1950's

Stuart Gerry Brown, 1961

Gifford Pinchot, Bull Moose Progressive

Martin L. Fausold, 1961

Henry A. Wallace: Quixotic Crusade 1948

Karl M. Schmidt, 1960

Oswald Garrison Villard, Liberal of the 1920's

D. Joy Humes, 1960

Big Bill Haywood and the Radical Union Movement

JOSEPH R. CONLIN

SYRACUSE UNIVERSITY PRESS

Syracuse, New York

FIRST EDITION

Library of Congress catalog card number: 69-80015

Manufactured in the United States of America

to Ag

Joseph R. Conlin is Assistant Professor of History at Chico State College, California. He is a member of the American Historical Association and the Organization of American Historians, and is the author of *American Antiwar Movements,* as well as several articles on this period. He holds an A.B. degree from Villanova University, and M.A. and Ph.D. degrees from the University of Wisconsin.

Preface

With the exception of Eugene V. Debs, who occupies a unique niche in American Socialist history, William Dudley Haywood was the best-known radical of his day. Born in Salt Lake City in 1869, Haywood was regionally famous as a militant leader of the Western Federation of Miners after 1900. He won national notoriety in 1906 as the principal defendant in a sensational murder trial which featured a former governor of Idaho as victim, a self-confessed multiple murderer become religious zealot as star witness, the nation's most famous detective as investigator, a United States Senator and a future governor as prosecutors, two of the era's foremost criminal lawyers as defense attorneys, and the tacit intervention of the President of the United States for the prosecution on the eve of the trial. Haywood remained a frequent subject of front-page copy for the next decade and a half until he defected to the Soviet Union and obscurity in 1921.

Debs has been accorded the usual posthumous respectability, and was received at the White House even during his lifetime, but Haywood lived and died notorious, untrusted, and hated. Throughout his career, his name was associated with murder, violence, and sabotage. Nor has time substantially altered the image. Even those historians who have sympathized with Haywood's motivations have been quick to demur at his alleged methods.

Haywood did look the villain's role. Well over six feet tall, big-boned and brawny, he was rarely photographed except when scowling ominously. One eye was blind (the result of a boyhood mishap and not a mining accident as radical apocrypha had it) and its immoble stare lent him an even more sinister cast. Anti-union employers and politically conventional Americans found it easy to fear such a man, and they did. The most despondent industrial workers, on the other hand, could see in Haywood a leader who was clearly "one of them," and this proletarian charisma stood Big Bill in good stead for many years. Certainly Haywood's prominence in the radical union movement owed nothing to his own insights into the social ills of the day. He was almost entirely self-educated, and an activist to the degree of obliviousness to ideology. But in an age of oratorical bombast, Haywood dominated a speaker's platform despite an unexciting manner. Children reveling in the bizarre new world of a strike-crippled community gathered about the "tall Cyclops" whenever he walked the streets and their parents idolized him. Friends refused to remember him other than cordially, even after his flight to Moscow betrayed their confidence.

The book cannot be written on the history of American labor or radicalism which does not take notice of Haywood, but little is really known of him. The most recent scholarship in the field portrays him either as sketchily as previous writers have done or through a romantic glass which distorts him even more. This book's aim is to remedy the obscurity and the myth. It is not properly a biography, for its material is strictly selected. It is a book about Big Bill Haywood's public career, intended to place him in proper perspective with his age.

The career was a busy one which coincided with one of America's most crucial eras and deserves study for that reason if for no other. Haywood was a man who knew the remnants of a once wild West from his boyhood; who truly rose "from the ranks" to the leadership of the most militant labor union of the day; who was acquitted of murder in an internationally celebrated case; who became the symbolic and real leader of the legendary Wobblies during their heyday; who was known well (if not with especial fondness) to the international socialist movement; who was the center of a dispute which foreshadowed the decline of the Socialist Party of America; who was the focus of the unfortunate Wobbly Sedition Trials of World War I; and who became a famous exile in the outcast Soviet Union. Those events which have been well chronicled elsewhere I have not narrated in great detail, but have concentrated on Haywood's role in them.

The conventional manner of expressing my acknowledgments will not, I hope, detract from the depth of my gratitude: to librarians and archivists at the State Historical Society of Wisconsin, the Tamiment Institute, the Labadie Collection of the University of Michigan Library, the Minnesota Historical Society, the IWW Collection at Wayne State University, the Socialist Party of America Collection at Duke University Library; the University of California at Berkeley, and the Hoover Institution of Stanford University; to Steven Anderson, and William Friedheim who read and criticized parts of the manuscript; to Professor Gregory Guroff who helped obtain for me sources on Haywood's Soviet years from the Lenin Library, Moscow, and to Patricia Coatsworth who helped with the translation of these; to Wobblies Fred Thompson, Carl Keller, and Richard Brazier who were kind enough to speak and write to me about the old IWW; and to Jean Harvey who prepared the final manuscript. Part of Chapter III, in considerably different form, appeared in the *Pacific Northwest Quarterly* (January, 1968); I am grateful to the editor of the journal, Robert Burke, for permission to include duplicate parts herein.

J.R.C.

Chico, California
April, 1968

Contents

1

Worker

When Big Bill Haywood was at the height of his infamy during the second decade of the twentieth century, his enemies often pictured him as the personification of all that was violent and disruptive in American industrial relations. They traced this alleged character to Haywood's youth; they said he had grown up in the old West where men reached for guns on impulse and that Haywood, unlike the nation, never outgrew this boyish unruliness. Bill Haywood himself occasionally reveled in the notoriety and reinforced their point by playing the son of the wild cayuse. In fact, while Haywood was no stranger to violence, the scene of his youth was not very wild at all. He spent all but a few of his first fifteen years in Salt Lake City, the placid capital of the Mormon Zion. Established in 1847, Salt Lake City was a physical monument to the disciplined mind of its founder, Brigham Young. The streets were broad boulevards, planned and straight, intersecting at regular intervals. Lots were uniform, and virtually every house was serviced by the Mormons' famous irrigation ditches.[1]

In its social life too, Salt Lake did not resemble the legendary town of the wild West so much as a prosperous and decidedly sedate midwestern city. A large number of permanent public buildings, including the famous Mormon Tabernacle, seemed to belie the fact that the town was barely two decades old. "Opportunities" listed in the city directory included the Mercantile Department of the University of Deseret, Morgan's Commercial College, Union Academy, and

Roger's Seminary. The city also boasted a midwestern assortment of debating clubs, female relief societies, Masons, Odd Fellows, Good Templars, and "Literary, Scientific, and Benevolent Lectures during winter months." [2]

Salt Lake City's version of sophistication would not have gratified an easterner of the day. But the town was neither Tombstone, Deadwood, nor Roaring Camp, thanks in part to the fact that Salt Lake was the most convenient resting place for transcontinental travelers between St. Joseph, Missouri, and California, and developed accordingly. More important, Salt Lake City was settled by families rather than by men alone. In a country where what was euphemistically called the "civilizing influence" of women was so considerable that a few could transform an ornery town overnight, more than half of Salt Lake's population was female, an extraordinary statistic for the West. The authoritarianism of the Mormon Elders also preserved the city's settled character, and a suspicious federal government was more obvious in Mormon Utah than was customary in the territories.[3]

Bill Haywood's youth in the Mormon Zion was typical of place and time. His father had been born near Columbus, Ohio. The family, Haywood guessed, was "so American that if traced back it would probably run to the Puritan bigots or the cavalier pirates." The elder William D. Haywood traveled westward with much of his generation, first to Iowa, and then to Salt Lake, working for a time as a Pony Express rider. (Big Bill must have inherited his ponderous physique from an earlier ancestor.) In Salt Lake Haywood's father took room and board with a recently immigrated South African family. There was a daughter and he married her; he was twenty-two, his bride fifteen.[4]

The marriage was brief. In 1872 or 1873, when young Bill Haywood was three, his father was stricken with pneumonia while mining at nearby Mercur, Utah. Bill and his mother left Salt Lake upon receiving the news, but by the time they reached the camp, the father was dead and buried. "When we visited his grave," Haywood recalled, "I remember digging down as far as my arm could reach." That incident and one earlier, vaguely recollected day, were Haywood's only memories of his father, although he later changed his name from William Richard to William Dudley in his memory. When Haywood was about seven his mother remarried, again to a miner, and the family traveled to the mining camp of Ophir, Utah, where Haywood's stepfather had a job. If Salt Lake City was relatively refined, Ophir, in the Oquirrh Mountains, provided young Bill with a small taste of the vanishing frontier. The town was located in a canyon at an altitude of almost 7,000 feet and the district was rich in copper, lead-zinc, gold, and silver ores. It was near the sites of the first precious metal strikes in Utah and also near the town of Mercur where Haywood's father had died.[5]

Ophir's brief history told the story of a thousand mining camps. During the sixties it did not exist. By 1871 it was one of the mining country's "hottest" districts as prospectors registered over five hundred locations within a few months. But the ore lasted only a few years. Haywood witnessed practically the whole meaningful history of the town during his two seasons there. A population of over a thousand during the early seventies shrunk to fifty ten years later. Of 2,500 ore locations during Ophir's heyday, fewer than 150 were even mapped by the middle eighties.[6]

For a boy, Ophir was an idyllic place to live. The canyon was steep on one side with lower hills opposite. The canyon floor was narrow, leaving room for only two or three streets at its widest point. Mines already abandoned by the early seventies provided sites where boys collected the crystals that served them the way marbles and baseball trading cards served later generations. Purple elderberries, maples, pansies, and other wildflowers blanketed the slopes in spring and summer. A network of picturesque brooks added to Ophir's beauty. And the town was isolated. A local woman recalled that "during the night we could hear the whine and growl of those mountain lions as they ventured nearer to the town of Ophir. The barking of the dogs seemed to keep them at a safe distance from the town."

What Haywood knew of violence in his boyhood he learned

in Ophir. Duke's Hotel was bombed one night and the suspected perpetrators were run out of town with summary frontier justice. Young Bill was witness to a "shooting scrape" in which "Slippery Dick" left "Manny Mills" dead on the street. And he saw the leavings of another gun battle in which three were killed. Later he wrote that "after the talk of massacres and killings at Salt Lake City," he accepted such sordid scenes "as a natural part of life." [7]

Although an older Haywood affected a proper revolutionist's nonchalance in recounting such episodes, another vignette showed a less cynical boy. Haywood told of the lynching of a Negro in Salt Lake. The victim's face was "ghastly," he wrote, "and although he was light colored, it was turning blue, with the eyes and tongue sticking out horribly. I looked at the swinging figure and thought over and over, 'What have they done—what have they done—.' It was as though a weight of cold lead settled in my stomach. . . . This was my first realization of what the insane cruelty of a mob could mean." [8]

After a few years the Haywoods returned to Salt Lake at a time when the town was bustling with business activity. The opening of hundreds of mines in Utah unleashed a hectic inflation, and prices rose to "almost fabulous levels." Young Bill had a small hand in the boom. Working at a fruit commission house, Haywood was often assigned to deliver his employer's perishable wares to the Mormon Tithing House. Sometimes the owner sold the fruit to Haywood, who hawked it on the streets. "Once he sold me ten or twelve bunches of bananas at twenty-five cents a bunch," Haywood recalled, "which I quickly disposed of at a dollar and a half a bunch; another time it was tomatoes at twenty-five cents a bushel: of these my mother and other women in the neighborhood made ketchup."

Haywood's recollection of such flush times could pass for the introduction to one of the successful businessmen's ghost-written autobiographies so popular at the time, but his career as a capitalist was destined to end somewhat shy of the Union League. In fact, the striking characteristic of Haywood's youth is that he worked for wages from a very early age. His parents were both of modest means—pioneers who made the long trek from their homes to the West of opportunity. His father died in the mines when Bill was three. His mother, remarried to another miner, of necessity sent her son out to work as soon as he could find it. Bill took his first job in the mines of Ophir when he was nine years old. The town's school closed for a term for lack of a teacher, and Haywood got a job through his stepfather. Later in Salt Lake he was a "boy-of-all-work," bound out for a period of six months at a dollar a month to a farmer named Holden. At other times he chopped wood, carried luggage in a Salt Lake City hotel, ushered in the Salt Lake Theatre, and was a messenger boy.[9]

Beyond patently working-class origins, there was little in Bill Haywood's youth to indicate the genesis of one of the most militant revolutionaries of the era. Haywood was a Gentile in the Mormon Zion (they comprised only 5 per cent of the population) during years when animosity between Mormon and Gentile was reciprocally bitter. But, interestingly for a man both combative and unreluctant to commit himself, Haywood retained little antipathy for the Latter Day Saints. He described polygamy unemotionally, in the bemused manner of the travelogue narrator come upon a quaint localism; it was a fact of life. On other aspects of Utah's submerged conflict, Haywood was noncommittal. While he implied that the Mormons were chiefly responsible for the troubles, he also proffered mild congratulations to the Saints for their just treatment of Indians. The fact is that Haywood got along quite well in Salt Lake City and Ophir, and remembered his childhood fondly and in some detail; this revolutionary's alienation did not begin in Zion.[10]

Bill Haywood took his first man's job at fifteen. His stepfather had become superintendent at the Ohio Mine and Milling Company in Humboldt County, Nevada, and wrote to Salt Lake offering Bill a job. Haywood was excited at the prospect of full-time work; he bought a miner's gear, a pair of boxing gloves, and a set of chessmen. "You will be back in a few weeks," his mother told him as he set out on the long journey. The trip to the Ohio Mine was long and arduous, two days by the Central Pacific through the monotonous salt flats of northwestern Utah and Nevada to Winnemucca on the Humboldt River. From Winnemucca Haywood took a stagecoach line due north through country which even a Nevada chauvinist described as "to the average emigrant . . . repulsive in the extreme." But metal-bearing country in Nevada was not expected to be verdant, and Haywood had come to mine.[11]

Haywood worked at the Ohio Mine for three years, and when a financial crisis closed the operation in 1887 he remained behind to guard the property. It was a tedious life in an isolated place "where one side of a baseball team could not be scratched up in a long day's ride." His first job was wheeling rocks from the shaft, but he soon assumed other tasks and learned most of the miner's skills. He was an enthusiastic youth, congenial and gregarious. The isolation of the country made men sociable when they did get together, and many of Haywood's recollections of the Ohio Mine are of social occasions and personal friendships. Writing about Haywood in 1921, a critic described him as "a man who believes in men, not as you and I believe in them, but fervently, uncompromisingly, with an obstinate faith in the universal goodwill and constancy of the workers worthy of a great religious leader." Haywood's zealous humanism had its roots in his young manhood. There was a genuine sense of community at the Ohio Mine and Haywood made many good friends.

John Kane, the mine's ore sorter, took a liking to Haywood and taught him the fundamentals of assaying. Charley Day made Haywood a gift of the rights to an undeveloped mine, although Haywood never worked it as an owner. Pat Reynolds, the oldest man at the mine, was a member of the Knights of Labor. From him Haywood claimed he learned about "the need of working men organizing for mutual protection," although he conceded there was little need for a union in Humboldt County. Reynolds and Haywood discussed absentee ownership, the Virginia City Miners' Union, and the Haymarket Massacre in Chicago which was front-page copy during Haywood's stay at the Ohio Mine.[12]

As a young man Haywood also displayed a sensitivity to human misery which later friends never failed to note. He recounted with revulsion the story of a local massacre of five Piute Indians which he heard from both sides. The tale, typical of a dozen similar events, "seemed to pull a lot of the fringe off the buckskin clothes of the alluring Indian fighters I had read about in dime novels," Haywood wrote later.[13]

He was intelligent, full of curiosity, and ambitious. His formal education was negligible; he had only a few years of schooling in Ophir and at a Roman Catholic school in Salt Lake City. But Haywood had exploited Salt Lake's relatively broad cultural offerings, and became "an ardent reader of Shakespeare" as well as a passably competent chess player after seeing "Dr. Zuckertort" put on an exhibition. With few other diversions, the miners at the Ohio Mine were voracious readers. Magazines were regularly if tardily delivered, and four or five daily newspapers arrived a week late. The miners also owned many books which they passed around and discussed extensively. Haywood's stepfather was a lover of poetry and introduced young Bill to Voltaire, Byron, Burns, and Milton. Haywood showed a keen interest in learning about virtually everything new with which he came into contact. When John Kane introduced him to assaying, Haywood fancied learning the profession, secured some books on the subject, and wrote to the Houghton and Columbia University Schools of Mines to learn their requirements for admission. He was intrigued by everything from prehistoric mastodon tracks to Indian dances, and remained open-minded and curious throughout his life.[14]

In 1887 Haywood returned to Utah and took a job in the Brooklyn Mine near Salt Lake City. He learned new phases of the miner's trade, firing boilers and running the cars which carried ore and waste to the surface. In 1889 he returned to Humboldt County where he married Nevada Jane Minor, a girl he had met while working the Ohio Mine, and he resolved to escape underground work. For a time he worked at assaying and briefly tried his luck as a prospector. He had no luck. The closest William Haywood came to mine ownership was with the property Charley Day gave him, the Caledonia Mine. He neglected to exploit it himself, however, and after the rights expired he mined on the site for a subsequent owner. About 1890 Haywood took a job as a cowboy on the Hoppin Ranch in Humboldt County. Haywood always recalled his cowboy days with fond nostalgia. Although scarcely less tedious than mining, it was healthier work and Haywood was close to his wife. He formed a fast friendship with his brother-in-law and co-worker, Tom Minor. Fifteen years later, as the secretary-treasurer of the Western Federation of Miners, Haywood toyed with the idea of forming a union of ranch workers.[15]

After a season or two on the range, Haywood moved to Fort McDermitt, an abandoned army post near Nevada's northern line. He delivered his own daughter when his mother-in-law and a midwife fainted and, predictably, he recalled: "I have confronted many desperate situations but nothing so serious as this." It was the happiest period of Haywood's domestic life. For most of the rest of her years, Nevada Jane Haywood was an invalid, suffering from an arthritic affliction of the joints which caused her considerable pain and eventually crippled her completely. During the time the Haywoods lived at Fort McDermitt, he took her to Kyle Springs near Winnemucca for a month of treatments in the alum baths there. The cure was a failure, as were a host of Indian remedies such as snake oil and sage baths.[16]

Haywood worked at various jobs during the early nineties. He joined a government surveying corps near the Quin River Sink of Nevada, and cowboyed for one more season. He mined at the Caledonia and later at the Commonwealth Mine in Tuscarora. In 1894 he made a false start for California, and later started for Chicago on a cattle train. He also worked briefly for the Imperial Mining Company at Kennedy, Nevada. Amidst all the aimlessness there was only one glint of accomplishment, Haywood's attempt at homesteading. While he was working at the Caledonia Mine, Haywood's brother-in-law, Jim Minor, wrote him that Fort McDermitt had been thrown open to entry by homesteaders. Although it was late at night when we received the news, Haywood left immediately by horseback, abandoning even his wages. He knew the site well and it seemed an excellent opportunity; the land was already partially developed and of high quality. "I can remember the thoughts about having a home of my own," Haywood recalled. The fort was small and, with his father-in-law and Jim Minor, Haywood intended to monopolize it. "Life began to take on a new aspect," Haywood wrote, "every tap of work I did, building fences, digging ditches, was all for ourselves." Unfortunately, the homestead was a failure. Nevada Jane Haywood's health took a turn for the worse; lack of employment in nearby mines and ranches forced Haywood to work far from Fort McDermitt for income, and, finally, the government withdrew the land from homestead for an Indian reservation. "It seemed as if a black curtain had been pulled down on the future," Haywood wrote. "There was no ray of hope." [17]

The fact that Bill Haywood became a miner during the mid-1880's holds more than chronological significance. This was an age of a technological and societal revolution in the mining fields which fundamentally affected Haywood's career along with the lives of thousands of men who moiled metals from the earth. Miners a generation older than Haywood lived an utterly different kind of life than those a generation younger. Bill Haywood's generation experienced the painful and portentous transition.

Technologically, the early prospectors of Utah, Nevada, California, Idaho, and Colorado were "placer miners." That is, they sifted pure metals from the sands and gravels of creek beds and gulches with which millennia of erosion had mixed them. This process of separation involved arduous labor but next to no money. After sampling a creek bed for gold with nothing more than a wash pan, the prospector built a simple machine called a "rocker" from a few cheap items in his pack and wood he found in the area. It was a small-scale enterprise, protected from big business for the thousands of individuals and partnerships by technological, economic, and geographic limitations. Almost anyone could master the technique of placer mining in a short time, and the gold fields were flooded with aspirants. While chance made millionaires of a few, most placer miners made only "a living" from their work—enough for them but too little for investors. Finally, only a footloose individual was sufficiently mobile to pick up and move when a claim was exhausted or the news arrived of better prospects elsewhere. It was not the sort of endeavor which lent itself to "business." [18]

The prospector's age contributed a colorful chapter to the American romance of tent cities thrown up one night and blown away in another, of hirsute prospectors and their inevitable burros, of gamblers, sheriffs, marshalls, and golden-hearted saloon girls. But it was also the context in which a distinct subculture was created. The prospector's society combined militant individualism and loyal cooperation. When searching for gold he was secretive and jealous, combing the lonely hills alone. He was beyond the pale of government and law and appealed to neither. He did not own the land on which he prospected and, acting on the principle that gold belonged to him who found it, he squatted on public and private lands indiscriminately. When he exhausted a placer, he left the site behind, giving it hardly another thought. Gold dust in a canvas bag was the prospector's idea of property, and it was property which he had earned himself. Long months of self-dependence had its effect. As one observer perhaps overstated the point, "since the days of Tubal Cain, the arts of mining have fostered peculiar independence." [19]

The prospector was also a cooperationist. It required only one man (or even a burro pawing the ground) to make a strike, but efficient exploitation of placer mining required two, three, or even more men. Building a sluice and rocker box was not a minor task, and the completed mechanism provided work for several. But the miner could not hire assistants. There were too many mountains, gulches, and promising ridges, too many tales of fantastic wealth, and too much independence in the men for the prospector to expect another like himself to work for wages. "The richest miner in the camp was seldom able to hire a servant," wrote the first systematic student of mining society. Men who would be employees in other pursuits "were digging in their own claims." [20]

The egalitarian partnership was only one manifestation of the miners' spirit of cooperation. The miners did not legally own their claims and could not exclude others from the scene of a strike. In California, the prototype of prospector society, the discoverer rarely took more than ten feet of frontage on a gold-bearing creek. It was about the maximum he could work efficiently and, excited by the prospect of riches for all, he was nonplussed by later arrivals who squatted nearby. An observant early miner recalled that the prospectors "seldom attempted to determine the superficial extent of the placer, and then divide it up among themselves. They seemed rather to wish to ascertain how much surface ground would give an operator a full season's work; they chose the richest spots they could find, marked out their small claims, and left to later comers the ascertaining of the limits of the auriferrous deposits of the district." Discovery earned choice of claim but possession also required work.[21]

The typical placer mining site was a community of several men or partnerships. Far beyond the realm of institutionalized law, the camps devised codes to keep order among themselves. Comprised of individualists, the society was necessarily democratic. Moreover, as Charles O. Shinn wrote, "the mines put all men for once upon a level. Clothes, money, manners, family connections, letters of introduction, never before counted for so little. The whole community was given substantially an even start in the race. Gold was so abundant, and its sources seemed for a time so inexhaustible, that the aggrandizing power of wealth was momentarily annihilated. Social and financial inequalities between man and man were together swept out of sight." Even a later spokesman for the corporate mining interests, Senator William M. Stewart of Nevada, commented on the egalitarian and cooperative atmosphere of the pre-industrial mining camps. "Regulations were thoroughly democratic in their character, guarding against every form of monopoly, and requiring continued work and occupation in good faith to constitute a valid possession." [22]

One of the most remarkable peculiarities of this society in which everyone expected imminent fortune was the nearly complete absence of theft as a social problem. It was "a crime of peculiar turpitude." An army colonel commented of the California mining camps that theft was unheard of despite the fact that some men daily left small fortunes unguarded in their tents. An early miner remembered that "a man could go into a miner's cabin, cut a slice of bacon, cook a meal, roll up in a blanket, certain to be welcomed kindly when the owner returned." An episode of 1895 which Haywood recounted in his autobiography illustrated both the tenacity and the death of that wholesome tradition. Leaving his cabin for a time, Haywood returned to find it had been robbed. "This outraged our feelings more than the loss injured us," he wrote, "because in the mining camps and on the ranches it had never been necessary to turn the key in the lock. We would leave home, even for days, and hang the key on the doorpost. If a stranger came by, he might go in and feed himself or sleep in the house, clean up afterward, and go on his way after hanging the key up in its place. No one ever stole."

But times had changed by the time Big Bill Haywood became a miner. The prospectors' social structure was torn up by the displacement of the economy on which it rested. The catalyst in the process was the railroad which, in fact, held its most glorious celebration when Haywood was three months old, fewer than a hundred miles from his cradle. The news reached Salt Lake City from Promontory, Utah, by telegraph on May 10, 1869: "The last rail is laid! The last spike driven! The Pacific Railroad is completed!" [23]

Unlike their practise in the Midwest, where railroaders built their tracks through rich farming lands, they sought out mineral sites for their depots in the mountainous West. The result was economic revolution. The old prospectors rarely practiced "lode" or "quartz" mining (actually digging into the earth from which placer metals had eroded), because metal in lode was not naturally separated from surrounding rock and separation required machinery beyond their means. Nor could the light-traveling prospector transport machinery to the mines or the ores to a smelting center. As narrow-gauge railroads snaked into the metal-bearing canyons, however, the problems were simplified. The railroad created conditions favorable to the large-scale industrialization and capitalization of the mining industry. The federal government's basic mining laws of July, 1866, July, 1870, and May, 1872, established terms of mine ownership conducive to the same end. Mining corporations followed the locomotive just as surely as, in another context, the flag followed the cross. It rarely took long after a new strike and a rush before an alert investor chartered a company and put a mine in operation. Some capital was indigenous. Marcus Daly, one of the founders of the great Anaconda Copper Company, began his career as a prospector in Ophir. Horace Tabor of Leadville, Colorado, amassed a great deal of capital on the scene of his mine. John B. Stetson, who preferred manufacturing felt hats but also kept money in mining, gathered his first funds as a miner on the Columbia River.[24]

Investors whose resources derived from a hundred other industries were also close to the western developments. British investors especially were early on the scene, sponsoring twenty undertakings in Utah alone between 1871 and 1873, with an initial capitalization of over $15 million. The mine in which Haywood's father was working at the time of his death was British-owned. One British agent wrote home exultantly in 1872, "Nevada and the whole neighborhood of Mormon land has already absorbed so much British capital that the mines are more British than American." [25]

The industrialization and capitalization of mining revolutionized the way men lived and how they made a living. A few eccentric old-timers continued to wander about with pickaxe and pan as, indeed, they still do. But the majority of prospectors became miners in the employ of others, working for wages. William Haywood never knew the prospector's age firsthand, but its traditions were so deeply ingrained among the miners that he was profoundly affected by it. Writing when the prospector was still a significant figure, Charles Shinn ventured that even when, a century later, the mining area was divided into twenty states with a population of forty million, "the atmosphere and traditions of the mining camp will linger in the mountain gorges, and fragments of the miner's jurisprudence will yet remain firmly imbedded in local and state law." Shinn's glowing prediction was based on the fact that, when he wrote, the mores of the miner's society had been unchallenged for a generation. He could not foresee the societal revolution wrought by the industrialization and capitalization of mining.[26]

In another sense, however, Shinn was notably prescient. Despite the proletarianization of the miners during the 1880's and 1890's, their fierce self-reliance and recourse to cooperation continued to express itself, not in the state law which was the province of their employers but in the miners' unions. The history of the unionization of the hard-rock miners is essentially a story of the mining camp traditions adapted to changing times.

The miner who had himself enforced order in his camps without recourse to weak, nonexistent, or irrelevant government was later quick to take matters into his own hands when established authority seemed indifferent or hostile to his interests. He might have become a wage worker, but running a scab out of a mining town was not so very different from expelling a thief from the diggings. Nor was it a great step for the miner, bred on the principle of work and occupation as the criterion of ownership, to regard the absentee mine owner and the nonworking superintendent as usurpers. A common practice among employees in the mining towns of the turn of the century was "high-grading"—secreting nuggets in their clothing after each day's work. While the mine owners might have considered this theft of "peculiar turpitude," the miners regarded the pilfered ore as their just due. The socialism of the Western Federation of Miners was rooted in the traditions of the prospector, not in the tomes of Marx and Engels. "Is the report true that comes from Telluride," a banker asked Bill Haywood in 1901, "about the miners being in possession of the mines? If that is the case, what becomes of the men who have invested their money in these properties?" Haywood replied, "If we follow your question to its logical conclusion, you'd have to tell me where the owners got money to invest in the mines. Who has a better right to be in peaceful possession than the miners?" [27]

Unionization was itself a most natural response of the miners as they were reduced from independent operators to wage-workers. Cooperation was the rule of the placer camps; the miners banded together in order to regulate disputes among themselves and to secure their rights against outsiders. By the 1890's, the "outsiders" were the mine owners for whom the miners were economically forced to work. The union was a response rooted in the miners' past. There was no validity in looking, as the mine owners did, for outside agitators and alien subversives to explain their employees' bitterness.

If Haywood never knew the prospector's age, he was familiar with the transitional industry. In an article which Haywood might have written, the *Miners Magazine* commented in 1900: "The conditions that confront the miner today are entirely different than the conditions of a quarter of a century ago, when the mines of the West were owned largely by individuals who were not too proud or arrogant to live in the same community with their employees." It is a fairly accurate description of the Ohio Mine at which Haywood took his first job. The mine was located in the Santa Rosa District, a region only half-heartedly exploited because the railroad was still sixty miles away. Mining was done by hand and apparently ventured at all only because the veins of gold and silver were relatively well defined. A commentator in 1881 was grateful that the mines of northern Nevada were not "fabulously rich." "Though it might seem strange to relate," he wrote, "it is now a conceded fact that mines which are rich enough to attract the attention of millionaires do a country little good. The management is entrusted to agents who obtain labor and materials at the lowest rates, the profits going to some other place to be expended, perhaps in London or Paris, in 'creating a sensation.' "[28]

Haywood discovered the new industry when he went to work at the Brooklyn mine in 1877. It was absentee-owned, large, mechanized, and run strictly for profit. Haywood learned that some mine owners considered precautionary safety measures too expensive. As late as after the turn of the century a mine inspector reported on mines in which "there were few air blowers, or suction fans, and the stiffs worked in lung-choking, eye-smarting, powder gas for an hour or two after their shift went on." The Brooklyn Mine was at least as bad. Haywood saw for the first time the ravages of lead poisoning, a result of poor ventilation. "A crowd of lead miners presents a ghastly appearance, as their faces are ashen pale." Lead miners were chronically ill, and at the Brooklyn Mine they paid a dollar a month for access to the hospital. "Their transportation to and from the hospital the workers had to pay themselves," Haywood remarked dryly.[29]

Lode mining was dangerous by definition, but the drive for profits by owners who did not see the results of their economies made it worse. In addition to chronic rheumatism, tuberculosis, and lead poisoning, miners were frequently exposed to the danger of cave-ins. It was possible to reduce this hazardous situation through rudimentary precautions. The most common method of excavating hard metals was called stoping; Haywood worked on one called the Mormon Stope at the Brooklyn Mine. The method had been developed in Ophir, Utah, by a German, Philip Diedesheimer, to meet the problem of supporting the ceiling of a mine as the ore was removed.[30]

This was a minor problem if, as at the Ohio Mine, the vein

was narrow and surrounded by strong porphyry and granite. Neither was it a problem if due consideration for safety permitted the miners to leave large sturdy pillars throughout the shaft. As the drive for complete exploitation of resources developed, however, large pillars of ore were considered "wasteful." Theoretically, Diedesheimer's "cribs" solved the problem. As the miners excavated above their heads and from the walls of the shaft, they built box frames of heavy timber, usually six feet high, four wide, and four deep. As the shaft expanded up and out, waste quartzite was dumped into the frames at their feet to provide a rising floor. It was an ingenious method and, if properly employed, effective. Unfortunately, while the "cribs" solved the problem of soft ore pillars, they did not solve the problem of soft cheap timber or cribs built too skimpily to hold up the ceiling. When mines were small and the owners close to the miners (and themselves in the mines), such dangerous parsimony was unlikely. But as ownership came increasingly to be located in San Francisco, New York, and London, and the owner's acquaintance with his business restricted to cost sheets, on-the-spot management found itself pressured to increase profits at the expense of safe mining.

The impersonality of the absentee owner's philosophy was succinctly expressed in a technological report on methods in the Mercur, Utah, mines: "a premature cave often causes the loss of valuable pillars of ore." A handbook for mining investors was equally candid. "The rule usually followed in the choice of mine timber is, *use the cheapest* which is usually the most readily available." The guidelines became more cynically specific: "Yellow pine although of no great durability or strength is widely used." Sawed timber was described as "inferior to hewn or split timber as it is more liable to split." However, "as hewn timber is more expensive than sawed the latter is usually preferred." An old miner was less detached: "Men are cheaper than timber." [31]

Haywood's job at the Brooklyn Mine did not in itself make him a radical. It would take the accumulated experience of more years in other Brooklyn Mines to do that. But it introduced him to the existence of labor exploitation in the context of a group of men with a tradition hostile to it. Haywood's homesteading experience was also an interlude of far more than episodal significance. At the time of his death, *The Nation* called Haywood "as American as Bret Harte or Mark Twain." Haywood's bitterness at American society was also native. He was an able, industrious, intelligent, and ambitious young man, but the opportunities available to him were few. Prospecting was ludicrous in the age of the Anaconda Copper Company. Success at homesteading could have established Haywood on a farm or ranch which would have challenged his energies and ambitions and perhaps diverted him to private life. But a combination of bad luck, personal problems, an economic depression, and an impersonal decision in Washington exploded that dream and snatched the homestead, that durable symbol of American opportunity, from his grasp.[32]

The United States at the end of the nineteenth century remained a land in which the gospel of success was vitally current. In the West, a land of men seeking "opportunities," the impulse was strongest. The legends of the self-made man and the individualistic western pioneer have a rightful place in American History. Unfortunately, the stirring exploits of those who did "succeed" have crowded the reactions of those who "failed" from the pages of the histories. Not all those who "failed" did so because, in the jargon of the day, they were "unfit," or because, as a contemporary commentator said of the proletarianization of the miners, "the weak men sank into laborers for the new companies."[33]

Bill Haywood is the case in point. Many factors, few of which were under his control, sent him into a wage-earning job. Unlike many who reacted with purely personal bitterness, Haywood studied his milieu. Like many other American radicals, he was at first bewildered by the dashing of his illusions, and later scornful of the social system which appeared to be responsible. In a description Haywood liked, a critic called him a man who, "knowing deeply the wrongs of his class, sees nothing beyond; whose mind, groping helplessly for remedies, seizes eagerly upon a scheme like Socialism which so smoothly and perfectly solves all difficulties." Haywood himself dated his revolutionism to the period following the failure of the Fort McDermitt homestead, describing his embryonic radicalism in quasi-evangelical terms: "suddenly came a great rift of light." [34]

2

Unionist

In 1894 Haywood left his family with Nevada Jane's relatives and headed north on horseback to Silver City, Idaho. He haunted the employment agencies of the town, planning to hold out for a better paying miner's job. But, as elsewhere during the nineties, Silver City's mines were mechanizing and there were few jobs for skilled miners. When Haywood's stake was exhausted he settled for an opening as a car man at the Blaine Mine. It was unskilled and tedious work. The car men shoveled ore into cars and transported them to the mouth of the shaft, from where the ore was taken to a nearby mill.

Eventually a miner's job opened at the Blaine Mine and the extra fifty cents a day enabled Haywood to send for his wife and daughter. Another girl was born soon after their arrival. On June 19, 1896, Haywood was injured while riding a car to the surface. His hand was badly mangled and the doctor suggested a partial amputation. Haywood insisted that he try to save the hand: "I told him that I did not want to go through life doubly crippled. I was already handicapped by the loss of an eye." His hand was saved, but Haywood lost his income while convalescing. At about this time, in mid-August, 1896, Ed Boyce of the Western Federation of Miners visited Silver City and called two organizational rallies. To the harried union leader, Haywood was just one of several hundred weary miners who attended his meetings. But Haywood was impressed by Boyce's message. Perhaps because he was out of work at the time, Haywood was elected to the new local's finance committee and shortly became treasurer. He did an able job, kept clear and honest books, and "never missed a meeting of the Miners' Union except when I was working on the night shift." [1]

Haywood eventually held every position in the Silver City Union, and was largely responsible for its success. In 1898 the Local selected him as a delegate to the WFM's convention in Salt Lake City. It was, as Haywood called it, "a significant point in my life." He played only a passive role in the proceedings, but was recognized as a potential leader when he was named to the executive board of the Western Labor Union which met concurrently with the WFM. The title was little more than an honorific, for the WLU was merely the WFM with another hat on, its existence symbolizing the miners' commitment to a union including all workers in the West. But "Big Bill" was making a name.[2]

Beginning in 1898 Haywood contributed frequently to the WFM's *Miners Magazine,* and continued to attract attention at the WFM's headquarters in Butte by his efforts on behalf of the union. At one time he sent in ninety subscriptions to the union journal. Ed Boyce visited the thriving Silver City Local for a second time after the 1898 convention and took careful note of the thirty-year-old Haywood's work. He took Haywood on a brief organizing trip to a camp at nearby Delamar, apparently to gauge his protegé's effectiveness away from home. In 1899 Haywood was again a delegate to the WFM's convention. Again he was seen more than heard, a thoroughgoing union regular supporting Boyce's policies, suggesting a change in the design of the WFM's lapel button, and little more. Boyce rewarded the organization man with his support for Haywood's election to the WFM's executive board, a post which meant real power.[3]

It was a part-time job. Haywood attended several board meetings in Butte, where he lined up behind Boyce and was entrusted with the task of carrying greetings to striking miners in the Coeur d'Alene and reporting back on their situation. But when that was done he returned to his power drill in the

Blaine Mine. Only in 1900, when he attended the WFM's convention in Denver, did he leave the mines for the last time. In Denver, again with Boyce's indispensable support, Haywood was named the Federation's secretary-treasurer and shortly thereafter he moved his family to Denver, designated the WFM's new home at the same convention.[4]

Haywood served actively in that post for over five years. He administered the Federation's finances, and even edited the *Miners Magazine* for a time. He took an active, sometimes the leading role in directing a series of strikes which broke out in Colorado in 1901, which merged after 1903 into full-scale labor war centered in Cripple Creek. He negotiated with mine owners, wrangled with judges and senators, joined in a few fights with fists and guns, and was frequently arrested in the union's cause. He built a reputation as a militant and skillful, if not always successful labor unionist, and by 1905 he was nationally well known among labor leaders.

Haywood's social views continued to change throughout his life, but the seeds of virtually every idea and policy for which he became famous were planted during his years within the Western Federation of Miners—1896 to 1905. Through the influence of Ed Boyce, his experiences in Silver City, and as a strike leader for the WFM, Haywood derived his convictions that the structure of American society was basically faulty; that direct action was superior to political action as a means of changing that structure; that unions should be organized by industry rather than by craft; and that the union movement must include the unskilled masses of laborers. The origins of Haywood's equivocal relationship with violence also date from this formative period.

The years of Haywood's introduction to unionism and his rapid rise within the Western Federation of Miners were a time when the hard-metal miners took a radical turn. If their unionism derived from the miners' pre-industrial tradition of cooperation, the miners' radicalism derived from the rapidity with which their pre-industrial society was displaced by a new and alien system which reduced them to a subordinate and exploited position.

Technological innovations and corporate organizational methods introduced themselves to a frontier situation and submerged it within a period of a few decades at most. In specific areas such as the Coeur d'Alene and the Cripple Creek District of Colorado the transformation occurred almost overnight. But social adjustments lagged far behind technological change and the result was severe dislocation. Independent prospectors became wage-earners in mercilessly short time. Untold numbers of individuals saw their economic dreams sour with all the accompanying frustrations and resentments. And this was a labor force far less tractable than the insecure and heterogeneous immigrants of the East. The western miner was not uprooted; he was comfortable with his surroundings and occupation. He identified his way of life with mining and felt secure in his world until external forces impressed themselves upon him. It was the corporation which was the alien intruder. The miner saw himself as despoiled.[5]

With a few exceptions, the leaders of the Western Federation of Miners (and later, the Industrial Workers of the World) were native Americans. Curiously, while as internationalists they invariably disowned their American ancestry as irrelevant, they almost as invariably emphasized it with careful attention to detail. Bill Haywood spoke of his "old American family" and, despite his remark that his ancestors were either Puritan bigots or Cavalier pirates, evidently took pride in his American origins. Other union leaders boasted similar genealogies, and a large proportion of the hard-metal miners were native-born. There were many immigrants in the mining fields, of course, but even most of these were easily assimilable "old immigrants" such as the Cornish "Cousin Jacks" so conspicuous in mining fields all over the world. Even those from less familiar cultures adopted the American ethic of the native miners much more readily than their cousins in the East. Unlike the immigrants in the big cities, they were not ghetto-dwellers. Mining camps were small and isolated and unsuited to ethnic segregation. As a result, even the foreign-born miners shared the native American's sense of despoliation.[6]

The radicalism that developed among these men seized

upon Marxist terminology, but that was never much more than a gloss, hastily applied. Western radicalism was a peculiarly American phenomenon, and WFM leaders like Boyce and Haywood always preferred American precedent to European ideology. Ed Boyce spoke of the western miners with the same reverence the Jeffersonians applied to the sturdy yeoman. Haywood hearkened back to John Brown and Abraham Lincoln for historical corroboration. A favorite rhetorical device was to compare strikers to American Revolutionaries of 1776 and the police to "the hated redcoats." Western radicals nodded approvingly in the direction of Frederick Jackson Turner as well as Marx because the American historian seemed to articulate their conception of what had happened to them.[7]

A decade later, middle-class progressives would react politically to their loss of status in industrial America. In a sense, the miners of the 1890's also rebelled against a decline in status effected by the industrialization of the mines. And they did not need Marx's *Capital* for their theory of value; that was rooted in the old prospector's dictum that gold was his who found and worked it.

Ed Boyce was the logical man to lead miners in such a mood and, characteristically, it was not until 1896, after the WFM had languished for five years as little more than a "business union," that he was elected president. Combining zealous militance with administrative shrewdness—no common alliance—Boyce transformed the WFM within another five years from a deathbed case to the most dynamic and powerful radical union in the nation. Haywood's career in the union coincided with Boyce's presidency and the latecomer reflected the president's influence in steering the union toward greater aggressiveness in industrial actions, independence of and rivalry with the conservative eastern labor movement, and socialism. It would be difficult to overemphasize Haywood's debt to Ed Boyce. Not only did Boyce sponsor Haywood's rapid rise in the organization, he also provided Haywood with a sense of the history of miner unionism. Boyce had himself been one of the founders of the WFM while imprisoned during a violent strike in the Coeur d'Alene in 1891.[8]

Boyce also set an example for Haywood in his active, personal style of union management. Before 1896, the turgid annual convention and an exchange of gossip had comprised the sole intercourse among the WFM's locals, separated as they were by thousands of miles of difficult country. Boyce immediately set out to conquer the geography on a barnstorming tour from mining camp to smelter town, making inquiries, holding meetings, scouting potential leaders, chartering locals. The success at Silver City was only one fruit of his organizational talents.[9]

Boyce was also largely responsible for the WFM's independence from the eastern labor movement, a policy which eventually put the WFM in the business of organizing non-miners. Boyce did not take office with this policy in mind. In fact, the WFM first affiliated with the American Federation of Labor after Boyce was installed. The reasoning was that, just as a miners' federation could serve the cause of the locals by mustering large resources behind them, affiliation with the national movement would put a national power behind the WFM.

The alliance was foredoomed. The Western Federationists were beginning to translate their native radicalism into concrete policy at the very time that Samuel Gompers was permanently affixing his social conservatism on the AFL. The WFM was calling for a harder militance while Samuel Gompers was urging the AFL to collaborate with flexible employers. The industrial facts of the mining industry meant that the WFM was committed to industrial unionism (all workers associated with mining belonged to the same union local regardless of the nature of their jobs), while the AFL reaffirmed its commitment to organization by craft. The Western Federation counted thousands of unskilled laborers among its members, while the AFL declared the unskilled to be poor union risks. Many immigrants belonged to the WFM but were tacitly excluded from many sections of the AFL. The Western Federation was jealously democratic, while power within the AFL fell by default or contrivance to the union's leaders.

It was a sorry mismatch, and Boyce and Gompers were soon at loggerheads. The former accused the AFL of hesitation and stinginess in supporting the WFM's strikes, especially the one at Leadville, Colorado, in 1896. Boyce had wheedled a mild resolution of support from the AFL convention at Cincinnati in December, 1896, but when he wrote to Gompers the following February and asked for funds he received no reply. Deriving partly from this disappointment and further complicating matters, Boyce intensely disliked Gompers personally and the AFL president seemed to return the sentiment. Boyce was a western chauvinist to his marrow, viewing Gompers almost as a trade-union dude. In calling for severance from the AFL in 1897, Boyce denounced the undemocratic administration of the American Federation and attacked Gompers for his conservatism. To Boyce, the problem was clearly sectional. He wrote to Gompers:

> I think the laboring men of the West are one hundred years ahead of their brothers in the East. . . . I never was so surprised in my life . . . when I sat and listened to the delegates from the East talking about conservative action when 4,000,000 men and women are tramps upon the highway, made so by the vicious system of government that will continue to grind them further into the dust unless they have the manhood to get out and fight with the sword or use the ballot with intelligence. You know I am not a trade [craft] unionist; I am convinced that their [craft unions'] day of usefulness is past; and, furthermore, since last election there is little sympathy existing between the laboring men of the West and their Eastern brothers.[10]

The inconsistencies of Boyce's letter highlight the transitional nature of his role in WFM development. On the one hand, he reflected the WFM's early Populist Party politics, implying that a vote for Bryan in 1896 (in which act many mine owners heartily joined him) was a progressive action, and castigating eastern workers for their alleged support of William McKinley. On the other hand, Boyce characterized American government as "vicious" and called for "a fight with the sword," albeit as a rhetorical gesture. Boyce's own sympathies were leaning toward the revolutionary, but he never himself completely transcended the WFM's "pure and simple union" origins. Haywood, brought into the WFM when its radicalization was already underway, helped take the trend to its logical conclusion.[11]

Boyce was necessary, however, to point Haywood in this direction, for Haywood's Silver City experience was not the stuff which made radicals. The camp was typical of a dozen mining camps in appearance. It was built in a canyon wide enough for only two streets, and the usual saloons and prostitutes abounded. But the town was atypical in that it was dominated by no single company. This fact, combined with the energy of men like Haywood, paid bonuses to the WFM. Within a year after Boyce's organization rally, the town was almost completely unionized. Haywood remembered only two men who refused to take out cards voluntarily. One was forced to become a member and the other was harassed until he left town.

With such success so easily accomplished, the Silver City union functioned rather like any established union. Spared the necessity of struggling simply to maintain its existence, the union concentrated on maintaining nearly unanimous membership, collecting dues, maintaining internal discipline, and periodically negotiating specific grievances with the mine managers. There were enough of these to keep Haywood busy: the miner's job was hazardous in the best-managed mines. Haywood himself had barely escaped death in the accident that almost lost him his hand and killed his friend, Theodore Buckle. Another Silver City miner was killed when a fulminating cap (used for igniting fuses) exploded in his face. Such accidents were common and, when not the result of blatant management negligence, accepted as a fact of life. The results were often less tragic in towns such as Silver City where the union operated its own hospital, in the administration of which Haywood was instrumental.[12]

Haywood was a militant unionist in Silver City. He hardly shrank from direct confrontation with the mine managers, but he was also a rather conventional union administrator. The hospital, the necessity of maintaining membership, the periodic negotiations with operators—all required constant attention and the most mundane routine. Haywood was scrupulously accurate with his financial records and, unlike most of his revolutionary comrades later in life, he was familiar with and recognized the importance of methodical administrative procedure. He was never exactly orthodox in his methods (he would file the day's notes and receipts in his hatband), but at Silver City he learned how to run a large organization.[13]

If Haywood was part business union bureaucrat when he went to Denver in 1900, he also possessed a radical's indignation toward the mine owners. Boyce's example was partly the source of this but, in addition, Haywood had been a member of the executive committee of the union when, at the turn of the century, labor war renewed in the Coeur d'Alene. The WFM was firmly entrenched in the smaller mines which survived in the district's isolated canyons and, in fact, in all of the companies except the Bunker Hill and Sullivan, a subsidiary of Standard Oil. It was an important exception. The largest employer in the district, Bunker Hill and Sullivan dominated the economy of the Coeur d'Alene and was adamantly anti-union.

The company's truculence, confronted by the miners' surly mood and increasing aggressiveness, characterized labor relations in the Coeur d'Alene as an uneasy truce. Unsolved murders were routinely attributed to the union. For some of them, circumstantial cases could be made. For others, such as the shooting of Fred D. Whitney, a member of the Butte Miners Union, blaming the union was patently absurd and reflected the anti-unionist temper of some legal authorities. There was plenty of lesser violence. Union militants harassed out of the district men who "spotted" secret unionists for the Mine Owners Protective Association. A Socialist, Job Harriman, admitted that the union was guilty of an occasional flogging. From the employers' side, the Protective Association employed "goons" and, at the Bunker Hill Mine, saw to it that union members were immediately dismissed.[14]

The decade of the nineties was a time of armament. The employers, ironically allied with the man who had suggested the formation of the WFM, James Hawley, plotted ways of banishing the union from the canyons. The Federation, insecure as long as its enrollment was incomplete, plotted to organize the Bunker Hill and Sullivan. Ed Boyce never forgot the first strike in the Coeur d'Alene. Working with local leaders, he helped to devise a new method of organization. Two trusted men secretly signed up workers at the Bunker Hill facility. No meetings were held, members were instructed not to discuss the union with co-workers, and only the two organizers knew who belonged and who did not. The WFM hoped to present Bunker Hill with a *fait accompli,* leaving the Standard Oil company no recourse but to deal with the union, and the campaign appeared to be a success.

By the spring of 1899, the WFM had about 250 secret members among Bunker Hill's employees. At this point, on April 13, Boyce was convinced that the union was strong enough to come above ground and post public notices calling upon all mine and smelter workers to join the union. The response was gratifying; success seemed closer. The superintendent at Bunker Hill, Albert Burch, steadfastly refused to meet with the WFM but, on April 24, recognizing the union's strength, unilaterally increased wages to $3 per day for laborers and $3.50 for miners, the level generally accepted by the district's unionized employers. At the same time, however, Burch "invited" WFM members at the company's mine and mill to quit the union. To make his invitation attractive, he dismissed seventeen Federationists whose names he had learned. About a hundred members of the union walked out upon receiving the news.[15]

The lines were drawn and neither side seemed to have particular advantage. While the Bunker Hill Company was intransigent and well prepared, a decade of frustration had steeled the miners for a hard battle. The WFM was determined to win, and put all the Federation's resources behind the local. On April 29, however, an incident occurred which tipped the scales in favor of the employers. The union had scheduled a rally at Wardner, the site of Bunker Hill's huge smelting mill. Before the day was out, a ton and a half of dynamite was exploded in the mill, reducing it to a tangle of steel, wood, and rubble.

Charges and countercharges filled the air before the dust had settled. The Mine Owners Protective Association attributed the blast to an "inner circle" of the WFM. Union leaders, including Haywood in retrospect, felt that while the men were doubtlessly responsible for the explosion, they had been driven to their desperate action by employer tyranny. "The people of these dreadful mining camps were in a fever of revolt," Haywood wrote some years later. "There was no method of appeal." Of the Wardner explosion, he wrote, "The miners have released their pent-up resentment. There may have been some who regretted the destruction of that which the workers had built, but the constraint of the entire population was for the time being resolved." Some miners blamed the explosion on a conspiracy which involved a monopoly-hungry Standard Oil and even the governor who, they thought, required some pretext on which to order in strike-breaking troops.[16]

This, at any rate, was what happened. While pockets of strikers held out for several months, the strike passed a turning point with the Wardner explosion. Governor Frank Steunenberg, first elected as a Populist but a Democrat by 1899, asked for federal troops and declared martial law in the district. While the explosion provided solid grounds for his actions, the troops under General Merriam soon showed that they had intervened not on behalf of life and property so much as of the Mine Owners Protective Association. A "bull pen" served for a prison and, over the duration of the strike,

1,500 miners were imprisoned. Small guerrilla bands of miners held isolated reaches of the district from where they sniped at soldiers, and the soldiers blatantly terrorized the local population. Some settlements were literally besieged, with starvation of the inhabitants the object; several men from both sides were murdered. The strike eventually petered out, but not until it had infected the entire mining region with its warlike mood. Miners as far away as Nevada anxiously followed the news of 1899, and Haywood wrote of the WFM convention that year that he found "the shadow of the Coeur d'Alene pervading the convention. The delegates could think or talk of little else." [17]

Although fresh from the peace and stability of Silver City, Haywood was inevitably affected. The Coeur d'Alene appeared to be a harbinger of a bleak future in which the WFM would have to fight not for complete victory but for its very survival. "If this dreadful thing happened in Leadville, in the Coeur d'Alene," Haywood wrote, "How long before it happens in Butte, in the Black Hills, in Nevada?" The recently retired president of the Silver City Union was thinking of home as well. The Silver City Union would have to rely on the caprice of the same Governor Steunenberg in a similar situation.[18]

The Coeur d'Alene did not frighten the WFM into tractability, however. It converted indifferent members into radical militants and confirmed radicals in their beliefs. When blacklisted miners from the district drifted into other camps they carried bitterness in their baggage. When Coeur d'Alene scabs were discovered in other camps, they were indecorously received. Most important, for both Haywood and the WFM, the lesson of the Coeur d'Alene seemed to say at first that it was futile to work through established political organizations and, subsequently, not to put much trust at all in political action.

As leader of a local in Silver City, Haywood's concern with politics had been strictly parochial; the union saw to it that sympathizers were elected to offices affecting the miners such as sheriff and mayor. Beyond the immediate neighborhood, the successful union had minimal interests, passively supporting first Democratic and then Populist candidates as apparently the most likely to benefit mine workers. The Coeur d'Alene trouble provided a shock. If any politician should have been sympathetic to the miners it was Frank Steunenberg, who owed his position to miner votes. Yet he had unleashed the most overtly partisan strikebreakers Idaho had ever seen. Populist-Democrat Steunenberg was as inimical to the miners as his Republican predecessors; Populism had proved to be an illusion. More than any other single event, the military intervention in northern Idaho resolved Boyce, Haywood, and large numbers of the WFM rank and file to commit themselves to socialism. Boyce and Haywood joined the Socialist Party of America shortly after its unity convention of 1901; many of their members had already led the way.

Ultimately more significant than the turn toward socialism was the role of the Coeur d'Alene in disillusioning Haywood with the efficacy of political action in general. While Haywood never unequivocally repudiated working through political processes, he never thought that elections could accomplish appreciable social progress after the first years of the century. Steunenberg's actions proved to be only one example among many. With the lone exception of Colorado's Governor "Bloody Bridles" Waite, who used militia to protect strikers from company guards, the state governments of Idaho, Utah, Montana, Nevada, and Colorado were at best inordinately responsive to mining company wishes and at worst completely dominated by employers.

From the point of view of national political history, it is customary to define these states as "reformist" or "progressive" inasmuch as they supported the Populist and Free Silver Democratic movements and opposed the traditional national conservatives, the Republican "Gold Bugs." From the perspective of state history, these governments were something altogether different. Governors promiscuously dispatched militia to struck mining camps for the thinly disguised purpose of breaking strikes. Frequently the miners' unions controlled local governments—sheriffs, mayors, etc.—but pro-union sheriffs were impotent once state authority was introduced.[19]

If a lesson beyond the Coeur d'Alene was necessary, Haywood got it during his first years as the WFM's secretary-treasurer. One of the first tasks assigned him in that capacity was to spearhead an eventually successful membership drive among the smelter and mill workers around Denver. The rallying cry was the "eight hour day." The movement itself was not new. In 1895 a bill limiting daily hours to eight in mine-connected occupations was put before the Colorado state legislature, only to be ruled unconstitutional in advance by the State Supreme Court on the grounds that it was discriminatory. Supported primarily by the WFM, a movement was launched to amend the state constitution to permit such discriminatory laws. In 1902 a state-wide referendum approved the amendment by the overwhelming margin of 73,000 to 26,000. Despite the mandate, the mine-owner-dominated legislature wrangled unproductively throughout its session and adjourned without passing the legislation.[20]

Haywood was confirmed in his disgust for conventional politics and his distaste for politics of any sort. What was the use of winning referenda? Manipulative politicos in the employ of mine owners could thwart the will of a people no matter how emphatic their voice. Haywood had already been a member of the Socialist Party for a year when the political eight-hour movement ended in fiasco but, in practice, the WFM had continued to pressure and tacitly support sympathetic politicians of the major parties.[21]

But this too was passing. While Haywood's never-strong faith in political action waned, he became more resolute in the belief that unions could achieve their goals through their own direct action. At Silver City, Miners Union Number 62 had maintained wages, settled grievances to its satisfaction, achieved some measure of job security, and assuaged accidents and illnesses—the stuff of the miner's life—so long as the union's strength was maintained and political intervention withheld. "We have not got an agreement existing with any mine manager, superintendent, or operator at the present time," Haywood said of the WFM in a somewhat different context, "we have got a minimum scale of wages [and] the eight hour day, and we did not have a legislative lobby to accomplish it." While the political eight-hour movement had sloughed off into farce, the miners and smelter workers around the city reduced their own hours. Eight-hour strikes broke out in virtually every important mine and mill town in Colorado between 1901 and 1904. Some were successful, peaceful, and short. Others ranked among the most tragic industrial disputes of a stormy decade. But whatever the failure in some cases, the union did achieve its goal in most, and that was a great deal more than it gained for all its efforts and expenses in the political campaign.[22]

Haywood assumed a leadership second to none in the coordination of the strikes and benefited from the new experience. Labor relations at Silver City had been marked by negotiation, grudging but peaceful. Beginning in 1901 at Telluride, in 1903 at Idaho Springs, and later at Cripple Creek and Colorado Springs, Haywood met head-on the bloody labor relations for which the WFM has gone into legend. The strikes were similar in many ways. On the one side was a group of employers, generally dominated by one large company, determined at any cost not to yield an inch to the Western Federation. At Telluride, the Smuggler-Union Mine dominated the town. At Idaho Springs, the Sun and Moon Mine dictated policy for the smaller employers. The American Smelting and Refining Company, a Guggenheim interest, formulated company policy in a series of altercations around Denver and elsewhere beginning in July, 1903. At Cripple Creek, a twice-famous name in the history of the Western Federation, the Colorado Reduction and Refining Company was the major antagonist.

The employers, seemingly irrational in their opposition to any dealings with the union whatsoever, were often allied to local organizations of small businessmen, variously called the "Citizens Alliance" as in Telluride, or the "Citizens Protective

League" as in Idaho Springs. Ostensibly organizations to protect life and property during industrial disputes, these were actually little more than anti-union "fronts" for the employers which aimed to break strike and union alike and which employed any vigilante tactics to achieve their goals. A favorite tactic was the "deportation." At Idaho Springs, for example, on the night of July 29, 1903, a group of 500 men removed fourteen jailed miners from the Clear Creek County Jail, marched them to the edge of the county, gave them each a sum of money for immediate necessities, and instructed them: "Never show your faces in Clear Creek County again, for if you do we will not be responsible for what may happen to you." The Clear Creek vigilantes were more polite than most.[23]

Opposite the anti-unionists was the Western Federation, well organized in some areas such as Cripple Creek, weaker in others like the smelting towns around Denver. The locals were generally militant, strongly backed by the WFM administration in Denver, and often benefited from competent local leadership. One leader of the 1901 strike at Telluride was the redoubtable Vincent St. John, who later carried the WFM flag to Goldfield, Nevada, and who subsequently preceded Haywood as secretary-treasurer of the Industrial Workers of the World.[24]

The WFM's goals in the strikes were three. First, the union aimed to improve the lot of the miners and smelter workers along tangible "bread and butter" lines: more wages, fewer hours, and improved safety and medical facilities. Second, and thought essential to the first, was organization. From his experience in Silver City, Haywood was already in complete harmony with the WFM policy of working from the bottom up; that is, of concentrating on the organization of the unskilled workers around the mines—the men who shoveled ore and ran cars to the surface. There was generally a minimal difference between the wages of those men and the highly skilled miners (fifty cents a day was the nearly universal rule) and, as Haywood later wrote, the union "came to learn that when the unskilled worker got a wage upon which he could live decently there was no danger of the skilled men falling below this level." The miners, vulnerable to being bumped by technology into unskilled work, concurred enthusiastically.[25]

This not altogether altruistic solicitude for the unskilled workers became a major tenet of Haywood's radical unionism. He came to be contemptuous of the skilled workers in other industries because of their frequent refusal to aid the unskilled, but he never ceased to champion the cause of those who received the lowest wages. In the campaign of 1901–1905, this policy was at the forefront. Nor was the WFM interested solely in mine-connected laborers. Through the satellite American Labor Union (the projected nationwide successor to the Western Labor Union founded at Denver in 1901), the WFM sought to enlist all workers. The Socialist Commonwealth was the WFM's third goal. Haywood and the rest of the WFM leadership were more than merely nominal members of the SPA. Haywood had met Eugene V. Debs and Father Thomas Hagerty at the founding of the ALU in 1901, and consistently, if only on a part-time basis, supported the party after that time.

Like the employers and the "citizens" organizations, the WFM was usually ready to employ extralegal means to achieve its ends. Violence punctuated the strikes in which Haywood played such a large part between 1901 and 1905. Both sides expended a great deal of rhetoric in attributing violence to the opposition. The WFM generally pointed to marauding vigilante committees, company guards, hired goons, and mercenary troops as the instigators of destruction and bloodshed. Haywood wrote tongue-in-cheek of the Telluride Strike that "the union offered to guard the property without expense guaranteeing protection to the company." Employers at the same time sought (and usually received) the intervention of state militia and federal troops on the grounds that the union was liable to embark on a course of untrammeled murder and destruction at any time.

The nature of the employers' position necessitated a very

delicate reasoning. They sought to break the strikes and the union, to be sure, but they also wished to resume production as soon as possible. Therefore, while they required government intervention on their behalf, they could not afford to eliminate their labor supply by permanently imprisoning, deporting, or even seriously alienating the miners and mill workers. The solution to their dilemma was a fiction which served to poison labor relations even more and to prevent a rational discussion of industrial problems between union leader and employer. The employers posited the existence of an "inner circle" of villains in Denver—Haywood, Boyce, and later Charles Moyer who succeeded Boyce as president, John O'Neill, the editor of the *Miners Magazine,* and, at different times, other leaders—who stirred up trouble among otherwise contented workers, were responsible through hired thugs for the murders and explosions which made a tragedy of the Colorado strikes, and sought to affix their "anarchistic" power on the Rocky Mountain region.[26]

There was an "inner circle," of course, in the sense that the three or four principle leaders of the WFM had a large say in the formation of WFM policy. However, their influence was decidedly limited; the WFM was a more democratically run labor union than most. All officers had to stand for election annually. After 1902, the rules of initiative and referendum governed all amendments to the union's constitution. After 1903, all major policy decisions were submitted to the membership for referendum. Most important, the decision to strike was in the hands of the membership. Strikes were called not by any "inner circle" but by three-quarters, later two-thirds, of the members of the affected local.[27]

There were, of course, plenty of murders, floggings, destruction of property, and petty harassments from the union's side. At Telluride, at least one major gun battle was fought and the manager of the Smuggler-Union Company, Arthur Collins, was shotgunned to death through a window. At Idaho Springs, Colorado, on July 28, 1903, the transformer house at the Sun and Moon Mine was damaged by a gunpowder explosion.

Cripple Creek witnessed a spate of explosions, a major one at the Sunset Eclipse Mine on August 29, 1903. But to attribute these very real depredations to the "inner circle" was pure purpose-serving. Not that Haywood and the rest were angelically incapable of violence. To the man, the WFM's leadership had come out of the mines and, although Haywood's particular local experience was relatively placid, he shared the ways of the miners.

The point which the mine owners refused publicly to acknowledge was that violence—unfortunate as it might have been—was the way of the hard-metal miners. Their proximity in time to a violent frontier, their sense of despoliation, their bitterness toward the mine owners, their familiarity with and easy access to dynamite and other explosives, their frustration at a double standard of justice for mine owners and miners—these were the sources of WFM violence. It did not require a sinister directive from Denver to prompt miners at Telluride or Cripple Creek to shoot a foreman or set off a charge of dynamite. Such directives might have come, thugs may have been hired, but the "inner circle" was hardly responsible for violence in the midst of "docile" workers. The Denver office's protestations that acts of violence (which the WFM regretted) were the work of highly frustrated men rings closer to the truth.[28]

The differences between the goals of the Denver office and the local miners explain this. To the miners, their plight was a matter of wages, hours, and conditions. They faced an adamant mine manager, irresponsible groups of company-instigated "goons" and "citizens' committees," and often militia. Their enemy was specific and concrete, eminently personal, and they often lashed out spontaneously against it with the tools available to them.

The goals of the WFM's leaders, on the other hand, were larger. They hoped to create a viable union organization and it is important to note that, despite centers of seemingly impregnable strength such as Butte, the WFM had organized only about 14 per cent of the hard-metal miners as late as

1910. Haywood, Boyce, Moyer, and O'Neill were not Spanish *anarquistas* who believed that the murder of a king (or a mine owner) would accomplish unionization or socialization of the mines, or even any progressive change. The clear lesson of violence was that it provided the pretext for the introduction of troops who, in turn, crushed the strike and crippled the union. The examples of Butte and Silver City taught that airtight organization meant power and stability. The "union town was not an ultimately satisfactory solution to the socialist Western Federation of Miners, but it was inestimably preferable to the woes of the Coeur d'Alene.[29]

For all the mine owners' accusations that the "inner circle" directed miner terrorists, they could muster only the most impeachable of evidence and the most unreliable witnesses to substantiate their case. The finale of their campaign, the Steunenberg murder case of 1906–1907, resulted in the acquittal of all defendants. Moreover, the "inner circle" often cautioned against violence, not only in platitudes intended for public consumption but in earnest advice to the strikers as well. The violence of the Leadville strike of 1896 was a local defiance of the leadership's counsel. A striker in Telluride in 1901 later cursed Bill Haywood for the latter's order not to retaliate against force but to surrender no matter how unjust the charge.

The WFM leadership was not incapable of violence, but it was not responsible for the widespread bloodshed that characterized the union's strikes. That part of the violence that emanated from the union's side was generally the work of local hotheads who, while invariably defended by Denver, were not motivated by the "inner circle." Even this was but a small part of the turmoil that convulsed the mining region between 1901 and 1905. Armed guards, citizens' committees, and militiamen were responsible not only for deportations and similar harassments but also for a number of killings. How much of this depredation should be traced back to the mine managers who organized the citizens' alliances, their eastern employers, and the governors of states who ordered in militia on the flimsiest of grounds and for the worst reasons, is uncertain.[30]

The strikes which erupted helter-skelter throughout Colorado after 1901 merged into one great labor war after 1903, with the Cripple Creek District the major theatre. That strike, culminating a decade of conflict in the hard-metal mines, ended in failure and marked a significant milestone in Haywood's career. Charles Moyer, WFM president, spent much of his time in jail during the strike, and the responsibility of coordinating the union's battle fell to Haywood. Cripple Creek climaxed his apprenticeship as a union leader. He took a decisive part in no Western Federation strike after it, for many of the Federationists, including Moyer, blamed the union's defeats on his leadership.

Located southwest of Pike's Peak, the Cripple Creek District was one of the last great mining regions to be opened. Populated by only fifteen people around 1890, the district exploded when "a forlorn prospector whose view of the scenery was obscured by the hind end of a jackass, dug with a dull pick into a streak of rich ore." By 1892, the towns of Cripple Creek, Victor, Anaconda, and Altman had sprung up and boasted 2,000 inhabitants. For a time the region was accessible only by three wagon roads over which lumbered heavy six- and eight-horse-team drays. But incorporation came quickly during the 1890's and the railroads soon arrived, turning the district toward familiar industrial patterns. By 1900 over 50,000 miners and other people made Cripple Creek District their home.[31]

With a highly industrialized pattern of employer-employee relations fastened on the district, even the once-popular "local man made good," William Stratton, became a villain to the miners. Stratton named his mines after patriotic themes—Independence, John A. Logan, American Eagle, Plymouth Rock, White House, Yankee Girl—which a local booster claimed would "always remain as an enduring and lasting monument to his memory." Local miners, however, remembered Stratton as a former friend who turned on them when he allied with absentee capital. They observed wryly that

Stratton's much-vaunted philanthropy was exercised not in Cripple Creek but in more genteel Colorado Springs.[32]

A strike at Cripple Creek in 1893 had been typical of the time, but industrial stability reigned for ten years after its settlement. Miners and employers religiously observed a compromise settlement which maintained standard hours, good conditions, and fair wages. But union and employers were headed for a confrontation at century's turn. On the one side was a dominant company, the Colorado Reduction and Refining Company, which was determined in the spirit of the day to eliminate the union from the district. Managed by C. E. MacNeill, whom Haywood described as "a dapper little man, the quintessence of the capitalist class," the Colorado Company employed all the tactics native to the region: a "Citizens Alliance," maneuver of the state government, violence (several assaying offices believed to be buying ore stolen by the miners were dynamited), and *agents provocateurs.* One of the most effective of these ever employed against the WFM, A. K. Crane, worked his way up in the Cripple Creek local, revealed the names of secret unionists to MacNeill, and served on the union's strike committee until he was exposed and driven out of town.[33]

Opposite was the WFM, seemingly secure but vulnerable in that while it had the loyalty of most of the miners, few smelter workers belonged. Like the company, the miners were not above the use of violent coercion as the strike of 1903–1904 would demonstrate. While violence was hardly alien to the mining region, it seemed out of place in Cripple Creek. Despite the picturesque name, Cripple Creek was no rough-and-tumble town. It was thoroughly "de-westernized with neat brick buildings; small cottages painted green, yellow, and white; complete electrification; a fire department; several daily newspapers; churches, schools, and women's clubs; and a thriving business district. The WFM seemed soundly established, with a two-story building in each camp and a library of 8,000 volumes in Cripple Creek itself.[34]

Like most WFM strikes, the strike of 1903 was called in

Cripple Creek. The "eight-hour" fight in the Colorado legislature was Moyer's and Haywood's major concern in early 1903. They were somewhat surprised when the unionized smelters of Cripple Creek decided to make a stand. The men quickly wholly or partially shut down several mills. Manager MacNeill responded with a request for troops from Governor Peabody. By almost unanimous testimony, there was no need for governmental intervention. A few fist fights had marked the extent of violence, and no one except MacNeill and a few hirelings signed the statement notifying the governor of an illusory "mob and armed bodies of men . . . patrolling the territory, from which there is danger of a commission of a felony." No neutral citizens joined in the appeal and, when the governor dispatched militia with unseemly haste, the mayor, chief of police, and city attorney of Cripple Creek (all, of course, dependent on the miners for votes), protested the action.[35]

The militia soon demonstrated that its function was to break the strike. It arbitrarily raided unionists' homes, harassed the union headquarters, surrounded struck facilities, and broke up peaceful picket lines. Local anti-militia sentiment among small businessmen as well as miners forced second thoughts on Governor Peabody, and he issued a call for Western Federation and management leaders to meet in his office. All parties, including the beleaguered Haywood and Moyer, who had several strikes going at once, answered the appeal—except MacNeill of the important Colorado Company. Finally, even he relented and came to Denver on March 14. MacNeill again displayed his truculence when he walked out of the meeting but, after an all-night session, the WFM leaders worked out a settlement with the managers of the Portland and Telluride mills which provided for an eight-hour day, no discrimination against union men, reinstatement of strikers, and a provision to meet later with the union concerning wages. MacNeill still would not comply and Haywood commented, "Six men had come to an agreement. The governor had told us that he would withdraw the militia at once. One wretched little autocrat was able to strangle our efforts and his stubbornness was responsible for the strike that followed." [36]

Haywood and Moyer were not anxious for a strike in Cripple Creek. MacNeill, however, was determined to break the union, and Governor Peabody soon showed that if he could not effect industrial peace on compromise terms he would support MacNeill to the hilt. A gubernatorial "advisory board" finally prevailed upon the Colorado Company to make most of the concessions which the WFM requested, but by July it was clear that MacNeill had no intention of keeping the promise. Under pressure, the independent Telluride Mill cut its wages to MacNeill's level of $2 per day. By August the renewed strike was widespread but peaceful.

Before the end of that month, however, the district was again in turmoil. On August 29, a shaft house was burnt to the ground and, subsequently, a mine guard was arrested by a pro-union sheriff and fined for carrying a concealed weapon. The Mine Owners Association again called for troops but Peabody, mindful of the backfire of his earlier action, sent only an investigating committee. It was enough. Comprised of two military men and a state official, the committee flitted in and out of the struck towns almost secretly, with three exceptions spoke only to anti-unionists, and advised the governor that the National Guard was required in Cripple Creek.[37]

If the strike had been resolved on the basis of public sympathy, the WFM would have scored an early victory. The commander of the troops, General Sherman Bell, was quite unequivocal about his mission: "I came to do up this damned anarchistic federation. . . . Military necessity," he continued, "recognizes no laws, either civil or social." Even more candid was Major McClelland (a member of the "impartial" investigating committee), who returned to the District with troops and the slogan, "To Hell With The Constitution! We are not going by the Constitution, we are following the orders of Governor Peabody." Another officer, General Chase, twice refused to abide by the decision of a civil court which ordered some illegally arrested prisoners freed. The violence which hardly existed before the introduction of the troops became the order of the day after they arrived. A track-walker discovered spikes missing from a rail on a sharp curve on the Colorado Springs and Cripple Creek Railroad. The *Victor Record,* a pro-union newspaper, was raided by a company of militia, although a linotypist's wife, Emma Langdon, surprised them the next day by putting out an issue headed, "Slightly Disfigured but Still in the Ring." The "peacekeeping force" was not immune to internecine violence and a tragi-comedy nearly occurred when the two commanders, Generals Bell and Chase, drew guns on one another.[38]

On November 30, 1903, an explosion in the Vindicator Mine killed two supervisors and recriminatory charges filled the air. The usual deportations followed and, also as usual, the militia kept a bull pen for arrested strikers. But the greatest atrocity of all was the dynamiting of the Independence Station. The depot was wrecked, thirteen non-union workers were killed, and six others were injured. The incident led to a wave of arrests, deportations, and harassments which broke the back of the strike over the next several months.

It is difficult to assign the blame for the depredations which plagued once-peaceful Cripple Creek. Employers blamed the attempted train wreckings on the WFM, but none of the charges stood up in court. The explosion in the Vindicator Mine was also widely believed to be the union's work (Moyer was arrested and charged with complicity in the incident), but the WFM denied any knowledge and itself offered a reward for the capture of the guilty party. The companies attributed another accident which killed several scab miners at the Independence Mine to the WFM, but Haywood, with some basis, blamed it on the incompetence of a scab engineer. He pointed out that the mine, like the Vindicator, was surrounded by troops and hardly accessible to the strikers.[39]

A sometime miner named Harry Orchard later confessed to the Independence Station dynamiting and claimed that he was put up to it by Haywood and Moyer, but his word was not good enough to convict. Haywood told an equally uncorroborated story about the Independence affair which had a mine boss named Murphy telling the train-bound miners to wait fifteen minutes before they went to the station (and their deaths). "What did Murphy know?" Haywood asked. Whatever the truth, the violence legitimized what had been groundless —the presence of the militia—and created an atmosphere of anti-union opinion which helped to kill the strike.[40]

Haywood's role during the early stages of the strike involved little more than desk work. He coordinated publicity, organized legal defense, and solicited support from friendly officials like Judge Frank Owers and equivocal friends like Senator Patterson, the owner of the *Rocky Mountain News.* He put his organizational talents to good use when, under mine-owner pressure, Cripple Creek retailers suspended credit sales. With local assistance, Haywood purchased large lots of potatoes and flour in Denver and shipped them to struck towns where the union sold them at cost. He also organized a chain of grocery stores, and produce and meat markets which helped to maintain the strikers. "We had the merchants so worried that they were in a state of insomnia," Haywood wrote. "There was not a striker nor a working member of the union but was well pleased with the experiment. They realized an increase in real wages, through being able to buy necessities so much cheaper." [41]

As time wore on and the strike heated up, Haywood was drawn from his swivel chair into the maelstrom. One of the most bizarre episodes concerned his "desecration of the flag." Shortly after receiving news of the militia's first depredations at Cripple Creek, Haywood sat down at his dining room table and sketched a picture of the American flag headlined: "Is Colorado in America?" On each stripe of the flag he wrote a phrase:

Martial Law Declared in Colorado
Habeas Corpus Suspended in Colorado
Free Press Throttled in Colorado

Bull Pens for Union Men in Colorado
Free Speech Denied in Colorado
Soldiers Defy the Courts in Colorado
Wholesale Arrests Without Warrants in Colorado
Union Men Exiled From Homes and Families in Colorado
Constitutional Right to Bear Arms Questioned in Colorado
Corporations Corrupt and Control Administration in Colorado
Right of Fair, Impartial and Speedy Trial Abolished in Colorado
Citizens Alliance Resorts to Mob Law and Violence in Colorado
Militia Hired by Corporations to Break the Strikes in Colorado

Underneath, Haywood appealed for funds over his and Moyer's signatures.

Sometime later, on March 26, Charles Moyer was arrested at Ouray and charged with desecrating the flag. Haywood heard that there was a warrant issued for his arrest on the same charge and, after consulting wih an attorney, had a friendly judge swear out a similar charge against him in Denver. With a deputy at his side to play out the pretense of arrest, Haywood was able to go about his union affairs. His case was dismissed when he showed up in court with two dozen samples of advertisements using the flag: tobacco sacks, cigar boxes, tomato cans, the business card of the Pinkerton Agency, and the flag of a Negro men's fraternal organization.[42]

It was not Haywood's only arrest during the period. Other incidents, in fact, were more serious. On Election Day, 1903, Haywood and Moyer had a fight in Denver with several deputy sheriffs. Moyer was knocked unconscious and Dan MacDonald of the American Labor Union had his arm broken. Haywood managed to drive away the attackers when he shot one three times with a .38-caliber revolver. Although arrested, he was freed immediately when the deputies filed no charges. They were clearly to blame. Another brawl was Haywood's doing. He punched a military officer who had merely put his hand on Haywood's shoulder. This time it was Big Bill Haywood who was beaten into submission by a group of soldiers and, by his own account, was beaten again while in the soldiers' custody. Later, he was freed.[43]

Charles Moyer was not so fortunate. He passed much of 1904 in jail, including the days when the Western Federation held its annual convention. The charges against him were varied, culminating with "conspiracy" in the Vindicator Mine explosion. Moyer's imprisonment was, according to the military officers, "a military necessity," but the charges against him were flimsy and he was eventually released. The Mine Owners Association had tipped its hand. After Cripple Creek, the chief tactic in their campaign to destroy the WFM would not be long and expensive contest with the miners but selective attack on the union's leaders. The employers learned from the Cripple Creek affair that the elimination of Moyer was insufficient. Haywood, relatively unknown to them before the Colorado strikes, had proved an effective substitute, directing the strikes in a more militant fashion, if anything.

The WFM's hostility toward the AFL reached a new peak in 1905 when the United Mine Workers called off a sympathy strike in the Colorado coal fields. And Moyer and Haywood were now convinced that unionization must be extended not only beyond the mines to the mills, but beyond the mills to all wage workers. The WFM had organized and subsidized the Western Labor Union and the American Labor Union as a means of organizing non-mine and mill workers. While not unqualified failures, neither organization had shown the vitality of its parent. The ALU claimed almost 17,000 members in 1905 (in addition to the WFM's 27,000), but almost all of its locals existed chiefly on paper.[44]

The dream of establishing a national industrial union endured, however, and the WFM found increasing numbers of allies among radical unionists elsewhere who were also disenchanted with the AFL. The WFM considered the question again at its 1904 convention and, partly as the result of the discussion, a small circle of malcontents met secretly in Chicago in November of that year. Moyer was still fighting his legal battles, and Haywood was occupied with the direction of the Cripple Creek strike, but both were effectively represented by Clarence Smith and Father Thomas Hagerty of the American Labor Union. Others at the clandestine session included William E. Trautmann, editor of the United Brewery Workers' journal, *Brauer Zeitung,* W. L. Hall and George Estes of the United Brotherhood of Railway Employees, and Isaac Cowen of the British Amalgamated Society of Engineers. The six drafted a call for a public "Industrial Union Conference" to meet in Chicago on January 2, 1905. Their appeal was both socialist and industrial unionist, excoriating "craft divisions and political ignorance" as the bane of the working class. The radical community received the document enthusiastically. Twenty-three leading radicals and unionists attended, including Haywood, Moyer, and John M. O'Neill from the WFM.[45]

Haywood came into his own at the conference. Self-confidence based on a decade as a unionist enabled him to take a part in the proceedings second only to Trautmann and Hagerty. He was elected permanent chairman of the conference and later, regional secretary for the West. The Industrial Union Manifesto which the conference drafted reflected precisely his social views of the moment. Amalgamating Marxist ideology and WFM experience, the manifesto described the "social relations and groupings" which reflected the "mechanical and industrial conditions" of American society. The great fact of industry, the manifesto stated, was "the displacement of human skill by machines and the increase of capitalist power through concentration in the possession of the tools with which wealth is produced and distributed." [46]

The consolidation of industry had obliterated true craft divisions among laborers and competition among capitalists. The radicals felt that the workers in general failed to see that obsolete craft divisions destroyed their power and speeded their decline into "wage slavery," while capitalists "carefully adjust themselves to the new conditions. They wipe out all differences among themselves and present a united front in their war against labor." Their strategy was succeeding because of "the blindness and internal dissensions of the working class." This could be remedied only by the foundation of an all-encompassing, industrially organized, socialist labor union. The manifesto was the product of many men throughout the nation, but there was nothing in it strange to Haywood or the Western Federation. The miners had been quick to recognize the absurdity of craft divisions in their highly industrialized field. The artificial division between miners and smelter workers at Cripple Creek had been a major source of the disaster there.

Two hundred delegates responded to the manifesto and assembled in Chicago in June, 1905. They met at Brand's Hall on Lake Street, a favorite rendezvous for the anarchists of the Black International during the 1880's. Although Brand's was already twenty years past its heyday in 1905 it was still a favorite object of police surveillance, and they were busy on June 27. As chairman, Haywood walked to the platform at ten o'clock in the morning to rap a noisy crowd to order. He looked briefly for a gavel, found none, and substituted a length of board a carpenter had left on the platform. "Fellow workers," he shouted, "this is the Continental Congress of the Working Class."

This was the founding of the Industrial Workers of the World. The convention enabled Haywood to make or resume acquaintance with the nation's leading radicals. Practically "everyone" was there! Moyer, O'Neill, Hagerty, and MacDonald were almost daily associates. Mother Mary Jones and Eugene V. Debs were old friends. Haywood met Lucy Parsons, the widow of the Haymarket martyr, Albert Parsons, and he got his first look at Daniel DeLeon of the Socialist Labor Party. Here was a man Haywood eyed closely. DeLeon was "the theorizing professor," Haywood wrote in retrospect, whose "only contact with the workers was through the ideas with which he wished to 'indoctrinate' them." But Haywood was always fascinated by, as well as scornful of "idle intellectuals," and was somewhat taken by the head of the nation's oldest Socialist Party. Even after twenty years' estrangement from DeLeon, Haywood would grant him the compliment that DeLeon had "an understanding of the necessity of working-class seizure of power." [47]

Despite the presence of so many luminaries at the conference, Haywood shone brightly. He delivered a stirring address of welcome to the "continental congress of the working class," effectively damning the AFL for its refusal to admit Negroes and immigrants to membership. In a speech during the debate on ratification of the new union's constitution, he renewed the theme and emphasized other WFM ideas which the IWW adopted for its own. On the question of organizing the lowest paid and most miserable workers, Haywood told the meeting:

> We came out of the West to meet the textile workers of the East. We men of the West are getting more wages per day than these men are getting. We recognize the fact that unless we bring them up to our condition they of necessity will drag us down to theirs.

He hammered on the necessity of organizing all workers:

> We are going to get at the mass of the workers and bring them up to a decent plane of living. I do not care a snap of my finger whether or not the skilled workers join this industrial movement at the present time. When we get the unorganized and the unskilled laborer into this organization the skilled worker will of necessity come here for his own protection.[48]

Haywood's ideas did not dominate IWW thinking from the beginning. Much of the union's early effort, for example, aimed not so much at organizing the unorganized as at wooing AFL affiliates into the new fold. Nevertheless, Haywood—or, more precisely, the WFM—had a great deal to say about the policies of the Industrial Workers of the World. The WFM was by far the IWW's largest component. And, though he could not know it at the time, Haywood would find in the

IWW in later years his most congenial home. For the time, however, he was primarily a Western Federationist. There were some efforts to name him the IWW's first president but he declined the offer. Another critical chapter of his life was to be written before he would attach himself to the IWW.

3

Undesirable Citizen

Haywood had little time to ponder the IWW when he returned to Denver from Chicago. The Western Federation was pledged to join the new union but was not yet a part of it in 1905; official affiliation required the endorsement of the miners' convention. Moreover, while Haywood's interest in national industrial unionism did not flag, he was still secretary-treasurer of the WFM and there was more than enough business with the miners to keep him busy. The tragic Cripple Creek strike was limping toward its conclusion, and Haywood was concerned with assisting the many miners forced to look elsewhere for employment. During the autumn of 1905 he toyed briefly with the idea of organizing a cowboys' union for the Industrial Workers of the World through his brother-in-law, Tom Minor, but little came of the notion.

Haywood's relations with Charles Moyer were outwardly friendly, but the union's setback at Cripple Creek had caused tension between the two. Still, Haywood's position seemed secure when the episode occurred which, while it did not maintain Haywood's position in Denver, catapulted the burly westerner to national and even international prominence. In one sense it is a most easy tale to relate, for the undisputed facts are few. The broad implications of the case which made it a *cause célèbre,* the passions and the invective which it inspired, and its significant effects on the career of Big Bill Haywood, require more extensive discussion.

The chain of events known to posterity as "The Haywood Case" began late on the evening of December 30, 1905. Frank

Steunenberg, newspaper publisher, former governor of Idaho, and a locally popular sheep rancher in Caldwell, Idaho, returned to his home. He opened the front gate to which was attached a length of fishing line and a bomb "placed with such devilish ingenuity that a Russian anarchist might well shudder at the thought of employing such an agent of destruction." Steunenberg was killed instantly, blown to pieces.[1]

The local police soon arrested a likely suspect, a short, ordinary-looking man who gave his name as Harry Orchard. Orchard steadfastly maintained his innocence, but a routine investigation produced damning evidence. Orchard had been in Caldwell for much of the month of December, claiming to be a sheep buyer but buying no sheep. The keyhole of his hotel room had been covered and in the room the police found bits of plaster of paris like that used in the device that killed Steunenberg. Other clues in Orchard's room included a length of fishing line identical to that used in the detonator, crumbs of dynamite, chloride of potash, and sugar. In Orchard's trunk at the Caldwell railroad station police found a large quantity of explosives and a full set of burglar tools.[2]

Orchard was remarkably cool and insisted on his innocence until the arrival of a special investigator, a Pinkerton Agency detective named James McParland. McParland was a once-celebrated man whose fame had somewhat faded. He had cracked the famous "Molly Maguires conspiracy" in the Pennsylvania coalfields in 1877. Since that time he had moved about in the Pinkerton Detective Agency as a specialist in labor unions and, at the time of Steunenberg's murder, was assigned to its Denver office where he kept close watch on the Western Federation of Miners. The confession he got from Orchard was kept secret. Only Orchard, McParland, Governor Frank Gooding, and a few other confidants knew what had transpired. McParland, who had gained Orchard's full confidence, instructed him to continue protesting his innocence publicly, to his own attorney, and even to the Caldwell County prosecutor.

Events in Denver soon revealed the reason for the secrecy.

In February Haywood began to notice several known Pinkertons observing the Federation's office. The *Miners Magazine* published a short article on one of the "secret agents" and facetiously sent a copy to the Pinkerton office on St. Valentine's Day. But when the reason for the stepped-up surveillance was revealed three days later, it was not such a jolly occasion. About eleven-thirty on the night of February 17, 1906, Haywood was called to the door of his house by a deputy sheriff whom he knew. He was taken to the jail and discovered that Moyer (who had been taken off a train while waiting to leave on a business trip to several WFM locals), and George Pettibone, a blacklisted miner who had become a businessman in Denver, were already there. At about five in the morning, the three were driven in separate carriages to the railroad station. "We drove along the quietest streets," Haywood wrote, "we were marched to the depot, deserted at that hour of the morning. A train was ready and waiting. We stepped aboard and were off to Idaho." [3]

The train did not stop at regular stations but took on its coal and water and changed engines at isolated spots or small junctions. It was a well-planned itinerary, worthy of the collaboration of the two state governors who, it developed, were implicated. In Boise the three were taken to the penitentiary and put into cells in the death house. With the three safely and quite illegally in custody, the substance of Harry Orchard's confession was revealed. Not only had he murdered Steunenberg and seventeen other men as well, Orchard said, he had committed the crimes on orders from the "inner circle" of the WFM—Moyer, Haywood, Pettibone, and Jack Simpkins. Haywood, the state announced shortly, would be tried first.[4]

Almost a year and a half passed before the trial began on May 7, 1907. The chief prosecutor was James H. Hawley, who was locally well-reputed as both a defense and a prosecuting attorney and who would later be elected governor of Idaho. This was the same Hawley whose suggestion to the Coeur d'Alene miners of 1893 had precipitated the organization of the Western Federation. He had become an unstinting foe of the Federation. William E. Borah, already elected to the United States Senate where his illustrious career spanned four decades, assisted Hawley. The defense retained Edmund Richardson, the WFM's regular attorney, and Clarence Darrow, not yet at the peak of his fame but already a hero to the labor movement by virtue of his eloquent defense of Eugene V. Debs in the Pullman Strike case of 1894.[5]

The state's case relied almost entirely on Orchard's confession and circumstantial evidence. Orchard was a heinous criminal, to be sure, the prosecution argued, but he was only the pawn of a vicious conspiracy which sought to rule the West through terror and assassination, and Haywood was a major figure in this conspiracy. The jury was urged to act promptly in punishing those with such scant regard for the law and decent society before their policies spread.

Darrow and Richardson eloquently fought the indictment on every avenue open to them, legal and moral. Even before the trial opened they sought to have the men freed on the grounds that they had been illegally extradited. The case eventually went to the U.S. Supreme Court before their motion was finally denied. Once in the courtroom Darrow opened the defense by requesting that the case be dismissed for lack of corroborative evidence. This too was denied. The next and principal device was to impeach Orchard's testimony before the jury on the basis of Orchard's own confessed degeneracy. Darrow devoted a major part of his exhausting eleven-hour summation to an attack on Orchard. How, Darrow asked over and over, could a man who coolly spoke of murdering nineteen men be believed? He hammered at the preposterousness of convicting any man of the testimony of a Harry Orchard: "Gentlemen, I sometimes think I am dreaming in this case. I sometimes wonder . . . whether here in Idaho or anywhere in the country, broad and free, a man can be placed on trial and lawyers seriously ask to take away the life of a human being upon the testimony of Harry Orchard." [6]

"Let us take a short view of this fellow," Darrow pressed on. "I have sometimes thought I had a fair command of language, but it fails when I get to describing Harry Orchard. . . . He is unique in history. If he is not the biggest murderer who ever lived, he is the biggest liar, at least, who ever lived, and I undertake to say that the record of the English and American courts cannot show a single man who has been impeached by as many witnesses as Harry Orchard." Darrow listed Orchard's confessed crimes and, never one to miss a sentimental appeal, named as the greatest the fact that Orchard (who revealed his real name as Albert Horsley) had dragged into the gutter the good name of his relatives who had had no knowledge of him for years. He told of Orchard's desertion of his wife and daughter, of his brother, "a quiet, peaceful, honest man." Principally, Darrow pleaded, think of Orchard's daughter, "growing up neglected, uncared for." Her name was all that she had. "The honor of the grandfather and the grandmother sleeping in the Quaker graves, that is all she has. She has nothing from the father that deserted her." Then, suddenly comes back the story that her father is "the monumental criminal of the ages, . . . that this man, who went out from this quiet town, covered himself with crime and with infamy, so that every neighbor who goes through that quiet yard can point to the grave of this old Quaker couple and say, 'There lie the father and the mother of the greatest criminal of modern times.' "

"Think of that girl!" Darrow told the jury. "Every act of this villain's life pales into insignificance compared to the crime committed against that child." [7]

William E. Borah commented wryly of Darrow's attack on Orchard, "If Orchard had not turned state's evidence he would be on trial, and the eminent counsel from Chicago would be defending him with all the eloquence he possessed instead of denouncing him as the most despicable monster on earth." Indeed, it must have been a distasteful task for Darrow, who defended many "degenerates" on the grounds that society was responsible for their "degeneracy," to base Haywood's defense on a prosecution of Orchard. Darrow as much as admitted the truth of Borah's observation. "If the time should ever come that somebody pronounces against [Orchard] the decree of death and nobody else asks to save his life," Darrow said, "my petition will be there to save it." But the case at hand was Haywood's, and Darrow devoted his greatest eloquence to "Harry Orchard, an unspeakable scoundrel; Harry Orchard, a perjured villain; Harry Orchard, bigamist and murderer and coward; Harry Orchard, shifting the burdens of his sins upon these men to save his life." [8]

In keeping with his contention that the prosecution's defendant was not Haywood but the Western Federation of Miners, Darrow closed with a brief account of the WFM's running battle with the mine owners, predictably to the detriment of the latter. He listed the atrocities of the Mine Owners Association, the cruelties and inequities inflicted upon the miners, and the WFM's attempt to secure a decent life for its members. He closed with an appeal to defy this latest mine owners' conspiracy to wreck the union by finding Haywood innocent. Haywood called the defense speech "one of Clarence Darrow's greatest," and certainly the closing words support his observation. It was not for Haywood alone that he spoken Darrow said,

> I speak for the poor, the weak, for the weary, for that long line of men, who, in darkness and despair, have borne the labors of the human race. The eyes of the world are upon you—upon you twelve men of Idaho tonight. Wherever the English language is spoken and wherever any tongue makes known the thoughts of men in any portion of the civilized world, men are talking, and wondering and dreaming about the verdict of these twelve men that I see before me now. If you kill him your act will be applauded by many. If you should decree Bill Haywood's death, in the railroad offices of our great cities men will applaud your names. If you decree his death, amongst the spiders of Wall Street will go up paeans of praise for these twelve men good and true. In every bank in the world, where men hate Haywood because he fights for the poor and against that accursed system upon which the favored live and grow rich and fat—from all those you will receive blessings and unstinted praise.
>
> But if your verdict should be "Not Guilty," in this case,

> there are still those who will reverently bow their heads and thank these twelve for the life and reputation you have saved. Out on your broad prairies where men toil with their hands, out on the wide ocean where men are tossed and buffeted on the waves, through our mills and factories, and down deep under the earth, thousands of men, and of women and children—men who labor, men who suffer, women and children weary with care and toil—these men and these women and these children will kneel tonight and ask their God to guide your hearts—these men and these women and these little children, the poor, the weak, and the suffering of the world, are stretching out thier helpless hands to this jury in mute appeal for Bill Haywood's life.[9]

While Darrow's appeal might ring baroquely in today's ears, it was brilliant in its time and place. The references to railroads and banks and "spiders of Wall Street" were only indirectly related to the mine owners' conspiracy which Darrow posited, but they were magnificently calculated to win the jurors from populist Idaho. After an unexceptional summation for the prosecution and twenty hours' deliberation, the jury brought in a verdict of "Not Guilty." Haywood left the room a free man. George Pettibone was tried and acquitted perfunctorily the next January. Moyer was released on bail and never brought to trial. Harry Orchard lived out his life within the Idaho State Penitentiary walls.[10]

This is, in barebones outline, "The Haywood Case." It stands by itself as one of twentieth-century America's most fascinating criminal trials. But it was, in addition, a most significant episode in Haywood's career and in the history of American radicalism in general. The Haywood Case was more than a murder trial because its principal figures were actors in a bitter drama of several decades' duration. Moreover, the case generated further bitterness in American industrial relations. Virtually every radical and labor group in the nation rallied behind "Big Bill" as the symbol of themselves on trial. Virtually every large newspaper and magazine commented on the broad social significance of the case. The President of the United States tacitly intervened on behalf of the prosecution. Conservative and Progressive mainstream politicians called for his execution in the name of law and order. Darrow's references to Wall Street and the railroads may have seemed mere populist rhetoric, but the fiercely anti-Haywood statements emanating from those quarters both before and after the trial lend some credence to the statement.[11]

The Haywood Case was indeed a skirmish in the Western Federation's struggle with the mine owners. The murder victim, Frank Steunenberg, had originally been elected governor as a Populist with the support of most Idaho miners. He had campaigned as the friend of the little man. The "union printer," his advocates called him, and Steunenberg made much of the fact that he had, at the time of his election, less than $20 in cash to his name. In 1898 he was re-elected, his popularity undiminished. But 1899 brought the tragic strikes in the Coeur d'Alene, and Steunenberg, at the behest of the mine owners, called in troops who mistreated the miners and paralyzed the WFM in the region. The miners were bitter about "their" governor. When Steunenberg failed of re-election in 1900, the *Miners Magazine* rejoiced, describing him as "this Hessian descendant that would disgrace Ananias [who] resorted to deeds from which Nero would shrink." The union accused Steunenberg of selling out to the mine owners. "Your cheek has long since lost the blush of shame and your damnable deeds will never appeal to your manhood, for such you never possessed. . . . Your sole ambition was money, which in your estimation was superior to honor, but you are gone and upon your political tombstone shall be inscribed in indelible words, 'Here lies a hireling and a traitor.' "[12]

Whatever the implications of Steunenberg's intervention on behalf of the mine owners, the cries of "treason" were not altogether warranted. While it is true that miner votes were an integral part of Steunenberg's political success, the Populism of the silver states was by no means a class movement.

Rocky Mountain Populism enjoyed the support not only of farmers, sheepmen, and miners; it also drew heavily on the financial resources of the mine owners. It was almost exclusively a "free silver" pulism and the unlimited coinage of silver was a program which miner and mine owner both approved. As long as free silver dominated Idaho politics, Steunenberg, vociferous on the subject, was universally popular. But class conflict rent the "silver front," and Steunenberg had to choose between his financial angels and his popular support. He chose the former and was defeaed in his attempt at re-election in 1900.[13]

Steunenberg remained a popular man in Caldwell, where former governors were none too common. When he was murdered there was justified anguish. Many said immediately, "It's the miners getting even." A. B. Campbell of the Mine Owners Association was quoted as saying, "There is no doubt that Steunenberg's death was the penalty for his activity in doing his duty during the strike." Aware of this suspicion, and perhaps uneasy about their unfortunate choice of metaphor at the time of Steunenberg's "political passing," the WFM wrote soon after the killing: "We recognize that the assassination of Steunenberg is not a step forward in the march of organized labor toward the goal of economic freedom. . . . The man or men who may have been implicated . . . have but little grasp of the great unsolved problem. . . . The murder of a man who may be looked upon by labor men as a tyrant . . . does not destroy one iota of the system that has given birth to industrial slavery." [14]

But the events of the Haywood Case were already in quick motion, and the hostility between unionist and mine owner was too deeply rooted for the disclaimer to receive much attention. So deeply ingrained was the "heritage of conflict" that the fact that a man had been murdered was soon secondary to the social issues of the case. Both sides interpreted the murder in terms of conspiracy. To the mine owners and the prosecution, an "inner circle" of the Western Federation of Miners had killed Steunenberg partly in revenge for the Coeur d'Alene and partly as a lesson in their terroristic grammar. They submitted Harry Orchard's long and sordid confession as proof of their thesis. Led by attorneys Darrow and Richardson, Haywood's partisans claimed that the prosecution of Haywood was an attempt on the part of the Mine Owners Association and its hirelings to destroy unionism in the mines and smelters by executing the WFM's leadership. Steunenberg, they claimed, had been killed by a deranged misfit who had a personal grievance against the former governor. At the time of the strike, the defense showed, Orchard had been forced to flee the Coeur d'Alene, selling his one-sixteenth interest in the Hercules Mine which, he learned shortly before the murder, had become a rich ore-producer. Orchard, Haywood's partisans continued, had made a deal with the prosecution whereby he would be freed, or at least spared execution, if he helped the state implicate Moyer, Haywood, and Pettibone.

The case has been frequently studied since 1907 and investigators have usually adopted one of the two theories, adding little to what was known at the time. Those convinced of Haywood's guilt have relied on Harry Orchard's confession as undisputed fact; Haywood's partisans reiterate the case constructed by his defense attorneys in 1906 and 1907.[15] Occasionally a new theory has been conjectured. One suggested that Jerry Simpkins (a WFM official who was allegedly with Orchard in Caldwell and who disappeared forever after the murder), might have been a detective who worked his way up in the WFM, instigated Orchard in his deed, and then disappeared in order to give the prosecution a better case.[16] It is a preposterous theory, based on nothing other than the obvious fact that Pinkertons infiltrated unions. It further assumes that Steunenberg was murdered by the Mine Owners Association or the Pinkerton Agency, with the idea of framing the Western Federation in mind from the beginning. Even the bitterest anti-mine-owner demonologies did not posit a conspiracy before Steunenberg's murder; they maintained only that various anti-union individuals capitalized on his death as a godsend to their cause after the fact.[17]

A recent recounting of the case presents the most convincing argument to date on behalf of the case that Haywood was unsuccessfully framed.[18] In fact, the recent publication of the Pinkerton Records dealing with the manner in which Orchard's confession was extracted throws a pall of suspicion over the prosecution's behavior, and especially over that of the Pinkerton investigator, James McParland.

McParland was despised by both conservative and radical labor unionists. His role in the Molly Maguire case of 1877 was more that of union breaker than law enforcer. Indeed, McParland's specialty within the Pinkerton Agency became the obstruction of unions. In 1906 he was the head of the agency's Denver office, which meant to many that his standing assignment was to crush the Western Federation. It was with McParland's entrance into the case that "conspiracy" theories came to dominate the state's reasoning. Certainly, unionists thought, such an illustrious detective was not required to secure a confession from a petty villain such as Orchard who already had a damning case against him. It is impossible to tell whether McParland asked to be invited into the case or whether the Idaho authorities took the initiative. It is on the record, however, that the detective had conspiracy on the mind before he ever met Orchard. He was thinking in such terms on the train to Idaho.[19]

He arrived in Boise on the evening of January 9, 1906, and met almost immediately with the head of Pinkerton's Spokane office, Governor Frank Gooding, and Justice E. C. Stockslager of the Idaho Supreme Court. Sometime that night or early the next day, McParland wrote his first report for William Pinkerton. "I am satisfied that there were other people in this plot besides Orchard and feel almost sure that Orchard was the tool of others." To leave no doubt as to who was in on the plot, McParland continued, "This conspiracy is so widespread and so well and secretly conducted that it would not surprise me that the W.F. of M. has one or more men posing in Caldwell as bona fide residents, for the purpose of proving an alibi." McParland did not pursue this part of his intuition and never turned up the men who had their wives "or women posing as their wives, to help them out in the plot." But he "uncovered" a conspiracy even greater, and his manner of dealing with Orchard is intriguing.[20]

He first met with Orchard for three and a half hours on January 22. McParland emphasized that he had not come after Orchard's personal confession of the Steunenberg murder. The state had more than enough evidence to hang Orchard for that. What McParland wanted was Orchard's implication of the "inner circle" of the Western Federation. Orchard continued to maintain that he was innocent and mocked McParland's hint that by cooperating with the state he would receive special consideration. "Talk about acting square with the state," Orchard replied, "I never heard tell of a man that did but that he afterwards paid the penalty." [21]

McParland then related to Orchard "cases in which the state witnesses went entirely free," including that of "Kelly the Bum," who had been the key witness during the Molly Maguire Trials and who was freed despite his own admission that he was a murderer. Orchard replied: "McParland had all that fixed, and he saw to it that whatever promises he made were kept. . . . McParland would go to any extreme to convict a man, but as a rule he kept his word." McParland, then, by his own account, identified himself to Orchard.[22]

The question of McParland's reliability arose again. At their second meeting on January 25, 1906, Orchard's manner was "entirely changed" from the uncooperativeness of the first interview. Again he told McParland that "I know more about you than you suspect. I am well aware that if you made a promise to a man, no matter what crime he had committed, if he did his part, you have always seen that your promise was carried out." McParland again emphasized to Orchard that the state had enough evidence to convict him personally but, knowing that he was "but the tool of the power behind the throne, the Inner Circle," hanging Orchard would be of little satisfaction to the state. If Orchard "would come up and make a full confession of all that he knew in this case the State would no doubt take care of him." [23]

Orchard was, by McParland's account, a shrewd negotiator. He posed several further questions about his liability for crimes in Colorado, implying that, as with Kelly the Bum, McParland actually discussed the possibility of freedom. In addition, Orchard was concerned about the public pressure for execution from the people of Idaho which his confession would evoke. McParland assured him that he would not be prosecuted for any crimes he had committed in Colorado, and stated that "if he acted in good faith with the State that the sentiment that now existed would be reversed, that instead of looking upon him as a notorious murderer, [the people of Idaho] could look upon him as a saver, not only of the State of Idaho, but of all the states where the blight of the Inner Circle of the Western Federation had struck." Orchard then stood up and exclaimed, "My God, if I could only place confidence in you" and shortly thereafter he agreed to dictate his confession. Orchard told of rigging innumerable explosions and of killing seventeen men before Steunenberg, all commissioned by the "Inner Circle" of the WFM. George Pettibone had been his mentor, he said, instructing him in the methods of making "hell fire," a mixture of stick phosphorous, bisulphide of carbon, benzine, alcohol, and turpentine which, when thrown with force, broke into flame.[24]

Orchard's sensational confession is the key to the Haywood Case; the prosecution relied upon it almost entirely. Beyond this the prosecution introduced only circumstantial evidence. To Haywood's defenders, both contemporary and subsequent, the document was utterly fraudulent. The most recent student of the case, Philip S. Foner, states that Mc Parland "came to see Orchard with the express purpose of getting him to name the leaders of the W.F. of M. as the men responsible for the assassination . . . and this without having acquired the slightest evidence that this was the case. . . . McParland did not ask Orchard who might have been associated with him in the assassination. He told Orchard, without having any proof of the charge, that the leaders of the W.F. of M.—the so-called 'inner circle'—had hired him to do the job. Orchard was given a clear alternative: either name the leaders of the W.F. of M. as the instigators of the assassination or hang! Name them and the States of Idaho and Colorado would see that Orchard was not made to pay for his crimes.[25]

"McParland's Reports on how he got Orchard to 'confess' are probably not unique in the history of frameups," Foner continues. "What is unique is that these reports are at last made public, and it is possible to see the strategy used in the conspiracy to railroad the leaders of the W.F. of M. to their death." [26]

One other bit of evidence reinforces this analysis. This was the "confession" of Steve Adams, with which the prosecution hoped to corroborate part of Orchard's story. A sometime miner and roustabout, Adams was arrested at Haines, Oregon, on the same day that Orchard's confession was publicly released. According to Orchard, Adams had assisted him in some of his projects. Adams later confessed complicity, but subsequently repudiated his confession. During a trial at Wallace, Idaho, Adams said that he had been put into a cell with Orchard at Boise and introduced to McParland. The detective told him, Adams testified, about Kelley the Bum and other men who had turned state's evidence and were later freed. "McPartland [*sic*] told me that he wanted to convict Moyer, Haywood, Pettibone, [Vincent] St. John, and Simpkins whom he called 'cut-throats.' If I did not help I would be taken back to Colorado and either hanged or mobbed. If I did help I would only be taken to Colorado as a witness. When we parted McPartland told me he was my friend. They put me in a cell with Harry Orchard and talked with me about the need for backing up his story. I was frightened. The next day McPartland called again. I said I would do what he wanted me to do. . . . When the confession was made he led me on step by step and showed me all they wanted me to say. . . . He wanted the names of the officers of the Federation used as much as possible all through the confession." Adams was acquitted of several charges and eventually freed.[27]

McParland's "Reports" are the story of a "deal." It is clear that McParland offered freedom or leniency in return for a confession implicating Haywood, Moyer, and Pettibone. But the Reports do not *prove* that Orchard *falsely* implicated the three only because it was that fabrication or the gallows. McParland was a skillfull detective who had mastered all his trade's devices (including, no doubt, the less savory ones) . It is possible to read his Reports as merely the work of a clever detective manipulating a criminal into revealing the full story of his crime. McParland's conviction that Orchard was the "tool" of the "inner circle," expressed to Orchard from the beginning, can be seen in that light. That is, McParland was simply making clear to Orchard "how much" McParland "knew" and what the prisoner's end of the bargain was to be.

There are, however, troublesome aspects to the McParland Reports. The detective's psychological manipulation of the prisoner and Orchard's susceptibility to it is one. Once again this may be considered merely as good detective work of which McParland was especially proud. But it increases the suspicion that Orchard was indeed manipulated into supporting McParland's previously formed hypotheses. Orchard was an unstable sort. Even setting aside the murder of Steunenberg (of which Orchard was certainly guilty) and the other atrocities to which he confessed (the assignment of guilt for which is not at all certain), Orchard was a wife-deserter, a bigamist, apparently a claim-jumper, and a ne'er-do-well who had suffered more than his share of misfortune and inflicted a pretty amount of it on others in misplaced revenge.[28]

There is evidence that he did not want to escape capture for Steunenberg's murder. He made no effort to escape Caldwell after the murder although, as a stranger in a small town, he must have known that he was automatically suspect. Moreover, he was unbelievably sloppy in leaving clues strewn about his hotel room and in his trunk, both of which the police could be expected to search routinely.

During his first months in prison Orchard was in an unsettled state of mind. He had a religious experience, for example, when Steunenberg's widow visited him and converted him to the Seventh Day Adventist Church. Darrow made much of Orchard's sudden embrace of Christianity, picturing the unsavory McParland as an unlikely evangelist indeed. McParland did indeed sense Orchard's frame of mind, and exploited it with a flattery which would have been blatantly obvious to a balanced man. "I told Orchard that the reason the guard watched him more than he did the condemned man," McParland wrote of their first meeting, "was that he—Orchard—was such a great criminal that the guard was hypnotized and simply had to watch him instead of the other prisoner." [29]

Sometime later McParland wrote to his chief: "I found that he prides himself on being very intellectual and I catered to his vanity in that respect all through the conversation." For example, on January 25, when McParland and Orchard discussed the various possibilities of the case, McParland told the prisoner that "a man of his intelligence and reasoning power, as his forehead would indicate, had the ability of doing a large amount of good, as well as evil. As I stated to him on Monday, if he had formed associations of law-abiding citizens when he first started out in the world instead of a crowd of socialists, anarchists, and murderers, he would have become a shining light in any community instead of now occupying the cell of a condemned felon, and relying on his intelligence when the right path was pointed out to him." [30]

McParland established a bizarre relationship with Orchard. "My God, if I could only place confidence in you," Orchard exclaimed after a long early interview. "I want to talk; I ought to place confidence in you. Your talk is right. I know every word you have said is true. You cannot live a hundred years longer. You certainly have got to build a reputation as a detective and I am satisfied that all you have said is for my good." Later Orchard told McParland, "I think you are honest, and if I was only with you a while I know that I would have confidence in you." [31]

On February 9 Orchard told the detective that "I look upon you as my father at the present time" and, in parting, held

McParland's hand for a long time and promised him that if Steve Adams were put into the cell with him, Orchard would make him confess "without using any force." McParland repeatedly had to keep the prisoner's spirits up during the long wait until the trial, and urged prosecutor Hawley to visit Orchard frequently toward this end. McParland himself spent considerable time with the prisoner and wrote to him regularly, if sometimes with annoyance, when the detective was out of town.[32]

That McParland was a clever psychologist and an artful flatterer (he managed to include extravagant praise of Governor Gooding in all his dispatches to the governor) does not prove, once again, that he manipulated Orchard into making a *false* confession. Psychologists are not historians for the precise reason that the past does not permit them laboratory conditions. But the profile of Orchard's state of mind in McParland's reports throws suspicion on his competence and credibility as a witness.

The question remains: was Haywood guilty as charged? Barring the unlikely discovery of new sources, that must remain a riddle. At best it is possible to list probabilities. On the other hand, Orchard's confession—the sole concrete evidence of Haywood's complicity—was acquired under impeachable circumstances. On the other, Orchard's testimony standing alone was convincing. It was knowledgeable, filled with corroborative details about his confessed acts, coherent, and consistently repeated. The most arduous cross-examination did not shake Orchard from his story. "Probably there has never been a witness in a criminal trial who was ever subjected to such merciless cross-examination as this man Orchard," wrote a Boise newspaper, "and yet he emerges from the ordeal without as much as having one single essential point in his testimony either shaken or discredited." Moreover, Orchard was adamant until his death many years later. At the age of seventy-four he gratuitously observed to a visitor that "Haywood was no friend of the working class."[33]

But Haywood also insisted upon his innocence long after it

was necessary for him to do so, and in company where maintaining his innocence was of no particular social benefit. He continued to claim no responsibility for the crime in his autobiography written twenty years later in the security of his exile in the Soviet Union, and he always insisted the same in private conversations with friends. He told one during World War I that Orchard "confessed to so many blood-curdling crimes that he was beyond belief." [34]

It is conceivable that the William D. Haywood of the WFM period of his life could have been involved in a murder. While his past was unexceptional for one of his station and time, his experience in the union had exposed him to an unruly way of life. It is conceivable that he could have commissioned someone like Orchard to destroy a mineshaft or railroad depot. The hard-rock miners were accustomed to such tactics and they were in a surly mood in 1905. Haywood's defenders never attempted to deny his rough-and-ready image. Darrow submitted to the jury that "labor unions are often brutal, they are often cruel, they are often unjust." But this, as he pointed out, was hardly cause to convict for Steunenberg's murder.[35]

It must also be emphasized, however, that Haywood was before anything else a unionist whose first priority was the construction of a powerful and effective Western Federation of Miners, and that in other cases he had warned against violence for the very reason that it weakened the union. But even assuming that in 1905 he did accept violence as a means to a desired end, there was no rational reason to desire the elimination of Frank Steunenberg. The former governor had neither political power nor political future at the time he was killed. Anti-Haywood partisans spoke of revenge for the Coeur d'Alene disaster as the motive, but the argument is unconvincing. There is no evidence to suggest that either Moyer or Haywood were either careless or personal enough to risk execution for the sake of a six-year-old grudge. If the question of revenge is to be introduced as a likely motive for Steunenberg's murder, it is more credible that the beaten, bitter, and possibly deranged Orchard did the deed because of Orchard's lost fortune than to attribute the crime to Haywood who, for all his setbacks, was established in a comfortable position of power in Denver.

Orchard said at one point that a motive behind the crime was that the newly formed Industrial Workers of the World had adopted terror as a policy. The IWW, Orchard said Haywood had told him, planned to eliminate strikes by assassinating recalcitrant employers and their political supporters. As there would be no benefits to pay out of the treasury, "the emergency fund would soon be filled to overflowing and the employers or capitalists would soon learn that if the demand of their employees were not granted, they would be removed; also their friends would be removed." [36]

This was complete nonsense, and potentially impeaches the rest of Orchard's testimony. The allegation would seem to tie in with the attacks on Haywood's honesty as an administrator. The latter were easily disproved and the prosecution never emphasized Orchard's comments about the IWW. Haywood never held such views, nor did the other men instrumental in the founding of the IWW; it has the ring of the sort of story regularly circulated by the Pinkertons and the Mine Owners Association. The IWW was a striking union from the first. One of the major reasons for organizing the union was its founders' disgust at the American Federation's refusal to strike effectively, if at all. Moreover, throughout its history the IWW deliberately discouraged the growth of large strike funds, which it regarded as inducing timidity and conservatism among union leaders. Finally, the IWW was clearly innocent of tactics such as the "removal" of opponents.

In addition to the fact of Orchard's direct responsibility, the only thing about the Haywood case which can be said with certainty is that the verdict was a just one. Whatever the possibility of Haywood's complicity, the prosecution did not prove it by any rules of jurisprudence. Orchard's testimony was besmirched by his own past and uncorroborated. In view of the manner in which the confession was obtained, the verdict seems even more justified. While many Americans continued to regard Haywood as an accidentally freed murderer, the jury's action was their only honorable and just alternative. Beyond jurisprudence, the acquittal was also fortuitous. If Haywood had been convicted and executed, a million American workers would not have marched as Eugene V. Debs urged in his famous manifesto, "Arise Ye Slaves!" But American History would now have to wince at the presence of other Haymarket, Joe Hill, and Sacco-Vanzetti cases in its pages. The facts of the Steunenberg Case were fully as equivocal as the facts of these three which, most students have agreed, were unfortunate prosecutions ending in unwarranted sentences.[37]

It is possible that a tragically murdered man's killer went free in Boise during the summer of 1907. Nevertheless, the effect of Haywood's acquittal were far less adverse for posterity than the effects of the executions of the Haymarket anarchists, Joe Hill, and Sacco and Vanzetti. There was no wave of terroristic assassinations following the verdict, and William D. Haywood went on to help write an exciting chapter in the history of American organized labor.

For American radicals and the labor movement, the months between January, 1906, and August, 1907, represented a brief period of "popular front." The Western Federation, the Industrial Workers of the World, the Socialist Party of America, the Socialist Labor Party, anarchists of all persuasions, some progressives, and most of the American Federation of Labor all agreed that Haywood's arrest was a class action and they pulled together in defending him. They did not remain partners long; they managed to get in an occasional lick at one another even during the affair. But for the most part they cooperated in defending "Big Bill." [38]

This unusual solidarity was partly due to the highly irregular means by which Haywood, Moyer, and Pettibone were "extradited." The men were not legally fugitives from justice, since they were not in Idaho at the time of the crime. The question of whether or not they could have been legally taken to Idaho at all was very much in doubt. Had they been arrested openly in Denver, they would have won their freedom immediately on a writ of habeas corpus. McParland and Prosecutor James Hawley were well aware of their shaky ground when they traveled secretly to Denver. In Colorado they met at length with Governor Jesse McDonald and explained that they wished to avoid the usual channels which involved referral to the Attorney-General, whose deputy was a former member of the WFM. McParland was apprehensive, fearing that McDonald would not be willing to take the responsibility "for playing, as it were, the part of a kidnapper if he signed the papers without referring them to the Attorney-General." McDonald surprised him; he signed the papers willingly, and promised to delay recording his signature with the Secretary of State until the prisoners were in Idaho.[39]

The deputies then delayed apprehending Haywood and the others until late Saturday night when the courts were closed for the weekend. It was all quite extralegal. The arrest was made without a warrant, the three were denied counsel (Haywood was told that a messenger had been sent for his lawyer when, in fact, the police denied any arrest when WFM attorney Richardson called the jail in search of the three), and they were extradited without appeal to court. "Here we were in murderers row," Haywood wrote of the arrival in Boise, "arrested without warrant, extradited without warrant, and under the death watch!" After the arraignment, Pettibone instituted *habeas corpus* proceedings in Idaho, charging illegal arrest.

State, Federal District, and U.S. Supreme Courts ruled against the prisoners. The Supreme Court eventually ruled that the seizure had been illegal but, since the prisoners were in Idaho's custody, nothing could be done about it. Associate Justice McKenna dissented, writing that the "arrest" of the three was kidnaping pure and simple. "The foundation of extradition between the states," McKenna wrote, "is that the accused should be a fugitive from justice from the demanding state, and he may challenge the fact by habeas corpus, immediately upon his arrest." But the rest of the court prevailed, convincing labor men and radicals that even the highest court was involved in a vast conspiracy to crush the WFM by railroading its leaders to the gallows. When the press and prominent persons assumed Haywood's guilt publicly, Haywood's partisans hardened in their views. Most obnoxious was President Theodore Roosevelt's statement on the eve of the trial that Moyer, Haywood, and Debs were "undesirable citizens."[40]

There is no doubt that the prosecution's motives were mixed. While many doubtlessly looked upon their task as one of bringing a murderer to justice, that aim was often obscured by their palpable desire to emasculate the Western Federation. The governor of Colorado could not be expected to violate constitutional procedure and risk his career over a simple murder case, no rare occurrence in the mountain states. James McParland's aim was clear enough: his whole job revolved around the directive of "get" the WFM on something. James Hawley, the chief prosecutor, had also made a career of attacking the WFM. After serving as attorney for the miners between 1892 and 1894, Hawley had thrown in politically with the Idaho Democratic Party. In 1899, with William E. Borah, he had accepted from then-Governor Steunenberg an appointment as special prosecutor for the state in the indictments growing out of the WFM's strike in the Coeur d'Alene. He had adopted the mine owners' viewpoint that the state was not after rank-and-file unionists but the leaders who inspired local atrocities.[41]

Hawley was also quite explicit in his desire to destroy the union. "I am trying to develop a scheme to organize a Miners Protective Association which will take the place of the Miners Unions," he wrote to his legal partner. And again, regarding the trial of WFM leader Paul Corcoran, "No matter how [the trial] goes . . . we will win our fight by breaking the power of the Unions." The fact of Steunenberg's tragic death was also lost sight of in the press. The actual crime usually received no more than a sentence or two in the dozens of accounts of the trial, while the necessity of eliminating the blight of the Western Federation was tediously belabored.[42]

The *Idaho Daily Statesman*'s comment of June 30, 1907 provides an interesting insight into the trial's anti-WFM nature:

> Probably there has never been a witness in a criminal trial who was ever subjected to such merciless cross-examination as this man Orchard and yet he emerges from the ordeal without as much as having one single essential point in his testimony either shaken or discredited.

It is a most remarkable manner of writing about the self-confessed murderer of the state's former governor and the self-acknowledged murderer of seventeen other men. Terms such as "merciless cross-examination" and "ordeal" are unusually sympathetic toward such a man. The fact is that Orchard had indeed become something of a hero, fulfilling McParland's prediction to him that "instead of looking upon him as a notorious murderer they would look upon him as a saver." Nothing more clearly indicates the direction which the trial took.

For Haywood himself, the Boise trial was a watershed. "The eighteen months in prison could not be called a vacation," he wrote, but at least they were a rest. Throughout his life Haywood was a relentlessly driving man, full of nervous energy. At the time he was arrested he had not had an extended holiday from his desk in five years. Prison life was not difficult after the WFM's lawyers successfully insisted that the three defendants be removed from the death cells and transferred to the county jail at Caldwell. Then, after a change of venue, they were transferred to the Ada County Jail where conditions were almost pleasant. "Sheriff Mosely was a man of some feeling," Haywood wrote, "who tried to show us that in his opinion we were not guilty until convicted." [43]

There was room to walk about in the Ada County Jail, and in the daytime the prisoners were permitted access to a special cell where they could eat together. There was also an hour's exercise daily in the jailyard. Haywood was scrupulous with his health, bathing daily and exercising systematically. He fasted several times for days at a stretch so that by trial time he would be "as clear as crystal both physically and mentally." Haywood described his first months in jail as "the most quiet, peaceful period of my life." He spent much of his time on Western Federation affairs, writing articles, designing posters, and dispatching letters to conventions, rallies, and friends. Like many prisoners before and since, Haywood educated himself in a way for which he would have had no time had he not been imprisoned. He spent a great deal of time reading: Buckle's *History of Civilization,* Voltaire, classic English novels, Carlyle on the French Revolution, Marx, Upton Sinclair, and other revolutionaries. He also took a correspondence course in law at the suggestion of a lawyer friend, John Murphy, who had invited him to form a law partnership when he was released. During his first summer in Ada County, Haywood collected rose petals, dried them and stuffed a cushion for his wife. His second summer, before the trial, he cultivated a small garden of flowers and vegetables in the jailyard.[44]

During the trial Haywood's health slipped somewhat. The proceedings had to be delayed once when he was taken with a fit of stomach cramps and convulsions. Otherwise, he bore the strain well. He sat impassively throughout the proceedings, his daughter on his knee at times, never registering a response to the testimony of Orchard or other hostile witnesses. On the witness stand himself he was cool, deliberate, a good witness in his own defense. Borah for the prosecution did not rattle him, just as Darrow and Richardson failed to break Orchard. When the verdict was announced Haywood seemed visibly surprised and almost giddy in his elation. He autographed a miniation American flag for one of the jurors, quipping about the trouble his artwork on flags had caused him before, shook hands with the rest, and accepted an invitation from the foreman to visit him before he left Boise.[45]

After returning briefly to his cell to accept Moyer's and Pettibone's congratulations and to collect his belongings, Haywood emerged to the cheers of WFM members and sympathizers and went to the house where his wife and daughters had been staying. Haywood's mother had also come to Boise despite her declining health, and he visited her in the hospital. Then to another hospital where his friend Murphy was recuperating. Back at his temporary home, Haywood discovered a flood of congratulatory telegrams.[46]

The next evening Big Bill Haywood took the train to Denver.

4

The Eminent Man

Haywood titled the chapter of his autobiography which followed his version of the Steunenberg Trial, "The World Widens." In truth, the personal world into which he walked from the Ada County Courthouse little resembled the one he left eighteen months before in Denver. Before his arrest Haywood was a modestly salaried minor official of a large and powerful labor union who was popular with the miners and despised by the owners of the mines. But he was a figure of strictly local renown, almost unknown beyond the mining canyons and smelting towns. He had little to look forward to except, perhaps, advancement to the presidency of the Western Federation. But even that was in doubt as his relations with Charles Moyer and the other union leaders deteriorated. The trial changed everything. Although Haywood's role in the courtroom drama was passive, he became a symbol around which seethed an international protest movement of labor unionists and radicals. Widely publicized photographs of the burly miner brooding in the courtroom introduced millions to his unforgettable face. His name was emblazoned on red banners, featured in front-page headlines, cursed by the President, and cheered hoarsely in a dozen languages at rallies on his behalf. In the United States virtually all unionists and radicals leapt to his defense, including even a reluctant Samuel Gompers. Eugene V. Debs composed his most revolutionary tract on the issue, warning that "if they attempt to murder Moyer, Haywood, and their brothers, a million revolutionists will meet them with guns." Prominent writers such as Jack London and Maxim Gorky lent their names to Haywood's defense.[1]

Almost every major American city witnessed a rally supporting Haywood during the trial. Fifty thousand marched the streets in Boston, 20,000 in New York City, and similar numbers in other large cities. European unions contributed resolutions of support, and thousands of Continental workers heard Haywood's name cited as if he were a leader of the Workingmen's International. Indeed, the Socialist Congress meeting in Stuttgart sent Haywood "the congratulations of the Socialist movement of the world in view of the magnificent fight he put up in the interests of the organized workers of the United States." [2]

Thus was a provincial labor unionist transformed into a public figure. If Haywood's partisans were even partially correct in their accusations that the motive behind the trial was to discredit and destroy the leaders of the Western Federation of Miners, then the trial was a colossal boomerang. It created a hero.

Not that William D. Haywood left Idaho a celebrity of the first magnitude. Most Americans probably did not know Bill Haywood from the Vice-President of the United States any better after the trial than before. But among radicals, unionists, and the socially aware throughout the United States and Europe, his name and a somewhat romanticized account of his life were conversational commonplaces. Ironically (and fortuitously), these new horizons opened for Haywood at the same time that his position within the WFM was slowly deteriorating. Haywood's estrangement from Moyer and other WFM leaders such as John Kirwan and John O'Neill was well underway before his arrest in early 1906. As a relative latecomer to the Federation's central office, Haywood was never a completely secure member of the WFM "establishment."

Coming from the mines at a time when the miners were surly and restive, Haywood was more militant and aggressive than Moyer and his associates. He was more likely to make the inflammatory statement and mean it. Despite his proven ability to manage the finances of a union efficiently and honestly, Haywood was not cut from quite the same business-unionist cloth as Moyer, O'Neill, and Kirwan. He was more the activist, at home on an organizational drive in the field as well as in an office. He recorded his bemusement at finding himself in an office job in 1900: "I was more familiar with the stormy end of a number two shovel than I was with a pen!" [3]

His enthusiasm won Haywood warm welcome at WFM headquarters during the first few years of the century, when the militant spirit of Ed Boyce still held sway and President Moyer found good use for a firebrand. But wedges between the two soon developed. Haywood's ambition was one. It was clear by 1906 that he aspired to a higher position than he held, and Moyer was quite uninterested in retirement. Nor was Moyer oblivious to the fact that Haywood commanded a great deal of popularity among the miners. The chairwoman at the first convention of the Industrial Workers of the World inadvertently introduced Haywood as president of the Western Federation. While she corrected herself at Haywood's behest, she added, "you will all admit that while he has not been president he would make a good one." The *faux pas* was not calculated to improve Moyer's feelings toward his secretary-treasurer.[4]

It is difficult to determine the extent of this personal rivalry before the Steunenberg Trial. In his autobiography Haywood recorded several incidents which indicated disenchantment with Moyer predating the trial, but it is possible that they were convenient hindsights. At any rate, their personal relations worsened during their long imprisonment. The two did not speak with one another for long periods, disagreed violently on trial tactics, and were openly hostile by the time of Haywood's acquittal. When Big Bill returned to his cell to collect his personal effects after the verdict was returned Pettibone rose to congratulate him, "but Moyer did not rise from his seat although my acquittal had assured the probability of his. He only remarked laconically, 'That's good.'" Clarence

Darrow somewhat quizzically reported the same scene. "Haywood and Pettibone were happy and could not conceal their joy and did not try to," Darrow wrote. "Moyer was shaving. He said a word or two and kept on shaving. He was as calm and as cool as a glacier." [5]

Part of Moyer's aggravation derived from the fact that, as first to be tried, Haywood had garnered the major share of publicity, just as he had during the Cripple Creek Strike which Haywood directed while Moyer sat in jail. The excitement over the trial made Big Bill a *cause célèbre* while Moyer and Pettibone languished almost forgotten. But that, too, only partly explains the estrangement. Moyer also thought Haywood at fault in the disaster at Cripple Creek. While responsibility for the failure was hardly Haywood's alone, he had been the chief architect of strike policy. More important than the question of responsibility, however, the results of Cripple Creek led Moyer and his confidants to re-examine the policy militant aggressiveness which had characterized the strike, and they turned toward a more conciliatory unionism. The Steunenberg affair complicated the split over tactics. Whether Haywood alone was guilty, or all three were guilty, or none were, it was obvious that Haywood's outspoken revolutionism made the union more vulnerable to tactics like Idaho's.

The trial showed that the Mine Owners Association aimed to destroy the WFM on the question of violence and, rightly or wrongly, Haywood was their easiest target. He was the first of the three tried for that very reason. Moyer was badly shaken by the Steunenberg affair. The close brush with execution confirmed him and the Denver leadership in their opinion that future success called for retrenchment and a more cautious approach to industrial conflict. While Moyer was not yet in 1907 the conservative who would eventually lead the WFM back into the American Federation of Labor, he was already headed in that direction during his time in the Ada County Jail. Shortly after the affair was closed, Moyer said that "if to be conservative meant to stay out of prison, he was going to be conservative." Many of his associates in Denver were already considering some sort of alliance with the United Mine Workers which would necessitate jettisoning some of the WFMs radicalism. For this Haywood had no stomach.[6]

Events within the newly organized Industrial Workers of the World complicated the split. While Moyer and Haywood were awaiting trial, the IWW was suffering its first of several splits between "moderates" and "radicals." Through his representatives in Denver, Moyer aligned with the "moderate" faction behind president Charles O. Sherman. In his written messages to the 1906 convention of the WFM, Moyer roundly attacked Sherman's opponents, Daniel DeLeon and Vincent St. John. Haywood generally concurred in the criticism of DeLeon, but simultaneously took the more central position of conciliator (or, perhaps, fence-straddler). He wrote that his worst fear was a "useless and meaningless wrangle. . . . It must be prevented. Such policy is suicidal." And Haywood stopped short of attacking St. John. Vincent St. John was an organizer for the Western Federation who stood for the same sort of militance in the field that Haywood represented in Denver. St. John was Haywood's protegé in the same sense that Haywood had been Boyce's. Thus did the split within the IWW have repercussions in the WFM which speeded Haywood's passing from power.[7]

Neither Haywood nor Moyer's associates in Denver openly displayed their animosity when Haywood returned to the city after the trial. Haywood several times spoke to raise funds for Moyer's and Pettibone's defense, and traveled to Goldfield, Nevada, for the WFM in late 1907 in an effort to rally striking miners there. But he never returned to his desk after the trial, and his claim to a vacation after a year and a half in prison served only temporarily to mask the fact that he had been purged.[8]

Haywood's last official speech to the Western Federation was before the convention of 1908. He had just returned from New York and Chicago where large audiences greeted him wildly. He returned to Denver to visit his family and evaluate his status within the WFM. When he rose to deliver his address,

Moyer conspicuously left the hall. The delegates, wholeheartedly behind the union's president, were polite but unreceptive. Haywood knew what the chilliness meant. He had helped engineer a similar reception for representatives of the AFL at the 1900 convention when, by previous agreement, the miners returned the AFL's "fraternal greetings" with icy silence.[9]

Shortly after the incident, C. E. Mahoney, a vice-president of the Western Federation, visited Haywood in Chicago. Haywood had been traveling extensively and speaking to many radical groups. It was his tour—that is, his expenses and fees were paid by the various organizations that he addressed. Mahoney asked him amicably if he would write a notice for the *Miners Magazine* to the effect that he was not lecturing under the auspices of the WFM. Haywood conjectured that those among the union's leadership who were urging reaffiliation with the AFL "had probably gone over the reports of my speeches on the trip and had found that they were too revolutionary for their liking." He refused Mahoney, but to no avail. Shortly thereafter, effective April 8, 1908, the *Miners Magazine* announced that Haywood's capacity as "representative of the Western Federation of Miners in the field" was terminated. Haywood maintained his membership in the union and Denver as his address as late as 1913, long after he had ceased making frequent visits to Colorado. But he exercised no power in the union after 1906.[10] Years later, from the Soviet Union, Haywood sent his carefully retained WFM button to a friend in the United States.

Haywood enjoyed his physical prime in 1907. He was thirty-eight years of age and still close enough in time to the rigorous labor of the mines that his awesome bulk still meant strength and vitality. The months in prison had not hurt. In addition to the comfortable quarters, good diet, and opportunity for exercise, prison kept Haywood away from the liquor for which he had a periodic weakness. Haywood was never robust in the sense of freedom from illness, but his health was better in 1907 than it would ever be thereafter. He needed good health that year. His new-found status meant a hectic schedule of speech-making and public appearances. The crowd that welcomed him back to Denver was only the first. Almost at once he was off to the Midwest where he addressed huge crowds in Chicago and Milwaukee, and smaller groups at points between. Back in Denver only briefly, he swung through the mining regions to Goldfield, Nevada, and other mining camps. In January, 1908, Haywood took his first trip to New York, and then returned to Denver and the Far West.[11]

He visited Ed Boyce in Portland, Oregon, in 1908. Boyce's wife had inherited a large sum of money in 1900, and Boyce had become manager of a Portland Hotel after retiring from active leadership in the Federation. Haywood had a pleasant visit with his friend but it was not exactly like old times. "I looked at Boyce in his beautiful surroundings and thought of him as the petty manager of a hotel. It seemed to me that he had lost all the imagination he had ever had, that the contact with money had destroyed his vision. I knew him to have been an earnest revolutionist. But now in a few years he had become musty and was vegetating in his prosperity." [12]

Perhaps Haywood envied his old protector's financial security. Haywood never had more than an adequate income during the years immediately after the Idaho trial, or even later when he was the head of the Industrial Workers of the World. Money was his for the taking immediately after the trial but he actively rejected it. *McClure's Magazine* made a generous offer for an article while he was still under indictment. (Harry Orchard accepted a similar offer and drafted another version of his trial testimony.) Haywood turned it down and repeated his rejections to later solicitors. These included a contract from the Tuileries Garden of Denver for $7,000 for a week of lectures. A California promoter offered $15,000 for forty lectures, and the Star Circuit, a vaudeville booking agency, offered Haywood $4,000 a week for a two-month tour.

Haywood's rationale was simultaneously ideological and practical. While all were temptingly lucrative in the short run, they were, after all, proposals from "capitalist concerns." The price would gradually fall, Haywood told his uncomprehending wife, and with the price his prestige among the workers. Haywood always maintained that his acquittal owed little to abstract justice and only a little more to Clarence Darrow's eloquence. Rather, the acquittal was due to the solidarity of the working class behind him. In 1907, as later, he felt an obligation to carry his message to them in gratitude. He would not entertain vaudeville audiences.[13]

Like many revolutionaries, Haywood reserved his greatest scorn for radicals who, by his definition, "sold out." His disillusion with Boyce is a case in point; his later criticism of temporizing socialists like Victor Berger is another. This scorn was in part a personal compensation for impotence in changing the greater, inimical society. American radicals have, with few exceptions, been so effectively excluded from significant decision-making that, when their recourse has not been frustrated cynicism, it has been a cultist's conviction of rectitude which in turn breeds contempt for more accommodating (and successful) comrades.

Haywood, too, would modify his intransigence in later years when he began to exercise a genuine power within the larger society, but his rejection of the tempting offers of 1907 was sincerely based on his distaste for "selling out." He was a man of no mean talent, as he realized, who could have been successful in any one of many pursuits. But his low start in life and the vagaries of fortune had made him into a proletarian and a revolutionist. To exploit his "revolutionary" fame to make a fortune would be a cardinal sin. In a very real sense, Haywood elected to remain loyal to the revolutionary union movement in 1907 for the same reasons that employees of a company which has paid them a salary their entire lives feel a "loyalty to the firm."

If Haywood chose "the cause" in 1907, the cause was good to him in other than the financial sphere. His instant fame generated a momentum which provided Haywood with receptive audiences and a zealous personal following for over five years. He briefly entertained ideas of seeking the Socialist Party's presidential nomination in 1908, and campaigned widely on the "Red Special" when the party chose Eugene V. Debs. He lectured widely, crisscrossing the continent several times, and he took a minor part in the leadership of the Socialist Party's revolutionist wing in intra-party squabbles. The party's leftists seized anxiously on Haywood's support, and elected him a delegate to the International Socialist Congress at Copenhagen in 1910. In 1911 he was named to the party's General Executive Committee. Radical periodicals sought Haywood's writings; Charles H. Kerr eventually made him an editor of the *International Socialist Review*. And, increasingly, Haywood was the hero of the rank and file of the slowly emerging Industrial Workers of the World, who looked to him as their most famous partisan.

Haywood's eminence between 1907 and 1913 owed nothing to any official position; he held none. He was lionized because of his central role in the Steunenberg Trial; he had been the major figure in a rare radical victory. Haywood maintained and entrenched his personal fame, however, by virtue of his talents and presence as a public speaker. Haywood's speaking skills were effective only with mass audiences, however. He was generally unimpressive in small groups, whether the occasion were social, a radical seminar, or a committee meeting. There were exceptions to this; with preparation he could acquit himself satisfactorily. He was a good witness in his own defense in Idaho, although a reluctant one. (He did not wish to take the stand and only pressure from Darrow, Pettibone, and Moyer forced him to testify.) His story was consistent and credible, and he withstood a rigorous cross-examination. Haywood proudly related that prosecutor Borah had been impressed by his coolness under pressure. When he appeared before the Industrial Relations Commission in 1915, Haywood also testified effectively. Then, also, he was meticulously prepared. During the wartime sedition trials Haywood had brilliant moments, but weakened at times as well. Never enthusiastic about the IWW's opposition to the war, Haywood's failing health had been aggravated by a long imprisonment.[14]

On rare occasion Haywood was capable of the *bon mot*. He

was at his best during an exchange with Commissioner Harris Weinstock before the Industrial Relations Commission in 1915, "slipping a sizzler across" several times, as the friendly *New York Call* described it. In part Haywood sparkled due to the overly zealous Weinstock's blunders. The commissioner quoted two particularly offensive IWW slogans, which Haywood promptly identified as a chorus from the *Marseillaise* and an item derived from Abraham Lincoln.

Weinstock later criticized the IWW's recommendation that workers make inferior goods as a means of sabotage. Haywood responded: "that's a complaint we have against the capitalist system." He stated that he did not advise workers to sabotage by making inferior goods. They should sabotage by ignoring the employer's instructions to do so and thus cut his profits. To the laughter of the audience Weinstock weakly rejoined, "Well, we'll cut out that part about inferior goods." The *New York Call* commented that "Haywood had Weinstock fighting for wind." [15]

Haywood's best moment occurred when Weinstock asked him, "Let me see if I understand the distinction correctly between socialism and the I.W.W.'s. As I understand it, I.W.W.ism is socialism with this difference—" Haywood interrupted him: "—with its working clothes on." But it was not a spontaneous quip. Describing the Industrial Workers of the World as "socialism with its working clothes on" was indeed Haywood's own slogan but he had coined it earlier, not *ad lib* in response to Weinstock's question.[16]

Haywood was generally neither quick nor articulate in such circumstances. Outside a close circle of friends he was no glib conversationalist. Mabel Dodge recalled one of her "evenings" during the pre-World War I period when Big Bill was asked to explain the differences between anarchism, socialism, and the IWW idealogy of revolutionary industrial unionism. Haywood, who could and did explain the distinctions clearly in prepared speeches and on paper, "talked as though he were wading blindfold in sand." A sympathetic Walter Lippmann attempted to assist Haywood by playing interrogator. Lippmann asked several leading questions about the policies of the IWW. "Useless," Mabel Dodge wrote. "Bill's lid dropped over his blind eye and his heavy cheeks sagged lower." Andre Tridon, Haywood's good friend, related a similar story about a debate in which Haywood engaged. He was as powerless, Tridon wrote, "as the bull in a bullfight." Formally uneducated and uncomfortable with theory or abstractions, Haywood was insecure in situations such as debates which required facile thought and expression. He wrote very little in his autobiography about his Greenwich Village experiences between 1910 and 1919 although they marked the epitome of his eminence.[17]

Haywood spent much of his time in New York City during 1912 and 1913, especially when the IWW was waging strikes at nearby Paterson, New Jersey. In New York he was drawn compulsively to the Greenwich Village society that gathered in Mabel Dodge's salons at 23 Fifth Avenue. While he often chafed in the company and withdrew surlily into himself with a glass of red wine in his hand, or sometimes to Emma Goldman's apartment on the Lower East Side, Haywood was also fascinated by the sophistication with which he was completely unfamiliar until he was in his forties.[18]

The Village crowd was likewise fascinated with radicalism, and Haywood basked in the adulation. "Bill Haywood, like a large, soft, overripe Buddha with one eye and the smile of an Eminent Man, reclined in the yellow chaise lounge with two or three maidens at his feet," Mabel Dodge remembered. "They were young public schoolteachers who were circumspect and blameless from 9 to 4 every day but radical in the evening. The young admired Bill Haywood greatly. He was a hero." But the New Yorkers did not really like Haywood so much as they were fascinated by the presence of "the giant Arimaspian . . . pounding the seat of the brocaded sofa with his great fist." He was the fad of the moment, the hero of the radical labor movement. To the Greenwich Village literati he represented the western man of action, a Rousseauvian natural man. "Miners, garment-workers, and silk-weavers were the honoured guests in those days," remembered Carl Van Vechten, "The artists still came but the centre of interest had shifted." [19]

Mabel Dodge maintained her reputation by staffing her salons with individuals like Emma Goldman and Bill Haywood. She had them around in something of the same spirit that cocktail hostesses of the 1950's would "hire a beatnik" to mix with the guests. Haywood obliged for the liquor, company, and adulation, lending the salon "a new consecration . . . , reinforcing his points by crushing the heels of his huge boots into the Shirvan rug or digging his great hands into the mauve tapestry with which the divan was upholstered." The evening was complete when Haywood regaled the guests with a statement on "violence," although Anarchists like Hippolyte Havel, who passed the evening muttering "goddamned bourgeois," were more exciting.

> Violence, yes, we advocate violence of the most violent sort, violence that consists in keeping your mouth shut and your hands in your pockets. Don't fold your arms, I say to the men, but keep your hands in your pockets to keep hired thugs and detectives from putting bombs there. In doing this and staying on strike you are comitting the most violent acts in the world, for you are stopping industry and keeping it stopped until the millowners grant your demands, an eight-hour day, two looms to a worker, and higher wages.[20]

Sometimes Haywood played his part too well. At one gathering he chided a group of artists for thinking of themselves as an elite. Someday, he told them, there would be a proletarian art. In the new society everyone would be an artist because everyone would have the time to be an artist. That was going too far, natural man or no.[21]

It was a revealing statement. Hutchins Hapgood and Lincoln Steffens felt that Bill Haywood never made "a convincing and impassionate speech against capitalism" after he mixed in Mabel Dodge's circle. Mabel Dodge herself wrote that Haywood "hated capitalists until he knew them. When he knew us he couldn't hate us very much." Haywood, of course, continued to deliver quite passionate anti-capitalist speeches after Greenwich Village, and he never ceased to be a Socialist. But it is true that he was intrigued by the erudition of the intellectuals of New York and was drawn to them. He returned time and again to Greenwich Village when in the East, and enjoyed counterpointing his busy days of agitation with the easy social life of the Village crowd. He remained convinced, however, that only time and education separated him and the workers in general from what he regarded as "art." [22]

There was another aspect to Haywood's association with the "parlor socialists"—the financial support which they could provide him and his generally penurious causes. The Industrial Workers of the World shunned large strike funds as gates to conservatism, but the union was often embroiled in large strikes with taxing financial demands. In the years immediately preceding World War I, wealthy, middle-class radicals were a dependable source of support. Thus, along with an organization of Quaker women from Philadelphia, it was the Greenwich Village group which supported the dramatic "children's exodus" from Lawrence, Massachusetts, in 1912. The same small group of patrons mustered the monies and publicity necessary to stage the Paterson Pageant in Madison Square Garden in 1913. Mabel Dodge's friends provided the financial support, and her companion of the moment, John Reed, organized the artistic and technical assistance required. Haywood also drew personally on the goodwill. Taken seriously ill during his arduous year of 1913, he made a recuperative journey to Europe financed by an unnamed "friend." [23]

If Haywood did not quite go "soft" on capitalism as a result of his New York experiences, he did come closest to being an Establishment figure through his acquaintances there. John Collier of the People's Institute, who was a confidant of Frank Walsh of the Industrial Relations Commission, wrote to Mabel Dodge that "the Commission exists because of the revolutionary movement. It was directly occasioned by the Paterson and Little Falls strikes and the Homestead War." Walsh, Collier continued, wanted to "go the limit" with the commission but was handicapped by the conservatism of the representatives of labor and business. The actual situation invited dramatic hearings and fundamental statement, and Walsh wants this kind of thing and wants help in getting it." Collier then suggested that the "revolutionaries" work together and plan their testimony in advance. "And let me say," he concluded, "that it is Chairman Walsh himself who suggested the arrangement, and he has repeated the suggestion urgently." [24]

Mabel Dodge was unsure of her credentials for organizing such a project and sent Collier's letter to some thirty friends including Haywood, Lincoln Steffens, Max Eastman, William English Walling, George Creel, Hutchins Hapgood, Walter Lippmann, Clarence Darrow, Emma Goldman, Frances Perkins, and Alexander Berkman. The seemingly disparate group met and arranged that they, or others selected by them, would present carefully prepared testimony to the commission. Haywood was assigned along with William E. B. DuBois and Paul Kennaday to speak on discrimination against Negroes, foreigners, and women. ("Call as witnesses, Gompers, Mitchell, etc., Refugees Defense League, Liberal Immigration League," the minutes noted.) Haywood also signed up for "Unemployment and the Disemployed." [25]

Thus, several discreet steps removed, Haywood found himself a collaborator with a progressive agent of the federal government in exposing what both saw as glaring abuses in American industrial society. It was not a proper position for a revolutionist of Haywood's alleged extremism but, as his testimony showed, Haywood was quite willing to win gains for the working classes through even the most conventional means at his disposal. As events developed, Haywood spoke on neither "Unemployment," as was originally planned, nor "Socialism and Unionism," as was later suggested. He was ill during mid-1914 when the Commission investigated these matters, and Joseph Ettor spoke in Haywood's place. When he finally appeared on May 12 and 13, 1915, the commission had passed on to "Labor and the Law"—not exactly Haywood's forte and originally assigned by the revolutionary" cabal to George Creel. There was no problem, however. It was Big Bill Haywood in whom the commissioners were interested, not his expertise in legal minutiae.

The commission convened as usual at 10:00 A.M. on May 12. Walsh, Harris Weinstock of the employer's panel, and two conservative unionists of the labor panel heard a professor of political economy from Columbia University until midafternoon. Then Haywood took the stand. He was the fifth Wobbly leader to appear before the commission; others had testified regarding specific incidents, like Adolph Lessig who spoke on the Paterson strike. Vincent St. John had spoken a year before on May 21, 1914, and caused a mild sensation with his nonchalance about violence. His statements had been pounced upon (and somewhat distorted) by the press, and Joseph Ettor, speaking for Haywood the next day, had attempted to soften the impression left by St. John. One commissioner mentioned that she had asked St. John if he advocated violence and that he had replied "yes" without qualification. Ettor interrupted her: "I openly disagree with you. I know he did qualify it."

"In what way," Chairman Walsh asked.

Ettor: "He qualified it by saying that he did not believe in violence as a method in itself."

"Did you hear that?" Mrs. Harriman rejoined.

"Of course I did. I know his position," Ettor snapped.[26]

George Speed, an important Wobbly organizer in the West, had also testified before the commission when it sat in San Francisco. His testimony was chiefly concerned with a discussion of the problems of seasonal labor, IWW organization work among transient workers, AFL impotence in dealing with seasonal labor, and a discussion of "Jap," "Hindu," and "Chink" labor on the West Coast. James P. Thompson appeared before the commission during the same month in his home town of Seattle. Thompson compared the IWW with the AFL, outlined why the Wobblies regarded industrial unionism as a necessity, attacked parliamentary socialism ("they devote their energies chiefly to the patching up of capitalism"), and discussed sabotage.[27]

With the exception of St. John, who testified at some length, the Wobblies had been given little time before the commission. In the Commissioners' minds, as in the public's, Haywood was *the* Wobbly leader. Before them at last, he began by telling briefly of his early life, how he went into the mines first at the age of nine, and permanently at fifteen. He spoke of his wanderings and finally of settling at Silver City. Next Haywood described briefly the founding of the Western Federation and listed its major strikes: Leadville, Telluride, Cripple Creek. Then he described several IWW strikes at McKee's Rocks, Lawrence, Little Falls, and Wheatland. All of these incidents, Haywood emphasized, portrayed "a condition that this commission should understand, and that there is a class struggle in society with workers on one side of the struggle and the capitalists on the other; that the workers have nothing but their labor power and the capitalists have the control and the influence of all branches of government . . . , that they have on their side of the question all of the forces of law." [28]

The emphasis of conflict which Haywood, the other Wobblies, and some socialists presented to the commission was an issue to which the commissioners paid close attention. The Industrial Relations Commission was designed as much to give the impression that there was no essential conflict in American industrial society as it was to suggest means of alleviating it. Most of the commissioners, including the conservative labor panel, hammered home the point time and again that employer and employee had essentially identical interests, and that with ameliorative progressive legislation the eruptions which marked the era could be eliminated. The commissioners took special pains to rebut witnesses who disagreed.

First they questioned Haywood about his views on political action. Personally, Haywood replied, he did not think the workers' lot could be improved by political means. Wage earners, the producing class, were a minority in the United States and, just as important, the workers were not educated in politics. "Their life is altogether industrial," Haywood stated. It was in the industrial arena that their fate would be decided. Commissioner O'Connell of the labor panel broke in and asked Haywood how the workers' lot could be improved if political action was inadequate. By direct action, Haywood replied. Consider the United Mine Workers, he told O'Connell, a conservative leader of the UMW: they have about half of the coal miners organized, enough virtually to control the industry. The UMW could easily ignore politics and say to the owners, "You must put these mines in order, in proper shape, or we won't work in them." The UMW could "compel" the installation of proper safety devices, reduction of hours, better working and living conditions, merely by refusing to work if their demands were not met. They could likewise compel the owners to relinquish their ownership, Haywood added.[29]

Despite O'Connell's and railwayman Austin Garretson's conservatism, Haywood was more congenial with them than he was with his principal interrogator, Harris Weinstock, a progressive California merchant. He repeatedly cited examples to the two unionists from their own experiences. With O'Connell he brought up the UMW; with Garretson Haywood spoke of the railroads. His approach with them suggested the manner of a proselytizer, while with Weinstock Haywood remained courteous but combative. Weinstock dominated the interrogation of Haywood. English-Jewish in background, Weinstock was also formally uneducated, but like Haywood, had read extensively and published various articles on labor relations. In Sacramento, Weinstock's home, he was a partner in a large department store and had large real estate holdings. Weinstock was a progressive through and through. He campaigned tirelessly against the graft-ridden politicos of San Francisco, and supported both Hiram Johnson and Theodore Roosevelt. He had written a comprehensive report on the IWW free-speech fight at San Diego in 1914, and was widely recognized as an authority on the Wobblies.[30]

At first Weinstock discussed the question of the number of

laborers in the United States. Did they not comprise a number sufficiently large, the commissioner asked, that they held the political balance of power, like the Irish delegates in the British Parliament a generation before? Haywood conceded that they did. Then, Weinstock continued, with such progressive measures as the initiative, referendum, and recall, could not the workers secure their goals through political action? Haywood said he could not recall where the political reforms had brought any tangible benefits to the working class. Unemployment in Portland, Oregon, remained unspeakably high despite the state's pioneering progressive measures. The exchange was fruitless; the two men spoke in different terms.[31]

Weinstock recognized the impasse and moved to another topic: what were the IWW's policies? Vincent St. John had already taken these up a year before but, despite its policy against duplicate testimony, the commission thought Haywood a more likely expositor. The commission might find itself in a position to recommend that Congress encourage IWW organization, Weinstock hypothesized. "I think that would militate against the IWW's if you did such a thing," Haywood retorted, "It seems to me a recommendation like that, coming from you gentlemen, would militate against the organization and have a tendency to dilute it and dilute its revolutionary strength." [32]

Weinstock then turned to a stack of IWW pamphlets which had been given to the commission by St. John and read a line or two from each. He quoted St. John on expediency as the rule for selecting methods, and a militant verse from the *Marseillaise* which appeared in the IWW's "Little Red Songbook." From Arnold Roller's pamphlet, "The Social General Strike," Weinstock quoted a paragraph advocating a "help yourself" program for the workers when the proper moment had come. From William E. Trautmann's "Industrial Union Methods" the commissioner extracted statements disavowing signed agreements, advocating sabotage in the sense of producing inferior goods, and stating that there was no such thing as an "inviolable agreement with employers." A paragraph from

Haywood's "The General Strike" told of the day when the workers would own the factories, and one from a pamphlet by William Thurston Brown provided a nondescript stock revolutionary slogan. Are these representative of IWW ideas, Weinstock asked.[33]

Haywood replied that they were, but pointed out that some of the pamphlets were not by IWW members. He singled out the verse from the *Marseillaise,* and compared Roller's advocacy of "help yourself" to a statement by Lincoln during the Civil War, when Lincoln said that if food prices became too high in New York City working people should take their pickaxes and raid speculators' warehouses. "I think that is good I.W.W. doctrine," Haywood underscored the Lincoln quote. "I do not see much there I would take issue with." [34]

Weinstock then read his own summary of IWW teachings as he understood them from the quoted passages. Any and all tactics were accepted; "the question of right and wrong was not to be considered"; the "avenging sword is to be unsheathed, with all hearts resolved on victory or death"; the workers were to help themselves when the time came; no inviolable contracts; inferior goods were to be produced "by a silent understanding" of the workers; they should look forward to the revolution and prepare for it; and strikers were "to disobey and treat with contempt all judicial injunction." Would the American people stand for this? Weinstock was incredulous. Haywood took issue with Weinstock's definition of sabotage and Weinstock's list. "I look forward to a day with no child labor, full employment for men, the equality of women, and an age of security so that old people could at least live in peace." Weinstock murmured that he thought all present were agreed that those were admirable goals.[35]

The inquisitor took up each of his points. Did Haywood regard "any tactics" acceptable? He did, Haywood replied, and began to elaborate when Weinstock interrupted him. Did Haywood think there was no right or wrong in industrial relations? Haywood was equivocal: "What is right and wrong? What I think is right in my mind or what you think is right in your mind?" Weinstock moved on: What about "the avenging sword"? "What that means is a general strike," Haywood replied. What about driving employers out of their factories? "I would drive them in instead of out. . . . I would make an arrangement to take every owner on the inside and give him a job alongside of me. . . . Well, I have been plastered up with injunctions until I do not need a suit of clothes," Haywood answered, "and have treated them with contempt. . . . I do not believe in that kind of law at all. I think that it is a usurpation on the part of the courts of a function that was never vested in the courts by the Constitution."[36]

Weinstock and Haywood began to discuss the rights of property, but the exchange bogged down like their discussion of the laborer's political power. On questions on which the two were so diametrically opposed, coherent communication was impossible. Inasmuch as the interrogation was a debate, Haywood came out better on the question of property, just as Weinstock had scored points on political action. The commissioner insisted on equating property in a watch or suitcoat with John D. Rockefeller's coal interests in Colorado, a specious device, and Haywood had little trouble in winning the point.[37]

Haywood then compared the AFL with the IWW, emphasizing the AFL's time contracts and their craft structure. As always, he placed great emphasis on the "One Big Union" aspect of the IWW. "Granting an organization so colossal in its character would have great power for good," Weinstock asked, "would it not have great power for ill?" "Yes, it would have great power for ill—that is, it would be ill for the capitalists," Haywood replied, "Every one of them would have to go to work."[38]

From there the discussion disintegrated further. Weinstock's questions on the organization of the "new society" were pointed and Haywood's answers vague and stumbling. Would there not have to be bosses in the new factories? Haywood replied that these would not be bosses in the usual sense; decisions would be made democratically. What about regulations? These would be strictly a matter of common sense. The fact was that Haywood, no articulate utopian, had only the vaguest idea of his new society. He was a revolutionary in the sense that he wanted a fundamental change. But, like many revolutionaries, he had only half an idea of what would follow; he drifted off into unrealistic ramblings. Weinstock maneuvered Haywood into some specific prognostications and Haywood made his most ludicrous statements. Communities would be about 50,000 to 60,000 in population, Haywood said. There would be no great cities for there would be "no lawyers or preachers or stockholders" such as those who built New York. Weinstock asked what could be done with New York. "Tear it down, or leave it as a monument to the foolishness of the present day," Haywood replied.[39]

When Haywood realized he was being successfully baited, he cut short the topic by saying that specific measures would be settled as they came about. He should have said it earlier. He was, most of the time, a realist who confronted specific situations as they happened and left blueprints alone. His weakness toward dreams and designs was by no means completely out of character, but he generally recognized the fantasy in them. Weinstock discovered Haywood's romantic streak and turned it to his own advantage.

Doubtless Haywood's errors were pointed out to him that evening, for the next morning he did not allow himself to be diverted to reverie and came prepared to offer an antidote to Weinstock's distorted description of IWW policy. Weinstock examined Haywood again but then turned over the floor to the labor panel and Mrs. Borden Harriman, representing "the public." She brought up her pet topic of violence. Did Haywood believe in using it? "Yes," Haywood replied, "but I don't want it to be taken for granted without giving me an opportunity to explain what violence means. I think you will agree that there is nothing more violent that you can do to the capitalist than to drain his pocketbook. In that sort of violence I believe, and we are trying to make it impossible for the growth of more capitalists, and to make useful citizens of the existing capitalists." [40]

As an example of what he meant by violence Haywood described the free-speech fight which the Wobblies had directed at Sioux City, Iowa, in April, 1915. There the IWW's had refused to cooperate with the police, would not work on the rock pile once arrested, and, according to IWW custom, flooded the town and its jails with reinforcements. Haywood was describing nonviolent civil disobedience. "That I regard as action more violent than the discharge of bombs in St. Patrick's Cathedral in New York, because they enforced the rights that this country gave to them; they compelled the authorities who are supposed to uphold these rights in seeing that they were granted. I believe in that kind of violence, and as I said yesterday, when the workers are organized, it matters not to me what becomes necessary, if they are to get control of the means of life." After a few incidental exhanges, Haywood asked and Walsh agreed that the preamble of the IWW constitution be read into the record "in view of the attempt on the part of Commissioner Weinstock yesterday to create an erroneous impression relative to the methods and aims of the I.W.W."[41]

What was accomplished by Haywood's appearance? Ironically, a great deal, from the widely disparate points of view of the several parties involved. Chairman Walsh, who had wanted to "go the limit," did not quite do it with Haywood, but he had wanted the revolutionist position presented to the nation and Haywood served the conservative purpose by virtue of his personal infamy. From the point of view of most of the rest of the commission, Haywood was a nearly ideal witness. The business and labor panels, and Mrs. Harriman and professor John Rogers Commons of the "public" panel, were all members of the National Civic Federation, and approached their task with two goals in mind. First, they were militantly anti-socialist. They saw socialism as a genuine threat to an essentially sound system which should be preserved. But, while they sought to avert socialism, they were almost as interested in defeating or converting to the progessivism the stand-pat, anti-union conservatives such as those gathered about the National Association of Manufacturers.

The National Civic Federation was in many ways a lineal ancestor of the New Deal inasmuch as it sought to preserve the social structure by, among other innovations, recognizing and dealing with pro-capitalist unions like the AFL and granting them concessions which would insure their conservatism and cooperation. Haywood presented an "alternative" which they could point out to hard-line anti-union employers as the result if they did not soon come to terms with more congenial unionists. It is moot to suggest that the IWW and the Socialist Party were never a serious threat to American capitalism. Many Americans, including both Wobblies and industrial reactionaries, believed at the time that they were. Thus, Haywood, the more fire-eating the better, was a perfect "exhibit." The testimony of moderate socialists like Victor Berger and Morris Hillquit would not quite do; they sounded like progressives, which was the last thing the progressive commissioners wanted. When even Haywood began to sound too "reasonable," his testimony was cut off.

For Haywood, the opportunity to testify before the IRC meant publicity. He saw the wide newspaper coverage of the hearings as beneficial to the union's development. Moreover, the occasion presented another opportunity to pose as the eminent man. If he was not necessarily less radical by 1915, Haywood had mellowed. He lacked much of the erratic bitterness which characterized earlier years, and had taken the position of secretary-treasurer with the IWW in part because it promised an easier life.

He might have hoped that testifying before the IRC would present to the nation a more genuine picture of the IWW than it was accustomed to seeing. When the commission was first established in 1913, Haywood had said it was "a tragic joke." Before the commission he had made it clear that "in spite of anything that this commission can do or anything that you may recommend to Congress, the class struggle will go on." But his final words took the form of rather "New Dealish" recommendations. Haywood did not think that the commission could accomplish any real gains any more than he thought Socialist legislators could effect the revolution. But he was still as much a unionist as anything and willing to explore any open avenue toward improving the lot of the working class.[42]

What Haywood symbolized maintained his position in New York City, but in other small groups where his radicalism could not speak for itself, Haywood was personally ineffective. Despite his preparation for the IRC hearings Haywood was nervous, and spoke so softly that Chairman Frank Walsh several times had to ask him to pitch his voice higher. He was frequently inaudible at the Sedition Trial during World War I. In 1910, at the International Socialist Conference at Copenhagen, Haywood was utterly ineffective. He served without distinction on the labor commission and delivered an indifferent speech criticizing the American Federation of Labor. At one point he had an altercation with Victor Berger. He also met several prominent European Socialists, including "Red" Rosa Luxembourg and Georg Ledebour. He made no impression. Ramsay MacDonald was one of the few who later remembered him, and then not favorably. "He is useless on committee," MacDonald wrote, "I saw him at Copenhagen, amidst the leaders of the working class movements drawn from the whole world, and there he was dumb and unnoticed." [43]

But MacDonald also knew Haywood's strengths. "He is a torch amongst a crowd of uncritical, credulous workmen. . . . I saw him addressing a crowd in England and there his crude appeals moved his listeners to wild applause. He made them see things, and their hearts bounded to be up and doing." Mabel Dodge conceded the same point, describing Haywood as "so impassioned a speaker out in the rain before a thousand strikers." Haywood's recollections of his trip to Europe in 1910, dour and fidgety in recounting the conference, come alive when he leaves the committee room for the speakers' platform. He spoke several times in Copenhagen, to miners at Malmo and Stockholm in Sweden, and before textile workers at Christiania (Oslo), Norway. Before his return to the United States he spoke in London and Glasgow, to the striking miners in South Wales, and at Liverpool and Manchester. Again in 1913, when Haywood "vacationed" in France, England, and Ireland, it was the meetings and rallies that he remembered best. He spoke on behalf of the Irish labor leader and sometime Wobbly, Jim Larkin, in London, Dublin, and Belfast.[44]

In an age of great orators, Haywood's element was on the platform. W. J. Ghent later described him as "a forceful but by no means eloquent speaker." It depends on the definition of eloquence. Haywood was not an emotional or flamboyant speaker. He could not rival William Jennings Bryan or Eugene V. Debs in the spread-eagle style of oratory so popular at the time. He was not dramatic. "The platform from which he speaks never becomes a stage," one listener wrote, "and when he speaks from a stage, that stage becomes a platform." [45]

He missed or deliberately avoided "splendid opportunities for trashy melodrama." At Paterson during the 1913 strike a child was injured when the police cleared a street of picketers. The boy's mother was clubbed and, when a bystander attempted to help her to her feet, he was knocked down by a policeman. It was an incident with which many speakers would stir a crowd of strikers to hysteria. Haywood "recited the facts, bare, unimbellished, without comment, without tremolo." Speakers must not arouse their listeners to disastrous action. In 1914 he urged the anarchist Alexander Berkman to desist from staging a public funeral for three anarchists who killed themselves in an attempt to assassinate John D. Rockefeller. The funeral, Haywood told him, was "sure to cause another eleventh of November." [46]

The keys to Haywood's success as a speaker were simplicity and force. His style was ultimately sincere and lacking in affectation, for simplicity and force characterized Haywood himself. Hutchins Hapgood, who knew Haywood well during the second decade of the century, was struck "by the real marriage there is between Haywood's feeling and his active life. His is not a complex or split-up personality. His thought and action go together." This shrewd observation accounts not only for Haywood's discomfort among the easy erudition of Greenwich Village but also for his success as a labor orator. There was nothing hypnotic or grandiose in his monosyllabic vocabulary. His words were those of a partially educated union leader. He was no demagogue for the simple reason that his own stoicism, developed from years of personal hardship, did not lend itself to emotional rabble-rousing. The facts were there; one only had to know them in order to act. "See how he talks," an acquaintance wrote, "no rage, no emotion, a simple explanation of the humanities." [47]

Nor were his speeches profound or analytic. Haywood's repertory consisted of only a few speeches which he repeated with minor variations. To European audiences and on lecture tours Haywood narrated his experiences in the West and the history of the Western Federation of Miners, drawing from them a few rudimentary lessons such as the need to organize the unskilled, the obsolescence of craft unions, and so on. It was Ed Boyce's speech, appended but essentially unchanged. The first thirteen chapters of his autobiography were an expanded version of this standard speech.

To socialists and conventions he delivered a more or less standard exposition of his "ideology" of revolutionary industrial unionism and the necessity for it. To strikers the speech was a simple, direct manifesto calling for solidarity, militant action, and the necessity of not provoking the adversary to violence. The proportion of emphasis on each element varied according to the situation at hand. There were plenty of stock slogans, but Haywood relied on them less than most revolutionaries.

This simplicity of style, the charismatic presence of his physical stature, and Haywood's manifest sincerity made him one of the most effective labor agitators of modern times. Several observers noted incredulously that Haywood seemed possessed with the gift of tongues: he could communicate with a crowd of immigrant strikers even when a large majority of whom could understand no English. According to one writer, Haywood could make himself understood by a crowd that did not know a word he said, merely by waving his arms and shouting."

In fact, it had little to do with shouting and arm-waving and nothing to do with linguistic talents. (Haywood found even the fundamentals of Russian grammar difficult even after living in the Soviet Union for several years.) His success in communicating to immigrant workers was based on an ingenious feature more in keeping with his character. He was distrustful of interpreters, and passed on his secret to Elizabeth Gurley Flynn. He advised her to speak to immigrants as one would speak to children. The key was in speaking in short, clipped sentence fragments, and in using only the simplest words. The arm-waving was not designed to excite but to interpret his words. Thus, Haywood would extend five fingers and say, "A.F. of L." and then, after a brief pause, he would extend his fist and say, "I.W.W.: One Big Union of All the Workers."

Haywood knew how to speak to children. He often fled to their company in order to relax during trying strikes, regaling them with true and imagined stories about the Wild West. Children were fascinated by his great stature and often followed him about when he walked the streets of a strike-torn city. Haywood had a use for the children and young people as well. He found that they could be used as a common denominator by which to unify mutually hostile ethnic groups. Once, at a strike meeting, Haywood called for representatives of the twenty-five national groups participating to come to the platform and say a few words in their native tongues. Some rushed self-consciously to the front and shouted out stock slogans. Haywood encouraged them so as to give heart to the others. Some of the adults launched into a lecture and Haywood tactfully checked their speeches at a decent length. Some stuttered, and Haywood, with the help of an interpreter, repeated their words for the benefit of the last rows in the audience. Some were ridiculous, and the audience hooted and laughed. Haywood reminded the audience that "the hardest workers are not the best talkers."

The incident which most touched the observer of the remarkable meeting occurred when the Italian delegate, an adolescent girl, almost ran from the stage in a fit of fright. "Haywood, with the attitude of a father to his young daughter or of a courtier to a princess, came to her, took her hand and with a bow presented her to the audience. And the girl, feeling safe under the protection of the tall Cyclops, found something to say and the voice to say it." Thus was a potentially divisive situation averted. The IWW's strikes were often fought by a confusing melange of ethnic groups whose mutual relations were precarious at best. Just as abuse of the strikers' children by another ethnic group was most likely to split the tenuous alliances the IWW forged, common sympathies for children bound them closer together. Haywood, the amateur but shrewd psychologist, recognized the point and made the most of it.[48]

Haywood's relations with his own family were not so well resolved. During the same years that he impressed observers as "fatherly" with the children of strikers, Haywood was virtually estranged from his own family. His last close contact with his wife, Nevada Jane, and his daughters, Vernie and Henrietta, was during and immediately after the Idaho trial. Clarence Darrow, ever the legal tactician, suggested that he play the solid family man during the trial. Haywood's wife, daughters, and aged mother all traveled to Boise for the trial and Haywood passed the long days in court, notably the day when Darrow excoriated Orchard for deserting his own daughter, with either Vernie or Henrietta perched on his knee. In fact, Haywood and his family had already begun to drift apart.

The estrangement dated from late 1903 when Nevada Jane turned to religion for relief from her physical anguish. She suffered all her life from an arthritic affliction of the joints which caused her intense pain. Sporadic during the early years of her marriage, Nevada Jane's misery was aggravated by her second pregnancy, and by 1903 her suffering was almost constant. For his part, Haywood was always solicitous and tried every remedy available. He balked, however, when Nevada Jane turned to religion.

Indifferent to religion since his boyhood, Haywood had become anti-religious as he discovered that the churches generally stood in opposition to his unionism and radicalism. In 1903 his wife was converted to Christian Science. As Haywood reported it, one "charlatan" after another treated Nevada Jane "at so much per treatment." He regarded Christian Science as "the vagaries of a fanatical and ignorant old woman," Mary Baker Eddy. But, he protested, if the treatments provided his wife any solace, he was willing to tolerate them. It was the influence on his daughters he claimed most to resent.

Haywood hinted that "the thought of the superstition that was fastening my family in its meshes" drove him to heavy drinking. To be exact, he required no supernatural intervention to guide his steps to the saloon. Growing to manhood in isolated mines where liquor was one of the rare recreations, Big Bill was early a heavy drinker. He remained so except when imprisoned, during a few spells "on the wagon," and toward the end of his life when diabetes precluded indulgence. If domestic troubles encouraged him to drink and gamble in 1903 and 1904, however, the carousing likewise alienated his religious wife.

Haywood and his wife were never particularly close after the first years of their marriage when Haywood worked at the Hoppin Ranch and homesteaded at Fort McDermitt. Their conflicting ideas on drinking, gambling, and religion played a part. In addition, Haywood was possessed of demonic energy and Nevada Jane was an invalid. He chafed at working as a miner in Silver City. When the Western Federation came into town he threw himself wholeheartedly into union work and was home very little. He spent his days in the mines, evenings with the ledgers at the union office, and nights in the saloons. His sixteen-hour workdays continued after the family moved to WFM headquarters in Denver and, as secretary-treasurer, Haywood traveled a great deal. Family living was completely disrupted for eighteen months when Haywood was imprisoned for Steunenberg's murder, and he never resumed any sort of home life after acquittal. Haywood was off almost at once on the first of his interminable lecture tours and trips to Europe. He came increasingly to spend his time in Chicago and New York, while his family remained in Denver. Visits home became shorter and less frequent. When Haywood threw in his lot with the Industrial Workers of the World he divided his time between Chicago, New York, and the scene of the Wobblies' current strike.

Haywood's total immersion in work for unionism and socialism was partly an escape from an unhappy home life. Whatever the causes, however, his career in turn aggravated his estrangement from his wife. She did not share his radicalism and could not comprehend his rejection of a lucrative speaking career after the Idaho trial. Haywood's close friend of his Wobbly days, Ralph Chaplin, paid a courtesy call on Nevada Jane Haywood in Denver in later years. "I once thought the world of that man," she told Chaplin, "but nothing meant as much to him as the labor movement. For it, he gave up his God, his country, his wife and two children—everything!" [49]

Despite the physical and personal estrangement from his family, Haywood always provided materially for his wife until her death in 1920. Betraying a sentimentality out of character with his public gruffness, Haywood remained fond of his children despite his infrequent visits to them. His watch-chain was braided from their red hair. And he remained properly deferential to his family's sensibilities to the end. Traveling about the hard-metal mining towns with their contingents of saloons and whorehouses, Haywood shared in the mores of time and place. During his New York City period, at least, Haywood had several liaisons of a less ephemeral nature. Emma Goldman mentioned Haywood with a coy reference to his "many lady loves," although the implication that Big Bill was a lothario might have been overdrawn.

Haywood scrupulously and successfully avoided personal scandal at a time when he had many mortal enemies who would have wished for and capitalized on one. Only his close friends were aware of his personal affairs and Haywood omitted all mention of them in his autobiography. It is interesting that he should have been so circumspect in the matter, for he consistently maintained his unconcern for conventional morality with reference to friends who publicly flaunted it. He defended Maxim Gorky, who was hounded out of New York City and the United States in 1906 when newspapers discovered that his traveling companion was not his legal wife. And Haywood never looked askance at the personal relations of his friends—Emma Goldman and Alexander Berkman, John Reed and Louise Bryant, and Elizabeth Gurley Flynn and Carlo Tresca. Personally, however, he remained primly circumspect in public. He had a Victorian streak which he never lost; in the Soviet Union Haywood lived with a Russian woman with whom, in the fashion of a nineteenth-century novel, he regularized his relationship by marriage in the last month of his life.[50]

Like his speeches, Haywood's writings were characterized by simplicity of style and lack of either profundity or subtlety. He wrote in clear, straightforward terms, and extremely well for a man with only a few years of formal schooling. W. J. Ghent, a sometimes friend during the 1910's, described him as an "industrious writer," and his published works show signs of the labor. This held true whether his writing was polemical, narrative, or expository. Haywood preferred to avoid ideological disputes, both because he disliked disputation within the radical movement and because he had little interest in ideological hairsplitting.

On the few occasions when he was drawn into factional battles he vacillated between name-calling and conciliatory persuasion. With moderate Socialists such as Morris Hillquit and Victor Berger, Haywood was often scornful and summoned all the epithets in his repertory. At other times, such as in his dispute with British Syndicalist Tom Mann in 1914, Haywood was capable of cool, reasoned arguments without rancor, name-calling, or snideness. Big Bill's approach depended on his evaluation of the possibilities of future accord with his disputants. As long as he saw an opportunity for cooperation with the moderate Socialists, he was temperate in tone. Only when they made it clear that they inalterably opposed Haywood's brand of socialism and he sensed irreconcilability did he resort to name-calling in reply. With Mann he always hoped to see a rapprochement and never passed beyond courteous demurrer.[51]

Haywood was not cut out to be a factionalist. Although he read widely in history, novels, and social analysis, Haywood's radicalism was grounded in action. His thought illustrates no debt to Marx, Proudhon, Sorel, or any other revolutionary luminary. He never really understood the intricacies of the radical dogfights which raged so hotly during his lifetime. Haywood believed there were obvious injustices which required a remedy, and that all those who saw these injustices should pull together in curing them. He devoted his writings not to purifying the "brethren" but to converting the "heathen." His publications were based on his conception of himself as an organizer; he sought to win the workers to the revolutionary cause.

No detached intellectual, Haywood-the-writer was a pamphleteer and coiner of mottoes. He had learned to write first as a member of the Western Federation's executive committee and then as the union's secretary-treasurer. The latter position required him to contribute regularly to the *Miners Magazine,* and he even edited the journal for a short time. His contributions consisted of reports on union activities (he was a competent if unobjectional journalist), and standard calls for action, solidarity, and militance. Effectively out of the WFM after the Idaho trial, Haywood began to write for several radical journals, most notably the *International Socialist Review.*

The *Review* was published by Charles H. Kerr in Chicago, who was the owner of a small but profitable press specializing in translations of European socialist writers. Founded along with the Socialist Party of America at the turn of the century, the *Review* evolved into a serious (and turgid) scholarly journal under the editorship of Algie M. Simons, a prominent member of the SPA's moderate wing. While Simons drifted to the right, however, Publisher Kerr was smitten by the revolutionist wing of the party and he fired Simons. The new editors, Mary and Leslie Marcy, not only brought the journal a more radical bent but recast it in a slick format with abundant photography, and they eliminated the long scholarly disquisitions in favor of shorter, more topical articles. The *Review* lost its high tone and became a missionary magazine. With the change, Haywood found a congenial outlet for his writings.[52]

The new staff soon named him contributing editor. His articles were of several types, but journalistic accounts of labor disturbances and exhortatory messages dominated. His exhortations consisted of diatribes against the enemies of labor, which compensated in their shrill tone for Haywood's circumspection when writing of other radicals. In "A Detective," Haywood described his subject as "the lowest, meanest, most contemptible thing that either creeps or crawls, a thing to loath and despise." [53]

If no more edifying, his collections of aphorisms, or "Shots for the Workshop" as they were usually called, are more illuminating about Haywood himself. He coined several dozen of them over his years with the *Review:*

The manager's brains are under the workman's cap.
Twelve hours is a bad habit. Get the Eight Hour Habit. Get it Now.
To the Working Class there is no foreigner but the capitalist.
A shorter day means bigger pay.

And so on. It was not the sort of thing on which to build a writing career, but it was Haywood's way of spreading the gospel of socialism to the workers in simple, easily remembered terms. His aphorisms conformed nicely with Haywood's own method of learning through simplification, and illustrate his conviction that the job to be done was organization. The "Shots" were the work of an advertising man.[54]

A novelist who knew Haywood wrote that "he spurns eloquence and soapbox platitudes. He never gibbers about the brotherhood of man, the socialist commonwealth rising upon the ruins of the capitalist system, death to the exploiters, and all the other cliches of the ordinary labor agitator. Workers want simple homely facts regarding their trades and he gives them these facts." The description was wrong on all counts save the last. Haywood did believe in the presentation of simple facts just as he believed in speaking to immigrants as one speaks to children, but, as evidenced by the "Shots," he did not spurn simplification in platitudinous form. Moreover, Haywood sometimes "gibbered" about the brotherhood of man and the rising of the socialist commonwealth in fantastic terms. It is impossible to understand Haywood without recognizing that through this hard-nosed unionist ran a strong romantic streak which, if it showed itself only occasionally, literally erupted when it did. He spoke of the coming commonwealth before the Industrial Relations Commission in 1915: "And I have a dream that I have in the morning and at night and during the day, and that is that there well be a new society sometime in which there will be no battle between capitalist and wage earner, but that every man will have free access to land and its resources." [55]

He told children at Paterson, New Jersey, and elsewhere that he conceived of a city in the future where the people were all children and "there were no grown-ups to keep telling them: 'Don't, don't, don't.'" Nor were such rhapsodies for strictly juvenile consumption. Haywood sometimes visualized a future commonwealth smacking of "pie in the sky" as ethereal as any of the sermons of the "sky pilots" he claimed to abhor. The factory in the new society, he said,

> . . . will be utopian. There will be a wonderful dining room where you will enjoy the best food that can be purchased; your digestion will be aided by sweet music, which will be wafted to your ears by an unexcelled orchestra. There will be a gymnasium and a great swimming pool and private bathrooms of marble. One floor of the plant will be

> devoted to masterpieces of art, and you will have a collection even superior to that displayed in the Metropolitan Museum in New York. A first-class library will occupy another floor. The roof will be converted into a garden. There beautiful flowers will fill your eyes and their sweet perfume your nostrils. The workrooms will be superior to any you ever conceived. Your work chairs will be Morris Chairs, so that when you become fatigued you may relax in comfort.[56]

These were not exactly rare aberrations, but Haywood's two longer writings were as simple and direct as his "Shots." One piece, *The General Strike,* illustrates Haywood's unconcern for matters of ideology. The growth of the syndicalist movement in France and Italy during the early years of the twentieth century had made the question of *la grève générale* the unifying tenet of syndicalist ideology and a major topic of discussion among radicals. A spate of books and articles on the general strike were published around 1910. Haywood's contribution, however, did not rival George Sorel's. Haywood's *General Strike* largely ignored the ideological implications of the tactic although Haywood personally held views similar to those of the syndicalists. The book is a journalist's work, presenting the "simple homely facts" with which he always confronted working-class audiences. As a reviewer wrote, Haywood's "discussion of the general strike is far from theoretical. Generalized statements are few and far between. The account is, rather, a series of examples of the effectiveness of the tactic." [57]

His only other work of the period longer than an essay, *Industrial Socialism,* is more theoretical and a slim volume. It represents the development of Haywood's personal ideology to about 1913. It is more highly polished than his other writings of the period, a fact probably due to the collaboration of Frank Bohn, an articulate intellectual socialist who was associated with Haywood on the editorial board of the *International Socialist Review,* in the Socialist Party, and in the IWW.

Haywood's ideas were formed almost in their entirety by

1913. With the single exception of his late and equivocal adherence to Soviet Communism, he was remarkably consistent in ideology throughout his career. Some of his terminology derived from Marx, and in the broadest sense he was certainly a Marxist. He also employed terms generally identified with the French Syndicalists. But he mastered neither Marx nor George Sorel. He did not spice *Industrial Socialism* and his shorter "theoretical" writings with quotations to prove his points, for the substance of Haywood's thought derived from his personal experiences as a miner and a strike leader. His conclusions, even more than those of his contemporary, Debs, were moral and emotional judgments rather than intellectual deductions.

Haywood's "revolutionary industrial unionism" was rooted ultimately in his frustrations as a son of the dying western frontier. His early economic setbacks taught him the meaninglessness of the gospel of opportunity for his class and time. As a miner he learned the callousness of capital toward industrial workers, and it inspired in him his conception of the western miner as despoiled of his rightful inheritance by the possessors of wealth.

The idea of despoliation, extended somewhat haphazardly to all workers, runs through Haywood's career as an unbroken thread. In 1901 he told a Denver banker that the miners in Telluride had a right to be in possession of the mines. Trusts had robbed the American people of their heritage." In discussing the copper-mining region of Michigan in 1910, Haywood summed up his idea: "Copper was discovered in the upper peninsula of Michigan in 1843 by Jim Paull and Nick Minicleer, two frontiersmen, who facing many dangers made their way in the depth of winter through the wilderness from the southern part of Wisconsin and arrived at a place now located on the map as Houghton and Keewanaw Counties." Needless to say, Haywood continued "without tremolo," the mines were presently owned by interests comfortably ensconced in New York City offices, while the heirs of the frontiersmen toiled for miserly wages.[58]

Haywood generally avoided confrontation with the fact that many frontiersmen such as Paull and Minicleer had not been despoiled but had themselves capitalized on their good fortune and become as exploitative as any New York or London investor. Most of the self-made employers whom Haywood discussed he described as inestimably more reasonable and humane than the absentee investors and managers; those who were not, he generally forgot. Although Haywood implies that they had a right to their property, having earned it, there was no real place for them in Haywood's world, neatly summarized in a passage from his autobiography:

> The barbarous gold barons. They did not find the gold, they did not mine the gold, they did not mill the gold, but by some weird alchemy all the gold belonged to them.[59]

Haywood's westerner's sense of despoliation remained with him despite the fact that he wandered far from the mining region and spent most of his time in the eastern states organizing urban immigrants, who were not so much despoiled of their heritage as uprooted from it. He wrote of New York upon his first visit as if the people of the city were miners and the city itself an interloper. He "roamed around the streets of New York alone, more lonesome than I had ever been in my life." Only a tumultuous evening reception by the workers lifted the despair.[60]

Part of Haywood's disdain for the city was a romantic distaste for "progress" which he occasionally expressed. The undercurrent in Haywood's thought, that it was "progress" as much as capitalism which was responsible for the woes of the masses, emerged in a speech he delivered to striking rubber workers in Akron in 1913, "A Lesson in Rubber." He told of conditions on the rubber plantations of the Congo where slave labor was punished with medieval barbarism if its production was unsatisfactory. He traced the "blood-stained rubber" to Akron where it was made, under conditions only relatively better, into automobile tires. "But the function was not complete," Haywood concluded, "until it became smeared with the blood of some innocent little child that was run over and killed in the street."[61]

If Haywood's western heritage provided the frustration from which sprang his radicalism, the Western Federation of Miners showed him the remedy from which he never fundamentally deviated. Through union organization and, essentially, *only* through union organization could despoiled workers change their lot. To Haywood, the miner, this meant industrial unionism: all of the workers in an industry must belong to the same union regardless of their trade. The tenet that industrial unionism should be extended until all workers belonged to "One Big Union," the distinctive idea of the IWW, Haywood also derived from his WFM days. He had been an active member of the WFM when the union attempted, through the Western Labor Union (founded at the first convention Haywood attended) and the American Labor Union (organized when Haywood was already established in Denver), to extend industrial unionism beyond the mines and mills. The Western Federation eventually retreated to the mines and mills, but Haywood never abandoned the earlier vision. He reserved his sharpest epithets for Samuel Gompers and his craft-unionist devotion to the "aristocracy of labor," the skilled tradesmen. Haywood told the first IWW convention that they had not met to form a union rival to the American Federation because the IWW was to be "a labor organization."

While occasionally romantic, Haywood's revolutionism was also grounded in his unionism. The revolution itself, in fact, was to be accomplished by workers organized into unions. The fact that European syndicalists also conceived of the union as the agency of social change led many analysts of Haywood to confuse him with the European movements. In fact, Haywood's views derived from his experiences within the WFM, an eminently American phenomenon which predated the emergence of the French *Confédération Générale du Travail* and the writings of George Sorel. Haywood never conceded more than a remote and accidental kinship with the syndicalists.[62]

A final characteristic which can be traced to Haywood's WFM days was Haywood's low opinion of political action as a means of social revolution. The precipitant lesson was the Western Federation's experience with the eight-hour law, which they pushed through the Colorado legislature (and in several other western states) . An expensive political campaign finally won the law which the mine owners promptly evaded. What was the use of governmental action if industrialists seemed so clearly above the law? Haywood concluded, not from Marx but from Colorado, that the mechanism of the state was a pious ploy which capitalists would observe only so long as they controlled it. The workers' battlefield was the one they knew best—the point of production. Haywood said on several occasions that he would rather elect a shop foreman than a Senator of the United States. Not that Haywood rejected the value of political action completely. He attributed various functions to the Socialist politicians throughout his life. For him the point was that they could not accomplish the revolution; that depended on the union.

Haywood's ideas about violence changed after his career with the Western Federation. Fresh from the mines, Haywood had been easy with talk of dynamite and violence as possible means to the miners' ends. Just how much violence he was directly involved in is another matter; he seemed to realize it was at best an unproductive tool as early as 1900, and repeatedly urged striking miners to give no pretext for violent reprisals. His near-scrape with execution in Idaho confirmed him in this policy. The trial totally disillusioned Charles Moyer with unionist militance. Haywood would not go so far, but he discovered with Moyer that violence, whether the union's fault or not, could lead to an unhappy end.

After 1907 he rarely spoke publicly of the efficacy of violence. Partly this was due to his conviction that the workers needed only to lay down their tools to win their goals. Partly also it was due to Haywood's human fear of another Steunenberg case with a less salubrious outcome. Haywood delivered a speech in Grabow, Louisiana, for the Southern Timber Workers Union, and learned shortly afterwards from another town that there had been a riot in Grabow. He was greatly disturbed. "I don't know why something like that is always following me around the country," he observed to a friend, Covington Hall. Hall noted that Big Bill was nervous for the rest of the day and left abruptly after his last lecture. So far did he seek to divorce himself from labor violence that he refused to cooperate with his friends, Emma Goldman and Alexander Berkman, in arranging a funeral for the three anarchists who died in an attempt to assassinate John D. Rockefeller lest the commemoration be construed as condonation and lead to repression. "In late years he had repeatedly shown the white feather," Berkman commented some time later.[63]

By 1912 Haywood had developed an inarticulate version of the now-familiar idea that positive nonviolence often frustrated the adversary into the use of violence, and that the public's comparison of peaceful workers and demonstrators with violent employers, police, and militia would sweep the tide of public opinion to the workers' side. This was precisely what happened in Spokane, Washington, in 1909, and in Lawrence, Massachusetts, in 1912, when the brutality of police and the resultant public protest played a major role in IWW victories. At Paterson, New Jersey, site of a major strike in 1913, Haywood clarified his position when he shouted to a mass meeting of workers that their power was in their folded arms. "You have killed the mills; you have stopped production; you have broken off profits. Any other violence you commit is less than this, and it will only react upon yourselves." [64]

"The world is turning against war," Haywood said none too presciently in 1913. "People are sickened at the thought. Even labor wars of the old type are passing. I should never think of conducting a strike in the old way. There will never be another Coeur d'Alene, another Cripple Creek. I for one have turned my back on violence. It wins nothing. When we strike now, we strike with our hands in our pockets. We have a new kind of violence—the havoc we raise with money by laying down our tools. Our strength lies in the overwhelming power of our numbers." [65]

William Dudley Haywood, 1869–1928. (Culver Pictures, Inc.)

Mrs. Pettibone, George A. Pettibone, Haywood, Mrs. Moyer, and Charles A. Moyer. Taken during the Steunenberg murder trial in Boise, Idaho, in 1907, when the prosecution contended that the officials of the Western Federation of Miners were responsible for the murder. (Brown Brothers)

An unusual group photograph of the IWW leaders of the Paterson, New Jersey, silk workers strike in 1913. Left to right: Patrick Quinlan, Carlo Tresca, Elizabeth Gurley Flynn, Adolf Lessig, and Haywood. (Brown Brothers)

Mabel Dodge Luhan, wealthy patroness of many radical labor leaders, taken in Florence, Italy, during her stay at the Villa Curonia. (Bettmann Archive)

Haywood's sometime associates, the anarchists Emma Goldman and Alexander Berkman after their arrest in New York City in 1917, charged with conspiring against the U.S. Military Conscription Law. (Wide World Photos; print from State Historical Society of Wisconsin.)

Big Bill Haywood at the unveiling of the John Reed Monument in the Kremlin, *c.* 1920–25. Reed, a journalist, helped to organize the Paterson Pageant, led in the founding of the American Communist Labor Party in 1919, wrote the famous *Ten Days That Shook the World,* and purportedly was on his way back to the U.S. with money to reimburse Haywood's bondsmen when he died en route. (State Historical Society of

Emma Goldman and her lawyer Harry Weinberger, taken on Dec. 6, 1919, at Ellis Island, on the occasion of her deportation to the U.S.S.R. on the "Soviet Ark" with other anarchists and Communists. (Wide World Photos)

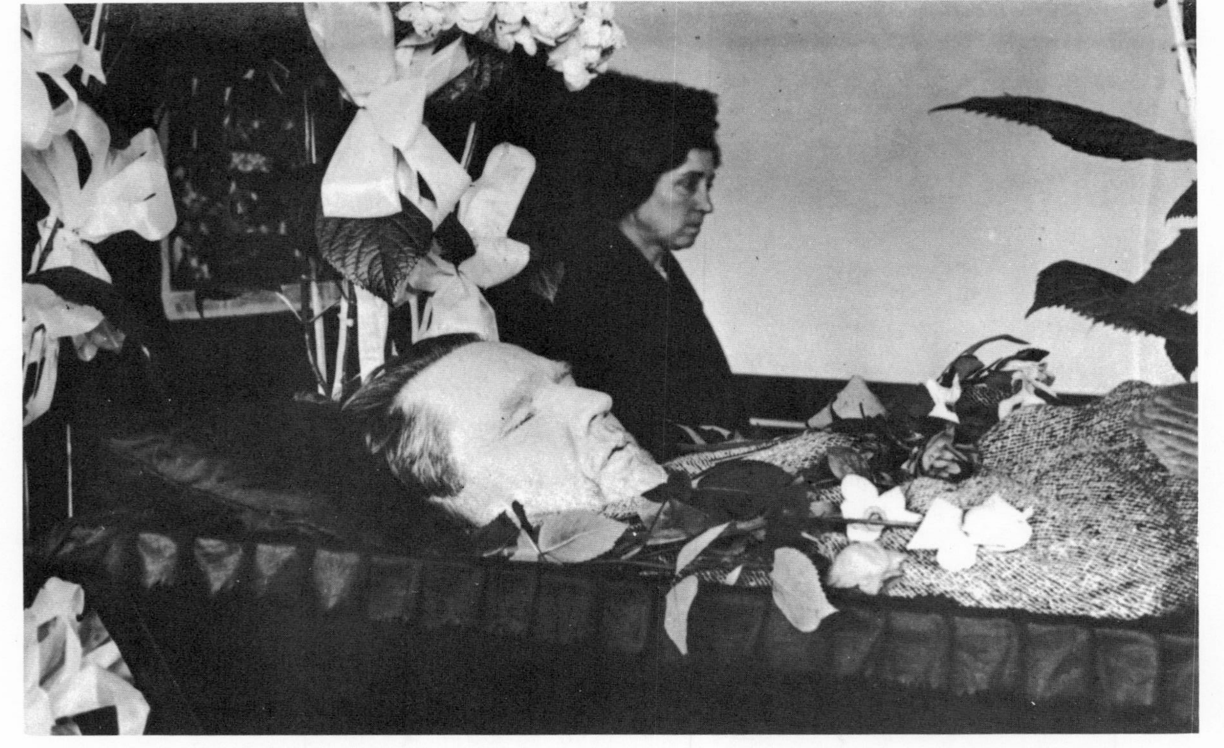

A rare photograph of Big Bill Haywood lying in state in the Clubhouse of Political Prisoners in Moscow, May 18, 1928. The woman in the background may be Haywood's little-known Russian wife. (Sovfoto)

With these ideas well under development in 1910, Haywood naturally drifted toward the union he helped to found—the Industrial Workers of the World. The IWW's inclinations were not identical to his own in that year, but its program was similar and, more important, the small union was like Haywood in that it preferred action to theory. The coincidence of the programs was partly the result of independent development. But, in addition, in 1910 Haywood was one of the few prominent American radicals who did not condemn the IWW, and as a result had never ceased to influence the organization. The similarity of ideas was also due to the fact that, after a lot of painful meandering, the IWW had anchored itself pretty much where it had stood at the time of its founding—when Haywood viewed the IWW as his beau ideal. Haywood did not, of course, cease to be the "eminent man" after he threw in with the IWW. His Greenwich Village period, the apogee of his social success as a *persona,* roughly spanned the same years as his Wobbly career. But the momentum of the fame won in Idaho which enabled him to live as a free-lance lecturer and journalist was finally dissipating as new *causes célèbres* caught the fancies of American radicals, and the memory of the small success of 1907 faded into history. In perhaps too glib a word, Haywood needed a "job," a basis of power—which the Socialist Party would eventually join the Western Federation in denying him.

5

Wobbly

The IWW's vitality in 1912 was a fresh experience for the union. Despite its founders' bouyancy in 1905, the Industrial Workers of the World did not immediately stride forth to a career of strikes and progress toward industrial democracy. Quite the contrary. The story of the IWW's activities until about 1909 is written in words of debilitating internal strife about which, an observer suggested, "it would require a Philadephia lawyer to determine which faction had the advantage." The IWW's problem was that its principal founders represented radical groups which, in the tragicomic manner of American radicalism, battled one another more zealously than they assailed their common enemy. The *personae* of the 1905 convention had been disputants for years; they had only rarely cooperated with one another, and their convention pledges of better future behavior meant little in view of these events. George Speed of the AFL's Seamen's Union called the convention "the greatest conglomeration of freaks that ever met."

Haywood saw this point in somewhat different terms and, in accepting the meeting's permanent chairmanship, hammered at the need for unity. "There is or should be no factions," he told the gathering, "and where you are all in hearty accord and are working for the same purpose, there should be no reason for wranglings or any personalities, and I hope there will be none indulged in." His plea could not have fallen on deafer ears. From the Ada County Jail, and on his tours, Haywood watched the IWW tear itself apart on two separate occasions.[1]

Unity might have been a realistic hope if the IWW had selected a president who could command through prestige. Eugene V. Debs' stature helped the Socialist Party of America to transcend its factional differences for many years, and the tiny Socialist Labor Party almost depended for its very existence on the force of Daniel DeLeon's personality. But persons of stature were at a premium on the American left in 1905 and none of the few were available to the IWW. Debs' personal policy prohibited accepting organizational positions. DeLeon's presence as a mere delegate to the convention was universally suspect; the unpopular radical could hardly stand for president. Victor Berger, of the large Social Democratic Party of Milwaukee, had refused to attend the meeting. Haywood turned down the office in order to devote full time to the Western Federation, and Charles Moyer was unavailable for the same reason. The convention finally settled on a nonentity of mediocre ability and dubious integrity, Charles O. Sherman of the United Metal Workers. To worsen matters, the secretary-treasurer was William E. Trautmann, an organizer of some accomplishment but personally incompatible with Sherman. Haywood regarded Trautmann as "honest and conscientious, but lacking in executive ability and entirely devoid of tact." He found Sherman satisfactory in 1905, but later described the IWW's first and only president as "incapable" and, "if not actually dishonest, he had used an enormous amount of the funds for unnecessary purposes." [2]

Three factions emerged after the founding convention. The first, which dominated in 1905, saw in the IWW a union allied to the Socialist Party. They did not require a formal connection between the two but, devoted to political action, conceived of the new union as a way of winning workers' votes to the Socialist Party as well as an agency of industrial struggle. Algie M. Simons, a Socialist editor, represented this persuasion. The Socialist Trades and Labor Alliance, ostensibly dissolved and merged into the IWW, comprised a second coterie.

Led and dominated by Daniel DeLeon, this group also visualized the IWW as a means of rallying the working class to radical political action, but it was the orthodox Marxist Socialist Labor Party which was to be the beneficiary. A third faction was but imperfectly emerged in 1905, but as events unraveled, this was a nonpolitical wing which conceived of the IWW as a strictly economic organization—the ideal to which all paid lip service in 1905—which would be free and independent of both the two socialist parties and political action.

The two latter factions began to assail Sherman almost as soon as the founding convention adjourned. The motives of his critics varied. DeLeon had been at loggerheads with the Socialist Party since its founding in 1900, and did not intend to let his old enemies control the IWW. He hoped the union might unite the two parties—but under his control. Trautmann disliked Sherman personally, and was increasingly appalled by the president's financial profligacy and mismanagement. Vincent St. John, a WFM organizer active in IWW affairs, hoped to free the IWW of all political influence, maintaining it as a nonpolitical revolutionary industrial union—a point of view which eventually dominated the IWW.

The St. John-Trautmann-DeLeonites controlled the IWW's 1906 convention and disposed of Sherman through both parliamentary and extra-parliamentary means. Their tactic was to destroy Sherman's power by abolishing the office of president. Trautmann, as secretary-treasurer, became the IWW's highest executive officer.[3]

Sherman continued to maintain that he represented the real IWW after the convention. In fact, he did retain the keys to the Chicago headquarters of a splinter organization to which there was little more of substance than keys. He also controlled the IWW's official organ, the *Industrial Worker,* and a small bank account. But it was all pretense. The small active membership of the union was behind DeLeon, Trautmann, and St. John. The anti-IWW Socialist, Max Hayes, rejoiced that "the I.W.W. received its death-blow at Chicago and will gradually disintegrate." In fact, the tiny union had enough life left to weather yet another split.[4]

St. John and Trautmann soon learned the old lesson that it was difficult to pull equally in harness with DeLeon. DeLeon did not share their view of the union as a purely economic organization, despite his professed agreement. In fact, DeLeon sought to tie the IWW to his Socialist Labor Party in much the same way that Socialist Party Wobblies like Algie M. Simons aimed to join it with the SPA. Like the SPA politicalists, Trautmann and St. John concluded, DeLeon would have to go. The key leader of the union, Vincent St. John, was understandably and increasingly apprehensive. The IWW was beginning to win strikes and a stable membership in 1908. St. John feared that to precipitate another split would destroy the union. An associate, Covington Hall, urged him on, arguing that "unless we take the Politicalists by the nape of the neck and seat of the britches and throw them out of the doors and windows, the I.W.W. is lost." St. John finally agreed, adding after the fact was accomplished, "I do not know if the organization can stand the strain, but it was the only thing left us to do if we were to save it." [5]

He smoked out DeLeon with a parliamentary maneuver as ingenious as DeLeon's in 1906. It centered on the deletion of the so-called "political clause" from the IWW preamble. The clause read:

> Between these two classes [employer and employee] a struggle must go on until all the toilers come together on the political, as well as on the industrial field, and take and hold that which they produce by their labor, through an economic organization of the working class without affiliation with any political party.[6]

St. John's group substituted for it a paragraph which omitted all mention of political action:

> Between these two classes a struggle must go on until the workers of the world organize as a class, take possession of the earth and the machinery of production, and abolish the wage system.

DeLeon responded by dubbing St. John's group "the bummery" and he claimed that the union had been captured by anti-political anarchists. He described the post-1908 union as "an anarchistic offshoot of the bona fide I.W.W." [7]

The IWW had become neither anarchist nor, as was later said, syndicalist. The deletion of the political clause was a tactic without much ideological import. It was not intended to align the Industrial Workers of the World with an antipolitical position any more than the abolition of the presidency in 1906 had been intended to destroy the union's centralized structure. In both 1906 and 1908, the actions of the victorious factions were based on expediency. The 1908 clause had a different, somewhat more militant ring than the 1905 version, but it was still nonpolitical rather than antipolitical. Its passage was intended to smoke out DeLeon's desire to subordinate the union to the Socialist Labor Party, and it succeeded handsomely.[8]

DeLeon was a remarkable figure, a brilliant Marxist scholar and an utterly incompetent politician. By the startlingly near-unanimous testimony of those who knew him, DeLeon was irascible and autocratic, impossible to collaborate with except from a posture of disciplined subordination. As Haywood wrote, "whether right or wrong, DeLeon always insisted that he was right. He made it impossible for any except his devotees to work with him. One able man after another had to leave him." DeLeon's insistence on his organizational and doctrinal supremacy within the Socialist Labor Party stunted the organization as well as its union affiliate, the Socialist Trades and Labor Alliance. He drove a succession of exceptional individuals out of the party, and in 1899 watched half of his party walk out and help organize the Socialist Party of America. Within the IWW after 1906 DeLeon was merely responding to old habits; he was out to turn the IWW into an STLA, a tail to the Socialist Labor Party's kite. It was this—his personality, more than any ideological issue—that caused the debacle of 1908.[9]

A union free of party influence ("without affiliation with

any political party" as the first preamble had it) was the IWW's original design. While the leaders of the IWW changed as if they were leapfrogging between 1905 and 1908, this was essentially where the IWW stood at the latter date. Moreover, the brand of unionism associated with the Western Federation of Miners—also a design of the original IWW—was restored with the ascendancy of Vincent St. John, who succeeded Trautmann as secretary-treasurer soon after DeLeon's exit and directed the union for the next several years.

"The Saint" is nearly a forgotten man in American labor history. Like Haywood, he was a westerner, born in 1876. His boyhood was uneventful and, again like Haywood, he went to work at an early age and wandered from job to job. He was in turn a delivery boy, a farmhand, a tinner, a printer, and an upholsterer. Finally, he went underground as a miner in the Coeur d'Alene District. In November, 1906, St. John traveled from Telluride, Colorado, to Goldfield, Nevada, where he emerged as the leader of the militants in the labor troubles which broke out during 1906 and 1907. The strike included workers of every type (it began with newsboys), but the miners were the backbone. It was both the IWW's and the WFM's show inasmuch as the two unions were affiliated at the time. The strike was crushed eventually, in part through the intervention of federal troops on President Theodore Roosevelt's orders. But in the meantime, St. John had made a name for himself as a crafty organizer.[10]

Disagreement among the strikers reflected the split between Haywood and Moyer in Boise and Denver. "Militants" looking to Haywood came increasingly to point to the IWW as their union, while "moderates" identified with the Moyer WFM. St. John, of course, was with the former. As a result, he found himself effectively excluded from the Moyer-dominated WFM and turned to the IWW as an outlet for his energies. He had his revenge in 1906, but Moyer, partly because of St. John's ascendency in the IWW, retaliated by taking the WFM out of it.

Haywood had little to do with the IWW between 1905 and

1908. He was imprisoned until 1907, and his lecture tours and European trip demanded most of his time as late as 1910. But he apparently maintained his membership in the IWW and frequently spoke to IWW groups on his swings about the country. In 1907 Haywood traveled to Goldfield and attempted to rally the frustrated strikers there. He recalled twenty years later that he recognized the split among the strikers as a division in part between "staunch I.W.W.'s" and "the reactionists in the W.F.M." At the time, however, he was clearly traveling under the aegis of the Western Federation, and he pleaded for unity, urging the strikers "to stand closer together, to avoid the outbreaks that were likely to occur among the members if contention continued." [11]

Haywood also lent his services to the IWW's colorful southern wing in Alexandria and Grabow, Louisiana. There the IWW had organized many lumberjacks and mill workers behind the leadership of the IWW poet, Covington Hall. Haywood played a major part in racially integrating the Louisiana unions, an unprecedented (and almost unduplicated) feat in that region. Haywood had been repelled by racism since boyhood, when he witnessed the lynching of a Negro and heard Senator "Pitchfork Ben" Tillman of South Carolina speak in Salt Lake City. "It was from him that I got my first outlook on the rights of Negroes," Haywood wrote.

> In the course of his lecture he showed his bitter antipathy toward the Negro as a man and as a race. A Negro sitting beside me asked him a question; his reply was a ferocious and insulting attack, with reflections on the colored man's mother. He referred to his questioner as a "saddle-colored son of Satan," and went on to tell him what his mother must have been for the Negro to have been the color he was; this because the Negro obviously was of mixed blood. I looked at the Negro and his pained expression caused me forever after to feel that he and his kind were the same as myself and other people. I saw him suffering the same resentment and anger that I should have suffered in his place;

I saw him helpless to express this resentment and anger. I feel that Ben Tillman's lectures must have made many people feel as I did. It seemed to me that I could look right into the breast of old Tillman and see his heart that was rotten with hate.[12]

Haywood did not forget, and when he discovered that Negro and white lumberjacks met separately in Alexandria he insisted that the practice cease. "You work in the same mills together," Haywood said. "Sometimes a black man and a white man down the same tree together. You are meeting now in a convention to discuss the conditions under which you labor. This can't be done intelligently by passing resolutions here and then sending them out to another room for the black men to act upon. Why not be sensible about this and call the Negroes into this convention? If it is against the law, this is one time when the law should be broken." There was no opposition to Haywood's suggestion in Alexandria and only faint murmurs in another town in the area. Both locals integrated before he left, and subsequently sent both white and black delegates to the IWW's national convention.[13]

Haywood spoke in Goldfield and Alexandria as a friend and not as an IWW official. He held no position in the union and his annoyance and hasty exit north when an IWW strike at Grabow, Louisiana, erupted in violence indicates that he did not wish to be considered a Wobbly leader at the time.

The factional bickering of 1906 and 1908 drove Eugene V. Debs from the IWW. Haywood remained a member but also a long arm's length from the battles. Like Debs, he did not like radical infighting, so he refused to take sides in either of the IWW's disputes. This was a disappointment to many, and Haywood's careful neutrality in 1906 probably aggravated his relations with cellmate Charles Moyer. While Moyer did not wholeheartedly throw in with Sherman's faction, his sympathies were there. In his message to the Western Federation's convention, he harshly condemned DeLeon, Trautmann, and St. John. Through his lieutenant in Denver, John O'Neill, he pressured the WFM to affiliate with the IWW only conditionally and to withhold all dues and assessments until it was determined who in the IWW held power. When St. John and his allies came out on top, the WFM withdrew from the Industrial Workers. Haywood had refused to attack St. John.

In 1907, aware of St. John's intentions for him, Daniel DeLeon attempted to enroll Haywood in his own camp. The SLP leader was well aware of his own unsavory reputation for factionalism, and thought of Haywood as a likely "front man" since Haywood had responded equivocally to the 1906 split while most of the Western Federationists damned DeLeon. Moreover, Haywood stood at the peak of his popularity among American radicals after the Steunenberg trial. He looked like an ideal ally to DeLeon, and in August, 1907, DeLeon wrote to Haywood to sound him out on his proposal.

It was a flatttering letter. DeLeon described Big Bill as the man who could "unify" the American left thanks to his acquittal in Idaho. "The capitalist class has thrown the ball into your hands," DeLeon wrote in uncharacteristically light metaphor, "You can kick it over the goal." DeLeon hinted at the possibility of a second split within the IWW, which was due to the fact that "however undeserved they were, those who have been early in the struggle have necessarily drawn upon themselves animosities." What was "worse yet," those animosities disqualified "such organizations and their spokesmen for the work of themselves speedily effecting unification." The organizations and spokesmen in point were, of course, the SLP and DeLeon. But all was not lost, DeLeon continued, for "the capitalist class, through this late persecution of you, has 'produced' the unifier." [14]

Haywood may well have been flattered by DeLeon's intimations that he was indispensable to the IWW, but during the summer of 1907 Haywood was the object of a great deal of attention and flattery. In addition, he was about to embark on a lecture tour when he received the letter, and DeLeon had already left the country to travel to the International Socialist Congress at Stuttgart. Haywood was also a member of the

Socialist Party of America at the time, and shared in the suspicion with which most of the SPA held the "ubiquitous Dan." He later wrote that "I was becoming more and more convinced that the Socialist Labor Party was so completely dominated by DeLeon's prejudices that it could not lend strength to any movement with which he associated." As he had done in 1906, Haywood remained neutral.[15]

With the factional splintering finally in its background, the IWW was revived in 1909 by two geographically separate and utterly dissimilar events. In the Far West the agent of Wobbly renascence was the "free-speech fight." The fights varied locally, but were generally called in response to local ordinances which forbade or crippled traditional practices of soapbox-speaking in the streets. The ordinances were usually designed to forestall IWW organization among the transient laborers who wintered in the towns and cities.[16]

The first significant free-speech fight broke out in Spokane, Washington, a favorite wintering place for thousands of migrant workers who seasonally manned the logging camps, sawmills, construction camps, and commercial farms of the Northwest. The migrant worker was poorly paid, his job was ephemeral, and he worked under some of the worst conditions in the United States. He was a natural prospect for the message of the Wobbly organizers, but geography made it difficult for the IWW to organize on the job. The IWW therefore relied heavily on the short winter season to propagandize the men. They found a fertile field. As Nels Anderson, the "hobo sociologist," noted of the IWW message, "no man, down and out, can hear this doctrine without a thrill." [17]

The Wobblies' theme during 1909 was the employment agencies. Ostensibly these were offices which, for a fee, placed the transient seeking work in a job at a lumber camp, construction site, or harvest camp. In practice, the offices were often perpetrators of fraud; they collected their fees efficiently enough but "placed" the worker, who had no avenue of recourse, in a nonexistant job. Another agency ruse required collusion between the office and the foreman on a job site.

The job would be sold, the worker given a week or two of work, and then fired by the foreman, who received for his services a share of the agency's fee. These frequent layoffs made room for another of the agency's clients who would himself be let go in a week or two. Labor was abundant and the work called for little or no skill. The IWW remarked ruefully that the "job sharks" had discovered perpetual motion, one "bindle stiff" leaving the job, one working on it, and another headed for it. Joe Hill's song, *Mr. Block,* immortalized the chicanery of the employment agencies and the unorganized workers' lack of recourse:

> Yes, Mr. Block is lucky; he found a job by gee!
> The shark got seven dollars for job and fare and fee.
> They shipped him to a desert and dumped him with his truck,
> But when he tried to find his job he sure was out of luck.
> He shouted, "That's too raw,
> I'll fix them with the law."

The law in Spokane was behind the sharks, of course. At their behest, the Spokane City Council issued an ordinance forbidding street speaking in the hobo area. Shortly afterward, under pressure from the Salvation Army, "religious bodies" were exempted.[18]

The IWW took up the challenge and their choice of weapons was civil disobedience. Their design was to shift the burden of enforcing the obnoxious law from the violator to the enforcer. By packing the jails with violators, each of whom when indicted would demand a separate jury trial, the Wobblies would render enforcement so expensive and troublesome that the ordinance would be suspended. Over a hundred "speakers," mostly Wobblies, were arrested on the first day the ordinance was enforced. By the end of November, 1909, between 500 and 600 separate arrests were recorded. There were, of course, many repeaters. Those earliest arrested were often quickly released on the assumption they had "learned their lesson." They had not, and were usually back on the soapbox after a bath, a shave, and a meal.[19]

The multiplication of a dozen active Wobblies into several hundred befuddled the Spokane authorities. They were the first to confront the Wobbly spirit which has earned the IWW a niche in American romantic legend. The hundreds of Wobblies came from two sources. First, many of those arrested had not been members of the organization before the campaign began but were swept up in the enthusiasm of the fight and joined the union. Second, anticipating the early depletion of their human resources, the Spokane IWW dispatched an alarm to nearby areas that all available members were needed to pack the town's jails. Those arrested in Spokane during the final days of the fight gave home addresses ranging from as far as Chicago and Milwaukee to Los Angeles, San Francisco, Seattle, Portland, various Montana towns, and even McKee's Rocks, Pennsylvania, where the IWW had recently led a successful strike. One Wobbly provided an excellent example of the IWW tradition of rank-and-file participation in a letter to the Spokane local:

> Fellow Worker:
>
> A Demonstration was just held in Sheep Camp No. 1 there being three present, a herder and two dogs. The following resolutions were adopted:
>
> Resolved: That we send $10.00 for the free speech fight in Spokane.[20]

The police at first responded to the Wobblies' surprise tactic by the use of torture but, despite at least three deaths of prisoners attributable to abuse in prison, the Free Speechers remained tenacious as ever. Partly due to their stamina, the Wobblies won the fight in Spokane. In addition, the national press publicized the tortures used by the Spokane police. There was an outcry of indignation on behalf of the Wobblies and the town was dubbed "Barbarous Spokane." The pressure increased when a Wobbly sued a city official named Burns, who panicked and threatened to implicate the city's "fat cats" in the tortures.[21]

The council relented and dropped the obnoxious ordinance

in return for the IWW's pledge not to prosecute any cases against the city. Most important for the Wobblies, the city turned on the employment agencies. A judge remarked that "I believe all this trouble is due to the employment agencies" and, by the spring of 1910, revoked the licenses of nineteen of the most fraudulent offices.[22]

Spokane was only one of the largest and most successful of the free-speech fights. Between 1909 and 1916 the union participated in at least twenty-six disputes on the same pattern. Most of them occurred among transient communities in the West like those in San Francisco, San Diego, Los Angeles, Fresno, Wheatland, Everett, Walla Walla, Aberdeen, Minot, and Missoula. Their larger effect was to revive (or, rather, to implant) the IWW in the West by attracting thousands of members and by attracting considerable publicity. Even before Spokane, however, the Eastern IWW, which dominated the organization during its brightest days and with which Haywood was most closely associated, was activated by the IWW's first great industrial victory.[23]

This was at McKee's Rocks, Pennsylvania, an industrial suburb of Pittsburgh a few miles northwest of the city on the Ohio River. The town was the site of the Pressed Steel Car Works, which was the largest local employer. The strike, which broke out in 1909, resulted from a labor-pooling arrangement which substantially lowered wages in the plant. In addition, workers were obliged to pay the premium rents customary in company towns in adjoining Schoenville (less poetically referred to by the workers as "Hunkeyville").[24]

The IWW did not initiate the strike in McKee's Rocks; the workers invited the union to organize them only after the dispute began. Nevertheless, the IWW's role was crucial; it welded the erratic, aimless, and often violent strikers into a well-disciplined front. After fifty-seven days, the company capitulated. The wage settlement was left to arbitration, but the most glaring abuses that had caused the trouble were resolved in the workers' favor.[25]

Thus had the IWW developed when Haywood cast his lot

with the union. In conception it was not a radically different organization from what it had been after the founding convention of 1905. There had been a series of changes in leadership and rhetoric during the intervening years but, in effect, they were gropings finally resolved into a union much like that originally intended. That is, the Industrial Workers of the World of 1910 was before all else a labor union with unionist goals and means. The historical image of the IWW as a colorful menagerie of misfits singing songs of varying quality, possessing a matchless spirit, and marching cheerily to oblivion is by no means false; the IWW was all these things. But that image also obscures the fact that, when William D. Haywood was at the union's helm, the IWW functioned quite successfully as a labor organization. There is a problem of definition: what a labor union is or should be. Certainly Bill Haywood's definition differed radically from that of Samuel Gompers. The point is that even by Gompers' definition of a union as an organization to achieve shorter hours, higher pay, better conditions of labor, and improved social services, the Haywood IWW qualified.

Haywood's part in forging the IWW's unionism was significant, but after McKee's Rocks the IWW was already headed in that direction. It was, in fact, the IWW's re-emphasized unionism which drew Haywood to it. Big Bill reveled in his personal eminence and never broke with the fashionable radical salons of New York City, but his background and disposition made him a labor unionist. No personal celebrity or political interests could take that out of him.

Haywood took an increasingly active part in IWW affairs after 1910, but the first incident in which he acted as a leader was the famous strike of textile workers at Lawrence, Massachusetts, in 1912. A city of 88,000 people, over 66,000 of Lawrence's residents depended directly on the city's cotton and woolen mills for their living. Most of the workers were immigrants but there was no single dominant ethnic group; Lawrence was not "Little Italy" or "Polack Town" with smatterings of other groups on the fringes. Rather, the population was distributed broadly among many nationalities. An informal study in 1912 revealed that Lawrence had about 9,000 English, 12,000 French Canadians, 2,100 Poles, 2,500 Jews, 2,700 Syrians, 3,000 Lithuanians, 2,300 Scots, 6,500 Germans, 8,000 Italians, 600 Armenians, 1,200 Franco-Belgians, and several thousand of other groups. *Harper's Weekly* noted ominously that there were no more than 8,000 people of "full American stock." [26]

The confused ethnic mixture presented a difficult organizational problem. Huddled together in ghetto neighborhoods, the different groups communicated little with one another. Indeed, maintaining the diversity of workers was part of the labor policy of the town's chief employer, the American Woolens Company. Owned principally by an astute Portuguese immigrant who adopted the name William Madison Wood, the company produced about 10 per cent of all the nation's woolens and owned thirty-four mills throughout New England.[27]

Wood was cut from the paternalistic cloth that characterized an earlier period of American industrialism. He was capable of issuing a sincere attack on profiteering retail merchants and establishing a chain of company stores which actually sold for cash and at cost. On another occasion Wood held a lawn party on his estate for his workers and called a half-day at full pay for the event. On the day of the party he paraded through the streets standing in an open car, smiling, and doffing his hat. He was severely depressed when as many jeered as cheered him and only a few hundred attended the affair. Part of the reason for Wood's social failure was that he was also capable of complicity in a plot to railroad troublesome unionists to jail, and that his largesse did not extend to his employees' daily life. Conditions in Lawrence were execrable. Charles P. Neil, the United States Commissioner of Labor, stated that during November, 1911—shortly before the strike—all textile employees in Lawrence (including relatively well-paid foremen and supervisors) averaged only $8.76 for a full week's work. Women's wages were less: some typical salaries cited ran as low as $4.92 per week for spinning and $5.84 for combing. Haywood might well have been startled by the figures; he had made almost four times as much when he left the mines twelve years before.[28]

Rents were disproportionately high, ranging up to $6 a week for small apartments in congested tenement buildings. This required that several members of a family work or take in lodgers, as 58 per cent of mill families did. As one result of crowding, infant mortality ran to 172 deaths under one year of age per 1,000 births. Life expectancy for mill operatives was 39.6 years, contrasted to a Lawrence middle-class average of over 60 years.[29]

The strike of 1912 derived from these accumulated grievances and was called in response to a wage cut in January. If he needed convincing at this late date, the circumstances helped to confirm Haywood in his conviction that the workers' future lay not in politics but in action at the factory site. The Massachusetts legislature had reduced the maximum hours for men and children in industry from 56 to 54 hours weekly. When the law went into effect, the Lawrence textile manufacturers reduced the subsistence-level wages proportionately.[30]

While the employers later blamed the IWW for fomenting the trouble at Lawrence, the strike was clearly a spontaneous affair. On the first day, workers in several unrelated shops walked out on their own initiative upon receiving their reduced wages. The IWW was called into the city only after the plants were closed. On the first evening of the strike, some workers held a meeting at the Franco-Belgian Hall, headquarters of a tiny IWW local. The inexperienced and divided immigrants were confused, "drowning men ready to grasp at a straw," as one worker later put it. As much because they had no alternative as anything else, they wired Joseph J. Ettor in New York. An Italian- and Polish-speaking general organizer for the IWW, Ettor had briefly visited the city some months before.[31]

Ettor was a remarkable individual, buoyantly optimistic, perpetually cheery, and a deliberate, effective organizer. Arriving in Lawrence within days, he established an IWW pattern by organizing a strike committee representing the different ethnic groups. The committee met every day and, to a surprising extent, they ran the strike. Their demands included no reprisals for strike activity or leadership and a 15 per cent raise in wages for the new work week with double pay for overtime. Ettor was so successful in welding an organization that the mill owners reasoned that if he were removed the strike would collapse.[32]

The first attempt to eliminate Ettor involved the planting of a cache of dynamite in a shoemaker's shop next to the house where Ettor received his mail. Although Ettor had actually ended a spate of violence when he arrived in Lawrence, the mill owners and some newspapers were quick to leap on the incident as an example of what Wobbly leadership meant.

Ettor and the IWW denied all knowledge of the dynamite and began their own investigation when they discovered that the Boston Hearst paper was already on sale in Lawrence with the news of the cache before it had actually been found. The police themselves discovered that the explosives were wrapped in old copies of a trade magazine, an undertaker's journal, from one copy of which the addressee's name had been imperfectly removed. He was John J. Breen, a minion of the mill-owner-dominated city government who had been county coroner and who was, at the time of the strike, a member of the Lawrence school board. After Breen's arrest, someone revealed that William M. Wood had recently made an unaccountable payment of money to Breen. Wood was not molested and Breen was fined $500 and immediately released. But, at least, Ettor and the IWW had been exonerated.[33]

The city attempted more successfully to eliminate Ettor after January 29, when a woman striker named Anna LoPizzo (or LaPisa) was shot to death in a clash between strikers and police. Despite the facts that the strikers had no guns, that Ettor was nowhere near the site of the spontaneous (if not police-instigated) clash, and that he had in fact acted positively to avoid violence with provocative militiamen on the same day, Ettor was indicted for the murder along with another organizer, Arturo Giovannitti, and an Italian immigrant who had nothing to do with the IWW, Giuseppe Caruso. In contrast to the delicate treatment of Breen and Wood in the dynamite affair, Ettor, Giovannitti, and Caruso were denied bail and imprisoned for almost a year before their trial began. It was obviously an attempt to break the strike by removing its leaders. But the mills and the city of Lawrence calculated on neither the effectiveness of Ettor's organizational work nor the IWW's determination not to be cowed. Soon after the jailing of the three, Carlo Tresca, Elizabeth Gurley Flynn (the "Joan of Arc of the Labor Movement"), Willian E. Trautmann, and William D. Haywood arrived in Lawrence to take command of the strike.

Haywood's was the principal role. Flynn, Tresca, and Trautmann were in and out of Lawrence, delivering speeches and rallying flagging enthusiasm, but Haywood's task was to take over Ettor's job. His task was the easier in that Ettor bequeathed him the strike machinery. It was more difficult in that enthusiasm lagged as the strike wore on, and in that Ettor's imprisonment and the addition of a demand to free him to the strikers' list of grievances complicated the dispute. In a sense, however, the latter handicap helped solve the former. The imprisonment of Ettor and Giovannitti proved to be a colossal blunder on the employers' part, for they had absolutely no case against the organizers and a national inquiry helped swing public opinion to the strikers' side.

Haywood continued Ettor's policies with little modification. The committee of ethnic group representatives continued to meet daily and direct the strike with only advice from Haywood. It organized mass picketing to preoccupy the idle workers and to maintain constant pressure on the companies. Mass rallies, designed to maintain the IWW's almost mythical "solidarity," met frequently and featured the popular Haywood as chief orator. And Haywood religiously emphasized Ettor's insistence on striker nonviolence as a prerequisite for victory.

One tactic, apparently of Haywood's device, marked (along with the dynamite case and Ettor's imprisonment) the turning point of the strike. Ettor's Relief Committee, Haywood learned, was inadequate to care for the needs of the 25,000 strikers. Drawing on a Wobbly precedent of 1910, when sympathetic Philadelphia Quakers and Wobblies took children of striking coal miners into their homes for the duration of the strike, Haywood and sympathizer Margaret Sanger sent over a hundred children to New York City on February 10. Haywood maintained that it was impossible to feed them all at Lawrence—which was true enough—and added that, with the militia so erratic, the IWW feared for the children's safety—no preposterous claim. In addition, although Haywood left it unsaid, the sight of a hundred children from Lawrence arriving in New York (accompanied by Wobbly ballyhoo) earned the strikers much public sympathy.[34]

On February 24, Haywood planned to repeat the little victory by sending 150 more children to Philadelphia, mostly to Quaker homes. When the procession arrived at the Lawrence railroad station, however, police and militia moved in and quite brutally, according to all accounts, arrested and loaded mothers and children into patrol wagons. Despite a judge's feeble attempt to excuse the police by accusing the parents of neglect, it was a blunder ranking with the sloppy dynamite plant and the arrest of Ettor and Giovannitti. Newspapers formerly hostile to the strike such as the *New York Sun* and the *Boston Herald* took Lawrence to task for the "embargo on children." Socialist Congressman Victor Berger, who had been maneuvering for an investigation of Lawrence conditions, pushed through his resolution in the aftermath of the raid.[35]

The American Woolens Company acceded to this increased pressure on March 12, the other mills following suit by the end of the month. Spinners received a 22 per cent increase, combers 19 per cent, winders 13 per cent, and so on. Ettor and Giovannitti were acquitted later in the year. There had been no case in the first place and, with the strike over, the companies lost interest in pushing the matter. Moreover, William M.

Wood's implication in the dynamite plant was republicized in August when a Lawrence contractor committed suicide after revealing that he had helped hatch the plot in Wood's office. Finally, the defendants attracted a great deal of public sympathy when the court tactlessly kept them in iron cages throughout the trial and, again under Haywood's direction, the IWW maintained constant agitation and was joined by almost every radical and Italian-American organization in the nation. The Wobblies and their sympathizers unleashed a rash of sympathy strikes, usually one-day affairs, throughout New England and in some other areas. The most dramatic of all was a general strike in Lawrence on September 30 when 15,000 workers walked out for a day. Protests poured in from as far away as the Italian *Confederazione Generale del Lavoro*.[36]

In addition to the workers' material gains, the victory at Lawrence won Haywood and the IWW a reputation as wizards among many eastern workmen. The American Federation of Labor had made it clear for years that it had little time for the organization of either immigrants or the unskilled. These groups, in the view of Samuel Gompers and his lieutenants, were either undesirable or ineffective because of their lack of skills with which to bargain. The IWW gave the lie, albeit temporarily, to the AFL writ. Its methods had organized and led some 23,000 to 25,000 unskilled immigrant workers and helped them to win a victory over an entrenched and powerful industry. When the victory at McKee's Rocks was topped by Lawrence, Haywood and the IWW seemed to many eastern workingmen a beam of hopeful light where there had been only fatalism and despair. Events were to prove that the IWW was not omnipotent and Haywood not omniscient, but after Lawrence both union and leader stood at the apogee of their success. The exhilaration of Lawrence tied Haywood closer to the IWW. He became general organizer of the union under his old protegé, Vincent St. John, and much more than the introverted "Saint," he was the public's image of the IWW's leader.[37]

The IWW's second great strike followed a year after Lawrence in Paterson, New Jersey, the traditional home of fine-silk weaving in the United States. Out of a population of about 125,000 in 1913, about 50,000 were employed in sixty silk mills. As late as 1913 Paterson claimed about 50 per cent of all the nation's silk production.[38]

But this monopoly had already been cracked, and by 1913 the city's share was declining. The problem lay in Paterson's traditional specialization in the finest grades of silk. During the 1890's, several mills were erected across the Delaware River in Pennsylvania. After a short but decisive competition with Paterson in the manufacture of cheaper-grade silks, the Pennsylvania mills won out completely. They employed a multiple-loom system which could be operated by women and children, whereas the Paterson mills relied on a single- or double-loom system operated by skilled silk weavers, many of whom had practised their craft before emigrating from Italy. Pennsylvania silk was decidedly inferior but profits were large. That was a fact which the Paterson owners had to consider before they took too much pride in the fine quality of their own product. Between 1907 and 1913 the Pennsylvania silk industry increased its business 97 per cent, while Paterson's output grew only 22 per cent. When some of the Paterson mill owners decided to rejoin competition in the cheap-silk market by adopting the multi-loom system, the result was a strike.[39]

The problem was purely economic to Paterson's employers: cheap-silk manufature necessitated a drastic cut in labor costs. This alarmed Paterson's weavers. They feared that, as in Pennsylvania, female and child labor would displace the skilled male weavers, and their fear had sound foundations. A Federal Report for 1908 showed an average weekly wage in the Paterson mills of $11.69, while in Pennsylvania the average was only $6.56. Moreover, inasmuch as the four-loom system would halve the number of workers required to tend two looms, many, especially the skilled, higher-paid workers, would be thrown out of work. In addition, tending four looms was more intense and exhausting work and foreboded an increase in an already high accident rate. Finally, the drive toward mass production offended the Old-World craftmanship of Paterson's weavers. They equated the conversion to shoddy silk manufacturing with "converting a vineyard to a hay-farm."[40]

As in Lawrence and McKee's Rocks, the IWW did not enter the Paterson strike until after it began. The walkout occurred spontaneously on January 27, 1913, when four members of an eight-hour league were fired after approaching the management of the Doherty Mills to discuss the four-loom system. In response, about 800 to 1,200 workers struck the plant.[41]

The AFL's United Textile Workers and Daniel DeLeon's "Detroit IWW" both had locals in Paterson, but John Golden of the UTW seemed more interested in winning the collaboration of the employers than in representing the workers, and the Detroit IWW was strangely lethargic. The stage was set for a grand entrance by the IWW, and on February 25 the union set out to win another Lawrence. If John Golden had come to Paterson, a progressive but anti-IWW magazine noted, "undoubtedly he could have organized workers in his union. Instead came Haywood, Elizabeth Flynn, Quinlan, Tresca—empty-handed, with neither money nor credit nor with the prestige of a 2,000,000 membership, but willing to work and go to jail."[42]

They did both. Elizabeth Gurley Flynn called a mass meeting on her first day in the town, and by the end of the day 25,000 workers left their jobs. Police Chief Bimson, who functioned throughout the strike much like a company employee, arrested her on the grounds that she attended "a meeting of tumultous persons and did make loud noises that struck fear into the hearts of all present against the peace and dignity of the state of New Jersey." He presented Flynn the alternatives of jail or leaving town. Stating that she had spoken within her rights and could use the sleep anyway, she elected jail. There, to the chagrin of the police, she calmly rolled up her coat for a pillow and fell asleep. Had Chief Bimson read the lessons of Lawrence, he would have known that jailing one Wobbly leader had a hydra-like effect. Within a few days, just as he had substituted for Ettor in Lawrence, Haywood arrived fresh from another IWW strike in Akron, Ohio.[43]

Haywood employed the methods which had won at Lawrence so far as they applied to a different situation. One difference was that whereas no ethnic group had dominated in Lawrence, Italians were a majority among Paterson's working class. Joseph Ettor was not available so Haywood relied heavily on Carlo Tresca, a professional anarchist and companion of Elizabeth Gurley Flynn, to organize the Italian workers. He established a strike committee patterned on Lawrence's and organized frequent mass rallies and mass picketing. Also as in Lawrence, Haywood urged the strikers to observe strict nonviolence and sit tight until the employers came to terms.[44]

The strike dragged on for several months and was reported even more comprehensively than Lawrence had been. Haywood courted public opinion through every means he knew, and devised new methods with the assistance of John Reed, who was reporting the strike for *Metropolitan Magazine*. It was probably Reed who conceived one of the most interesting episodes of the strike, the Paterson Pageant, a dramatization of the strike staged at Madison Square Garden on June 8, 1913. Through Mabel Dodge and the wealthy radicals who gathered at her "evenings," Reed raised a purse to finance the affair. Other money came from strike-relief funds, and all hoped that the Pageant would gross enough that the strike might carry on.[45]

Box seats sold for $20 and $10, with cheaper seats ranging down to $2 and $1.50. At the last moment, with thousands of seats empty and thousands of people milling outside (Haywood estimated one queue as twenty-eight blocks long), the Pageant Committee admitted spectators for whatever they could afford, sometimes ten cents and sometimes, for Wobblies, a flash of the "little red card." [46]

The IWW's foray into the world of *belles artes* bore Haywood's stamp. While John Reed and various radical professionals of the city handled the organization of the drama, the cast was authentically proletarian: 1,200 strikers from Paterson who preceded their performance with a march through New York City. Haywood was determined that the workers would "through their own simple action impress the crowd." He was demonstrating his brand of aesthetics to New York.[47]

The Pageant was presented in six scenes. The first portrayed a mill with distraught workers walking the streets before it. Suddenly whistles blew, someone shouted "Strike!" and the workers ran through the mill backdrop to join with the audience in singing the *Internationale.* In the second scene, the mills were quiet and the workers assembled peaceably to picket and sing strike songs. The police (portrayed by some reluctant strikers) attacked with clubs, a few shots were heard, and a striker fell. This represented Valentino Modestino, who had actually been shot by police in Paterson while seated on his porch with a child in his lap. Mabel Dodge, no mild critic, commented on the realism of the scene.[48]

Scene III duplicated Modestino's funeral. As at the original event, Flynn, Tresca, and Haywood delivered speeches. A critic noted, possibly to Haywood's pleasure, that the recreated talks, "efforts to give typical strike speeches, added nothing to the effect which the workers themselves spontaneously gave." It was the "simple movements of mill workers" which were the "inarticulate eloquence of the scene." Scene IV portrayed parents sending their children to another city. They departed singing *The Red Flag,* a favorite of the IWW. The Fifth Scene was a strike meeting which featured another speech by Haywood, and another rendition of the *Internationale* closed the Pageant.[49]

Ironically, the unionist Haywood's venture into the theatre was an artistic success and a unionist failure. The Pageant climaxed the strike; both the struggle at Paterson and the IWW's high hopes of a golden future in eastern industry dimmed with the klieg lights. First, the Pageant was a disastrous financial failure. The committee had only enough money to rent Madison Square Garden for one night, and the expense of a single performance proved too high for the gate. Even other entertainments on behalf of the strikers by celebrities like boxer Bob Fitzsimmons could not compensate for the deficit. Some newspapers accused the committee of pilfering the proceeds, but there is no evidence to substantiate a charge out of all character with the organizers. Mabel Dodge did not need it, and Haywood's record as a handler of monies was unblemished. There was no profit simply because there were too few paying customers.

The strikers' disillusionment at receiving no relief funds was fatal. Moreover, the Pageant caused dissension among the strike's leaders. Elizabeth Gurley Flynn, less the romantic and without Haywood's artistic friends, evidently opposed the Pageant from its inception and went along with it only reluctantly. At any rate, she was criticizing it—and soundly—soon after. John Reed left New York for Venice with Mabel Dodge almost immediately after the Pageant, and Haywood, who said he lost eighty pounds during the strike, also went to Europe to convalesce (financed, he scrupulously emphasized, by a friend). The ill-feeling implanted by the Pageant between Flynn and Haywood would eventually develop into an open split between the two friends which only common adversity during World War I and their membership in the Communist Party would heal.[50]

Finally, as Elizabeth Flynn pointed out, the fact that only about 1,200 of the strikers could go to New York caused considerable jealousy among the rank and file, and offended the solidarity which the IWW called its cardinal ideal. Moreover, the Pageant had absorbed almost the entire attention of the leadership and strikers during a period in which such energies could have been more effectively spent picketing. What Flynn saw which Haywood did not (or at least never admitted), was that the romantic allure of the Pageant briefly diverted Haywood from one of his own principles—that the worker's fight was at the point of production. Haywood prided himself by 1913 on the realization that the ballot box was of little use to the workers, but he was seduced by a far less substantial tactic.[51]

In Paterson during July, the skilled ribbon weavers broke

ranks and settled separately with the mills. Sensing a major breakthrough, the employers announced that they were prepared to deal with each of the 300 striking shops separately. Most of the workers soon returned to the same conditions they had left five months before. There were some small gains, but these were token gestures granted unilaterally by the employers and not IWW victories. While the IWW would fight and win many small strikes in the East during the years after Paterson, the union's short "golden age" of dramatic victories was over in 1913, four years after it began. The impression made at Lawrence, that the IWW was invincible, was dissipated when confronted by the sterner silk mill operators of New Jersey.[52]

Judged within the context of Haywood's career, the years he spent as a strike leader for the IWW rank with his years with the Western Federation as the most gratifying of his life. For Haywood was always, despite his revolutionism and enjoyment of eminence, more a unionist than even he sometimes seemed to realize. And the IWW provided him with the opportunity to do what he did best. With the revolutionary trappings set aside for the moment, Haywood conducted the IWW's great strikes at Lawrence, Paterson, Akron, and on the Mesabi Range in 1915 for the same pragmatic ends and in the same practical manner in which the AFL conducted its many strikes during the same period. He was more militant than any of the AFL's leaders, certainly more revolutionary in his rhetoric, and more willing to go to jail and risk a long sentence then the supporters of Samuel Gompers. But the aims of the Wobblies in each instance were immediate and pragmatic; they did not expect Lawrence and Paterson to lead directly to revolution; the IWW was there to get a somewhat better life for the workers in those cities.

Haywood's contemporaries never appreciated that unionism was at the heart of his actions. When Haywood appeared before the Industrial Relations Commission in 1915, the commissioners' chief interest was the IWW's revolutionism. But Haywood wanted to talk about the IWW's unionism and its concrete immediate accomplishments. Haywood did not attempt to conceal anything about the end which the IWW visualized and he answered all questions candidly, but he emphasized the movement's "bread and butter" accomplishments when he led the discussion. After discussing the revolutionary part of Wobbly ideology, Commissioner Weinstock asked Haywood if he thought that it would take a long time before the "whole world" adopted IWW principles. Haywood replied that "it does not make any difference to me if it is not for a hundred years." Surprised, Weinstock asked what Haywood and the IWW would do in the meantime.

Haywood replied: "The same thing we are doing now—plugging along and taking our part in the class struggle, fighting for better conditions and hoping to get them tomorrow, but fighting for them, if we do not get them for a century." When another commissioner asked Haywood what he would recommend to Congress if he were a member of the commission, Haywood replied that "I think I would advise to meet the needs of the people, employment, work, such as the government could do—reclamation, reforesting stations—such work as would meet the needs of the unemployed; that is, just as remedial measures." Commissioner O'Connell, a conservative unionist who seemed to react adversely to Haywood without listening, evidently misinterpreted Haywood's suggestions as visionary for he asked the witness the same question in his curious patois: "notwithstanding we probably feel that you are so imbued with your utopian ideas of things that they would not modernize down to the affairs of the day." "Really, Mr. McConnell," Haywood replied, "I don't think that I presented any utopian ideas. I talked for the necessities of life—food, clothing, shelter, and amusement. We can talk of Utopia afterwards. The greatest need is employment." [53]

All of which does not make Haywood a proto-New Dealer. He was a revolutionist; he sincerely and deeply hoped for the institution of a cooperative commonwealth and worked with that end always in mind. But neither was he an incessant dreamer. He was aware of the necessities of daily life, and sought to improve them for the working class with which he identified. With the revolution little more than a remote aspiration, it was the IWW's occasionally won immediate gains which sustained him during the years after 1910. And despite his interests in Greenwich Village, Haywood was no part-time laborer in the cause. When he was called to Lawrence he spent virtually every waking hour either in the town, speaking on fund-raising drives, or preparing the workers' presentation to the congressional investigating committee secured by Socialist Congressman Victor Berger. After Lawrence was settled, he sped from one New England textile town to another where smaller, shorter strikes had broken out.[54]

During 1913 Haywood alternated between Paterson and Akron, where the IWW was conducting a strike among rubber workers. His efforts cost him a stomach ulcer. Haywood became the IWW's secretary-treasurer soon after, and began to spend more of his time at the union's headquarters in Chicago. But he remained close to Wobbly strikes, speaking at them frequently, and maintaining close contact with the workers through his field organizers. It was a job much like that of secretary-treasurer of the Western Federation which he had held ten years before.[55]

Haywood's anarchist acquaintance, Alexander Berkman, grew disgusted with Big Bill after 1914 when Haywood proved reluctant to support several meetings and free-speech fights which the anarchists launched. He called Haywood "weak-kneed." But it was no loss of courage that alienated Haywood from his anarchist friends. Haywood showed no reluctance to face arrest and possible beatings during his Wobbly period. Although he was not arrested in Lawrence—thanks largely to the public reaction to the arrest of Ettor and Giovannitti—the Boston police tricked him into custody and indicted (but never tried) him on the occasion of a sympathy meeting for the confied Wobblies on Boston Common. In Paterson he was arrested for coming to town, and again for leaving it when he attempted to lead a group of strikers to neighboring Haledon for a rally. He was approached by the anarchists in Akron when he arrived to address strikers there. Haywood balked at backing their ventures because he regarded his unionist responsibilities as the most important, even to the point of excluding all others. He would risk arrest or even death to win a strike but not for the sake of an abstract libertarian principle, no matter how much Haywood-the-revolutionist concurred in it. This feature of his character neither Berkman nor Haywood's antiradical critics quite grasped.[56]

The IWW failed as a union, of course, and Haywood as a unionist along with it. Paramount among the reasons for the failure was the prosecution and persecution of the union during World War I. In addition, much of the blame for the IWW's failure must be attributed to Haywood's and the other Wobblies' belief that the workers would inevitably do "what was best for them," a foible common among Marxists before Lenin and Gramsci. Haywood placed too little emphasis on maintaining a viable and permanent union organization. He recognized this as a weakness and attempted to find the remedy, but too late to take advantage of the strikes of 1912 and 1913. Well over a million workers passed through the IWW at one time or another, but with the exceptions of Philadelphia longshoremen and some lumber workers' unions, the IWW never maintained a viable organization. In McKee's Rocks, Akron, Lawrence, and Paterson, where the Wobblies signed up tens of thousands of members, the locals folded within a few years. The reason was not the IWW's failure to win concrete victories. Even at Lawrence, where the IWW victory matched anything won by the American Federation of Labor during the era, a Wobbly local of over 20,000 members dissipated in a year to less than a few hundred.

The fault lay in the IWW's and Haywood's confidence in the capacity of the industrial proletariat to maintain an organization in the face of ethnic diversity and employer hostility. When Haywood, Ettor, and Flynn left Lawrence after the strike was won, they assumed that the strike committees which they had erected would continue to function with the crisis gone, maintaining the IWW's presence. They did not.

Haywood placed supreme confidence in "the workers" and he did not fully understand the vast differences between the western miners from whom he had come and the eastern industrial immigrants among whom he spent his IWW years. Western radical unionism had been deeply rooted in, and sprang spontaneously from, the miner's milieu. The Western Federation had been built from the ground up; the mining camps had produced their own leaders, Haywood foremost among them. But the immigrants of Lawrence, Paterson, Little Falls, McKee's Rocks, and even the Mesabi Range—however deep their aggrievance at the abuse they suffered and however heroic their efforts for the union in time of crisis—were essentially uneasy aliens in a hostile world. Despite the ringing Wobbly protestation that "We have no leaders; we are all leaders!" the eastern Wobbly experience proved otherwise. Divided immigrant workers could call a strike and stone scabs, but it took the IWW to impress on the disorganized mass a powerful union which won strikes on specific issues. When Haywood and the others left for other fronts there was nothing. And that was the IWW's failure.

Finally, the IWW failed because its fate was integrally connected with the fate of the other great radical organization of the day, the Socialist Party of America. And events within the SPA during 1912 and 1913 were showing that the Socialists did not realize the significance of the connection both to their party and to the IWW. The SPA's decision to sever all its connections with the IWW are of signal importance to Haywood's career, for he was the person who represented the alliance.

6

Socialist

William D. Haywood was a prominent member of the Socialist Party of America as well as the Industrial Workers of the World. Along with Ed Boyce and most of the other leaders of the Western Federation, he joined the party shortly after it was founded in 1901. He was inactive in the party's national affairs during these first years but won many members for it through his WFM leadership. In 1904 he wrote a pamphlet for Debs' presidential campaign called "The Wolf," in which he urged a Socialist vote as the way to eliminate "rascally government, poverty and crime" and the way to achieve collective ownership of the nation's resources. In 1906 Haywood stood as Socialist candidate for governor of Colorado while a prisoner in Idaho. He polled 16,000 votes, eight times as many as any previous Socialist candidate. In 1908 Haywood briefly considered seeking the party's presidential nomination when Eugene V. Debs hinted he would not run. When Debs finally did become the candidate, Haywood spoke widely on his behalf, rode the famous "Red Special" for part of its journey, and was a featured speaker at Debs' final rally.[1]

In terms of political success, American radicals enjoyed their happiest days with the Socialist Party. Pieced together by Bellamy Nationalists, Single Taxers, Populists, militant unionists, the Social Democratic Party of Milwaukee, and an offshoot from the Socialist Labor Party, the SPA won more votes than the older SLP in its first election campaign. Outright electoral victories were few, but in Massachusetts, where the party was informally allied with the Boot and Shoe Workers Union, the party figured prominently in two industrial cities. If growth was unspectacular, it was steady and promising. From nearly 100,000 votes in 1900, the quadrennial candidate Debs won 402,283 in 1904 and 420,718 in 1908. Compared to the major parties, the vote was a pittance but it was growing, and the Socialists' faith in the inevitability of their commonwealth helped to assuage the disappointment of defeat. Increasingly after 1910, moreover, the party won some immediate successes.[2]

Not all was promising, however. Even more than the IWW, the Socialist Party was an alliance of diverse and mutually hostile factions. The specific issues on which they differed shifted from year to year during the party's first decade, but one consistent denominator was the degree of conflict with which the factions interpreted their relationship with the capitalist enemy. Intra-party jargon reflected the distinction. The left wing of the party, which insisted on the necessity of social revolution, referred to themselves as "revolutionists" and their co-partisan rivals as "slowshulists." The name referred to the "reformists'" contention that socialism was possible through social evolution and that, in the meantime, a great deal could be accomplished through collaboration with pro-capitalist progressives within the system. They generally referred to the party left as "impossibilists" or "r-r-r-revolutionists."

By 1908 the specific party issues on which the SPA's factions divided were political opportunism and the nature of the party's relationship to the labor movement. The revolutionists held a singularly dim view of political action in general and the possibility of achieving socialism through political evolution in particular. Their interpretation of the Marxian definition of the state as the executive committee of the ruling class precluded for them any hope of changing society through the state. Jack London, who flitted in and out of radical circles at the time, wrote: "history shows that no master class is ever willing to let go without a quarrel. The capitalists own the government, the armies, and the militia. Don't you think capitalists will use these institutions to keep themselves in power?" Of course, responded the revolutionists, who added that the capitalists would also dissolve the same institutions if they failed to serve their design.[3]

Not that the revolutionists thought to dissolve the SPA. They reserved an important, albeit secondary, role for the political party. First, the Socialist Party was to prevent legislation adverse to the working class and prevent the use of the police and militia against strikers. In the phrase of the IWW, which was the vanguard of the SPA's left wing, Socialist politicians in power could withhold the policeman's club. According to a party revolutionist, the political party's major task was "to hamper the ruling class in the war it will be waging on the revolutionary unions." [4]

Second, the political party's function was to extort reform legislation from the capitalist-owned municipalities, states, and perhaps even the federal government. The revolutionists approved heartily of minimum wage laws, codes prohibiting the use of child labor, tenement legislation, and any concessions from the capitalist which might ameliorate the worker's life. They disagreed with those radicals who subscribed to the dictum, "the worse the better" because that meant the revolution was imminent. Deeply rooted in unionism, the revolutionists were happy to make any immediate gains just so the workers did not delude themselves into thinking that such "crumbs" were the goal.[5]

Third, the political party was invaluable as an educational agency. Through its political campaigns the party could transmit sound knowledge to the workers and educate them in the principles of revolutionary industrial unionism. All the better if the socialists won their elections; their victories would attract the curiosity of the workers. It was important, however, that socialist politicians recognize their limited role and not think they were accomplishing the revolution by holding office.[6]

Fourth, the SPA's vote would serve as a sort of popularity poll, a register of the degree of support the workers could expect in the event of a strike, a demonstration, or, ultimately, the revolution. The revolutionists subscribed to the old American Labor Union's view of voting that the party's vote was merely "public expression" so far as revolution was concerned.[7]

Fifth, when capitalism finally crumbled as a result of the general strike, the political socialists would help the political state to destroy itself. (In that socialist electoral success would increase as the revolution neared, this would be an easy task.) At a speech in Cooper Union in 1912, Haywood—who was, of course, in the revolutionist wing—emphasized that "with the success of socialism practically all the political offices now in existence will be put out of business" and socialist politicians would help in the liquidation.[8]

The crux of the matter was that the party could not establish socialism; that feat was within the competence only of the workers themselves, organized into revolutionary labor unions. Political action alone was ludicrous; the party should accept as its function that of auxiliary to the revolutionary union. "The Socialist Party and the labor union will come closer and closer together," Haywood wrote in *Industrial Socialism.* "The labor union will come to stand for Socialism. The Socialist Party will thus become a mere phase of the labor movement. The union and the party together make war upon the enemy, the capitalist class." [9]

To Haywood and the other SPA revolutionists, the "labor movement" meant the IWW. Disgustedly despairing of the conservative American Federation of Labor for many years, the revolutionists thought that a socialist party should ignore it (if not make war on it) and trust to a union which was unequivocally committed to a cooperative commonwealth. They did not seek a formal, explicit relationship between the two organizations. The IWW was to a large degree synonymous with the SPA's left wing anyway, and the IWW forbade affiliation with any political party. What the revolutionists sought was the party's recognition of the union as the heart of the class struggle and itself as an auxiliary. Hopefully, this would take the form of an SPA endorsement of the IWW. At the least, the revolutionists required that the AFL not receive the same.[10]

The reformists, however, still hoped to capture the AFL and the inevitable result in the deadlocked party was compromise. At the party's convention in 1908, a platitudinous resolution supporting the labor movement in general was introduced. "Forward," the Socialists called, "In one solid phalanx, under the banners of Organized Labor and the Socialist Party, to defeat capitalist aggressions, to win immediate relief for yourselves and your wives and children, and to hasten the day of complete emancipation from capitalist exploitation and misrule." Several revolutionist delegates criticized the resolution on the grounds that it did not single out industrial unionism for especial commendation. An amendment was offered which noted that socialists had a duty to point out to the workers that the industrial form of organization was the best suited to working-class solidarity. The amendment was voted down in favor of the neutralist resolution.[11]

The party's neutrality between the AFL and the IWW was as uncongenial to the reformists as to the revolutionists. The party's right wing was committed to a policy of attempting to win the AFL to the party's cause, and no one more emphatically than the titular leader of the reformist wing, Victor Berger, the head of the eminently successful Social Democratic Party of Milwaukee. Born in Austria in 1860 of a middle-class family, Berger was well educated at the Universities of Budapest and Vienna and emigrated to the United States while a young man. He was a schoolteacher for a time, but excited by socialist politics among Milwaukee's many German residents Berger became an editor, first of the daily *Vorwaerts,* and later of the English-language *Social Democratic Herald.*[12]

Berger was a highly pragmatic man who prized political office, and his program resembled the progressivism of his contemporary Wisconsinite, Robert Marion La Follette. Whether or not his "social democracy" was or was not "socialism" is a subjective question. But socialism or not, it won elections. Upon a "solid south" of German votes, Berger built a powerful coalition by wooing much of Milwaukee's middle class and the organized labor movement of the city. This required compromises. To win the labor movement, Berger was committed to support it in return, even though that sometimes meant supporting the American Federation's anti-socialist majority. To win the progressive sector of the middle class, Berger was required to play down the "socialistic" aspects of his program and emphasize the Social Democratic Party's reputation for "clean government." By 1902, for example, Berger was urging the national party to imitate his example and "make a clean sweep of stupid phrases and senseless catchwords" such as "social revolution."

In 1905 Berger risked expulsion from the Socialist Party of America for violating a party rule against supporting non-socialist candidates. He abstained from nominating a judicial candidate because the Progressive-Republican candidate was "a liberal, upright man," and Berger deeply resented the party's mild censure after the fact. During the campaign of 1906 in Milwaukee, when victory seemed imminent, Berger assured small employers that he could say "from actual experience that the Social Democrats of this city have opposed almost every strike that has been declared here." An aide claimed that "the business interests of Milwaukee will be safer in the hands of an administration made up of Social Democrats than they have been under Republican and Democratic administrations." As if the point were not clear, he added, "our party believes in all things that are for the business life of the city." [13]

All this was obnoxious to the revolutionists, of course, and they were not mollified by Berger's political success. When Berger was elected to the House of Representatives in 1910 and boasted to a New York newspaper that he was very popular on Capitol Hill, even with crusty Speaker "Uncle Joe" Cannon, the revolutionists observed that "frankly, it seems to us that a Socialist representative who has not earned the undying hatred of all the Joe Cannons, big and little, has not entirely succeeded in his mission. Is it possible for the spokesman of the millions who suffer every day of the year from monstrous oppression and injustice to give voice to their wrongs without arousing violent and bitter resentment in the breasts of those who are determined to continue these wrongs with all the means of oppression at their disposal." The revolutionists could not help but be dismayed by Berger's tacit denial of class conflict.[14]

But the impact of Berger's success on other Socialists was another matter. They were frankly impressed by his electoral success in Milwaukee and sought to duplicate it in their own bailiwicks. They saw that while Debs and local revolutionists ran no-compromise, revolutionary campaigns and went down to repeated defeat, Berger's party was actually governing a major city. Party leaders such as Algie Simons, John Spargo, Robert Hunter, Morris Hillquit, and many others increasingly looked to Berger for counsel and increasingly adopted his pragmatism.

With the exception of Debs, who abstained from an active role in the party's infighting, Haywood was the best-known party leader of revolutionist disposition, and certainly more than Debs the chief party advocate of IWW-SPA cooperation. Like the other revolutionists who gathered about the *International Socialist Review* and the short-lived *New Review,* Haywood was bitterly hostile to the AFL, a legacy of his experience with the Western Federation. Moreover, he boasted of having no illusions about the potential of political action for bringing about the revolution. "While a member of the Socialist Party and a believer in political action," he said repeatedly, "it is decidedly better in my opinion to be able to elect the superintendent in some branch of industry than to elect a congressman to the United States Congress."

Of the single socialist in Congress and his opportunism, Haywood was scornful, but he was willing to congratulate even Berger when the Milwaukeean functioned as Haywood thought he should. On the occasion of the Lawrence strike, when Berger agitated for and won a congressional investigation of working conditions in the city, Haywood beamed that the union and the party "worked shoulder to shoulder in presenting to the world and in assisting the Lawrence textile workers to win their fight." Haywood had no doubt that the unionized workers won the day, but he also recognized the assistance of the party. This was exactly how political socialists should function![15]

The revolutionists were vulnerable to cries that they opposed political action, but in actuality they never categorically denied the usefulness of elections, Haywood least among them. After his acquittal at Boise (which he pretended to attribute to working-class solidarity), Haywood thanked his audiences and urged them "to do for yourself what you have done for me," namely, "to organize politically as well as industrially." Under increasing reformist fire by 1910, Haywood stated his concept of union-party collaboration quite clearly. He was caught in a crossfire between the "purely political" Socialists and the antipolitical anarcho-syndicalists at a debate. To the IWW newspaper, *Solidarity,* it was "amusing and instructive" how Haywood, "with the easy confidence of a man who knows," held his balance between the two. "Do you believe in political action?" a socialist asked him. "Do you believe in direct action?" an anarchist interjected. Haywood replied, "as a socialist I believe in political action. As an industrialist I believe in political and direct action." Elizabeth Gurley Flynn recalled another Haywood gambit in another situation. "I'm a two-gun man from the West, you know," Haywood would say, and then pause while the audience waited "breathlessly." Then Haywood would take his union card from one pocket and his SPA card from the other.[16]

Even after the revolutionist wing lost out entirely to the reformists within the party, Haywood urged the Wobblies to support SPA political action at least as a stopgap measure. In August, 1912 he told an interviewer that "I . . . urge every workingman to use the ballot at every opportunity." At the party's convention in 1912 he announced that he had advocated at Lawrence that every worker who had the franchise exercise it to advance his economic interests. He also reported that "while only fifteen percent of the workers [in Lawrence] had the vote before the strike, since the strike we have taken into the Socialist Party as many as one hundred members at a meeting." In a debate with Morris Hillquit, Haywood explained his limited concept of political action. He repeated the IWWs refusal to affiliate officially with any political party, but pointed out that he and most Wobblies dutifully cast Socialist ballots at every election.[17]

In a sense, the revolutionist goal of an informal alliance of party and union was similar to Berger's "Milwaukee Idea": "a personal union of the workers [through] having the same persons take an active interest in both the trade union and the political labor movement. . . . Then we find the same men, with the same thoughts, aims, and ideals working in the economic and political field, thus forming a giant army moving on two roads for the abolition of the capitalist system." The signal difference was that where Berger and his allies saw the party as paramount, Haywood and the revolutionists reserved that role for the union. Just as important, Haywood's union was the IWW, Berger's the AFL. Berger and the other Socialist members of the AFL, like Max Hayes of the typographers union, did not wish to break from the Federation in part because they held positions of some power within it. Moreover, they assumed that the membership of the AFL would eventually come to its senses and overthrow Gompers' conservative administration, thus paving the way for the large union's alliance with the SPA.

This was by no means a fantasy. The socialists had controlled the AFL for one year during the 1890's and, while they were a minority within the Federation, they were well organized and it required all of Gompers' considerable acumen to keep them in line. The hope, of course, was for the AFL to adopt socialism. But when hopes for this grew dimmer, the reformists' distaste for the IWW and their habit of courting the AFL took them down an "unsocialist" path which led eventually to disaster for the party.[18]

Ironically, the Socialist who first initiated an attempt to merge the AFL and the SPA on a non-socialist basis was a founder of the IWW, Algie M. Simons. Simons was a graduate of the University of Wisconsin who had come to the Socialist Party through his interest in social causes during the late 1890's. He served as editor of various Socialist periodicals, and in 1905 was the head of Charles H. Kerr's *International Socialist Review*. Simons conceived of the IWW as the economic arm of the SPA, a magnet which would draw radical unions away from the AFL. This conception was at loggerheads with that of most of the IWW's founders, and Simons left the union soon after its founding when it became clear that the union would not be the SPA's adjunct. Simons continued with the *International Socialist Review* for three years, but he was moving away from the IWW as publisher Kerr grew increasingly enamored of the union and the party's revolutionist wing. Simons was dismissed, and by 1909 he had transcended his former distaste for AFL conservatism and launched an abortive campaign to join it to the SPA.[19]

In late 1909, after returning from an AFL meeting in Toronto, Simons dispatched a confidential circular letter to several prominent Socialists. Haywood was not included in the list and the reason for this was clearly implied in Simons' first proposal. "We must drive from our own ranks," Simons wrote, "the demagogical politicians who are seeking to raise rebellion against every person they cannot use for their own purpose." He was referring not only to his own dismissal from the *International Socialist Review* by revolutionist Kerr, but to the intentions of the revolutionists like Haywood who sought to replace the reformist members of the party's executive committee with more militant leaders. Simons continued that the members of the executive committee were "more than willing to surrender their positions if real workingmen are to take their place [but] they do not propose to surrender to those who have never worked save with their jaws and are tearing down every organization to which they belong." [20]

Second, Simons proposed, the party must become a true "labor party." As the SPA stood at the moment, to Simons' way of thinking, it was on the one hand "a bunch of intellectuals like MYSELF and Spargo and Hunter and Hillquit, on the other is a bunch of 'never-works,' demagogues and would-be intellectuals, a veritable 'lumpenproletariat.' . . . The actual wage earners, the men who are really FIGHTING the class struggle are outside." That meant the AFL. Simons concluded that he did not especially like the British Labour Party, but reorganizing the SPA along similar lines was the road to electoral success and the only alternative to a disastrous alliance with the IWW. Simons had learned at Toronto that some mildly socialist members of the AFL were pondering the possibilities of independent political action, and he offered this as a golden opportunity for the SPA. But to groom the party so that it would be acceptable to the majority of the AFL would require a further moderation of the party's program and probable abandonment of the name, "Socialist." The SPA must meet the AFL halfway.

Simons' proposal failed for a number of reasons. For one thing, the conspiratorial nature of the plan (Simons' hushing of his correspondents was ridiculous) was scuttled from the beginning by one addressee, William English Walling. A revolutionist by disposition—it is difficult to understand why he was on Simons' list—Walling published the letter on November 26, 1909. Walling excoriated Simons' attempt to organize a party which was, he added sarcastically, to be "more or less socialistic." Simons had written that the AFL came nearer to representing the working class than the SPA. Walling was ostensibly appalled: "no member of the Socialist Party, so far as I know, has ever dared to say in public that the A.F. of L., as at present constituted, comes nearer to representing the working class than the Socialist Party." To say so was to reject the essence of socialist principles, for the AFL was inalterably opposed to these.[21]

Haywood agreed completely with Walling's side in the dispute but he took no part in the brouhaha that ensued. He might well have paid better attention to it, for the issues which it dramatized determined his future in the party. The dispute illustrated that differences between party reformists and revolutionists were near the point of irreconcilability. The reformist desire for immediate electoral success, even at the cost of scrapping the socialist aspects of their program, was clearly stated. This meant an explicit repudiation of Haywood's IWW, whose very existence offended even socialist American Federationists. Walling and his supporters were not uncritical partisans of the IWW, to be sure. Walling described the Wobblies as sufficiently revolutionary but "not democratic." But he also felt that "certainly these people are far more sympathetic . . . to me, than the reformers." [22]

In addition to the premature publicity, the AFL's failure to act ended the short-lived movement. The extent of Simons' conversations in Toronto cannot be determined, but there was little activity within the AFL after the publication of the letter to indicate a substantial movement. Adolf Germer, a Socialist official of the United Mine Workers, continued to work for a liaison between the Federation and the party, but he had been doing so for years.

Third, there was a decided, if not necessarily determining, reaction among the SPA's rank and file. The revolutionists were briefly on the upsurge; they would elect Haywood to the National Executive Committee in 1910. All over the country, party locals censured Simons for his apparent desire to castrate the Party.[23]

Finally, the movement to disassociate from the IWW and ally with the AFL failed because the Party was diverted by a sudden rise in its fortunes without benefit of an AFL alliance. While this temporarily submerged the intensity of the factional struggle, however, it also sowed the seeds for its renewal. The increasingly reformist party came to a conclusion about its electoral successes which strengthened the position and policies of Victor Berger, and necessitated a policy which tore the SPA apart.

The SPA's brief but exhilarating period of electoral victory began in 1910, especially in Milwaukee where Victor Berger was elected to Congress and the party swept almost the entire city administration. In 1911 there were more municipal victories. When the results of both spring and fall elections were tabulated, the party announced that it had elected 56 mayors, 305 aldermen and councilmen, 22 police officials, 155 members of school boards, and 4 pound keepers. Then in 1912 the national ticket polled nearly a million votes, about 6 per cent of the total and fully twice the party's vote four years before. The number of socialists elected to local office had risen from 450 in 1911 to about 1,000.[24]

While elated by the victories, the reformists were also disappointed. Confronted by the evidence of Milwaukee, where Berger's party had succeeded in winning many progressively minded middle-class votes, the reformists reasoned that the nation lagged behind Milwaukee only because of the party's continued association in the public eye with the revolutionism and IWW-ism represented by Socialists like Haywood. Simons' plan to establish a détente with the AFL had failed because of the party's informal relationship with the Wobblies. Now, many middle-class votes which would have gone to the party were lost because such progressives abhorred the IWW's unsavory reputation for violence. The reformists had some evidence for the belief in addition to Berger's amazing success in Milwaukee. They pointed out that while the Democratic and Republican parties suffered net losses in votes between 1908 and 1912, the SPA had made an absolute gain of 476,873. Clearly, to the reformists, these votes were part of the same movement which created the Bull Moose Party. If the SPA could refurbish its reputation, it seemed logical that their share would be even greater.[25]

Enough progressives repeated the argument to the reformist

Socialists to confirm their analysis. Charles Sprague Smith wrote to Morris Hillquit that he saw the SPA as "a very important element in the whole progressive movement," and that for the sake of both the SPA and progressivism "it is imperative that [the SPA] be under the control of the intelligent, cool-headed, historically-informed, spiritually-consecrated men" like Hillquit. Reformist Robert Hunter exulted that the SPA was drawing increasing strength from the universities, the professional classes, the clergy, and even the business world. The implication was clear. The party could expect even more such support if it was disassociated from "disreputable" elements such as William D. Haywood.[26]

Middle-class progressives despised Haywood and the Wobblies because of their reputation for violence and sabotage. In the popular eye, the IWW was a conspiracy of desperate villains who set fires in wheatfields, drove spikes into sawmill-bound logs, derailed trains, destroyed industrial machinery, and killed policemen. That the IWW collectively was no more responsible for the industrial violence that plagued the United States in the period than Haywood was an advocate for it is beside the point. Most Americans thought so, and it was to "most Americans" that the SPA wished ultimately to appeal. The reformists were not concerned so much with the fact of the revolutionist position as with its image.

The specific issue on which the reformists joined issue with Haywood and the Wobblies was a term recently imported from France: *sabotage*. In its most popular connotation, sabotage stood for violent injury to machinery, crops, and other property of employers. With this definition in mind, the reformists watched aghast as the Wobblies seized upon the term and shouted it to the winds. In fact, to the IWW, the word meant a great deal more than violence alone. Another meaning was *ca' canny,* "go slowly." The French phrase was *à mauvaise paie, mauvais travail;* the Wobblies called it "striking on the job." As Elizabeth Gurley Flynn wrote in a Wobbly pamphlet on the subject, "sabotage means either to slacken up and interfere with the quantity, or to botch in your skill and interfere with the quality of capitalist production so as to give poor service. It is something that is fought out within the walls of the shop." She added, although reformists ignored the phrase, "sabotage is not physical violence, sabotage is an internal industrial process. It is simply another form of coercion." [27]

A third type of sabotage was obstructionist. It consisted in carrying out all orders literally, regardless of consequences. Many industries, in response to laws requiring safety devices, published long lists of safety regulations which, if violated, disqualified a man from compensation. The saboteur's device was to follow literally all the cumbersome rules which none ever expected to be observed. Employers soon agreed to compensate for injuries suffered in violation of the rules.[28]

A fourth form of sabotage was what the French called *la bouche ouverte*. It consisted simply of publicity; telling the truth to the customer despite its effects on the business. Most examples of the tactic in practice are European, but an IWW waiter's strike in New York City was settled in the workers' favor when the union threatened to release a list of hotels which maintained unsanitary kitchens or served adulterated, impure, or spoiled food.[29]

A final form of sabotage of which the IWW talked involved benefiting the customer contrary to the employer's instructions. Thus, wineshop workers instructed to dilute wines should secretly refrain from doing it. Cooks given margarine to use in products sold as butter-baked should use so much margarine that the product became just as expensive as if butter had been used. Grocery clerks must never shortweight customers although they might be told to do so. Apothecary clerks should always recommend the least expensive variety of a prescribed drug and they must not omit any high-priced ingredient, although that might be the employer's policy.[30]

Sabotage, then, meant a great deal more than violent action. In fact, Elizabeth Gurley Flynn explicitly warned against violence in her pamphlet on sabotage, and Arturo Giovannitti, who translated Emile Pouget's *Le Sabotage* into English, went to great pains in a lengthy introduction to disagree completely with the Frenchman's advocacy of damage to property. Haywood had relatively little to say on the subject, but talked about only the nonviolent varieties in his interview with the Industrial Relations Commission. Nevertheless, the popular image overrode the reality and it was on the issue of sabotage that the reformists finally resolved to eliminate the revolutionists. At the party's convention at Indianapolis in 1912, the reformists amended Article II, Section 6 of the party's constitution to read:

> Any member of the party who opposes political action or advocates crime, sabotage, or other methods of violence as a weapon of the working class to aid in its emancipation shall be expelled from membership in the party. Political action shall be construed to mean participation in elections for public office and practical legislative and administrative work along the lines of the Socialist Party platform.[31]

The predictable revolutionist uproar took on several aspects. Some critics pointed out that Section 1 of Article II already provided that one must subscribe to political action as a condition for joining the party. It did not require that one accept political action as the only, or even the most important function of the party, but Section 6 seemed intended to do precisely that. The pro-IWW *New Review* added that the ruling on sabotage and other means of direct action was not the proper concern of the SPA as the reformists themselves had defined it. Those were questions of internal union policy and tactics in which the reformists "had again and again pledged . . . not to intermeddle." But the chief and, in retrospect, most telling criticism of Section 6 was that through it the Socialist Party "surrendered the theoretical right of forcible revolution." Indeed, Section 6 marked the theoretical triumph of the reformist Socialists who had literally abandoned the notion of class conflict. To deny the right of violent revolution under *any* conditions literally undercut the ideological foundations of the movement and turned the SPA into a progressive party designed to reform capitalism from within.[32]

Of course, neither ideology nor the workability of Section 6 had much to do with the reformists' design. It would have been impossible, had the reformists sought to do so on any large scale, to expel more than a handful of Wobblies from the party for advocating violence. They simply did not advocate it. Nor could many be expelled for opposing political action. They would not have been in the party in the first place if they opposed it. Section 6 was designed, first of all, as a public relations ploy. It was necessary, as reformist C. E. Reeves wrote, for the party to shun "the very appearance of evil" if it were to win middle-class votes. By outlawing violence and sabotage on paper, the party could hope to appeal to middle-class voters offended by the party's revolutionist wing. Second, even if few could actually be expelled on the basis of Section 6, revolutionists who despised the "purely political" reformists could be expected to see that the party was firmly in reformist hands and leave it voluntarily. But to effect that end it was necessary to carry the reformist campaign one step further.[33]

Local Yuma, Arizona, had previously moved Haywood's recall from his seat on the National Executive Committee in March, 1912, on the basis of a speech Haywood made at Lawrence in which, purportedly, he made antipolitical statements. However, motions on party matters required seconds by locals comprising at least 5 per cent of the party membership before they could be submitted to a referendum. Morris Hillquit engineered a second at a meeting of the New York Central Committee on March 9, without debate and by the close vote of 14 to 11, but when, five days later, victory in the Lawrence strike enhanced Haywood's reputation, the New York committee meekly declared that it had acted in haste and withdrew its second.[34] That resolution of recall died without a vote, but with Section 6 in the party constitution the reformists moved again after the November election. Haywood's recall was proposed and passed easily, although only about 20 per cent of the membership bothered to vote in the referendum.

There were various attempts at reconciliation. Helen Keller, a member of the party and personal friend of Haywood who was widely respected because of her personal accomplishments, wrote an impassioned appeal for conciliation. "It fills me with amusement," she wrote, "to see such a narrow spirit, such an ignoble strife between two factions which should be one, and that too, at a most critical period in the struggle of the proletariat." She felt that the issue was a matter of disagreement on tactics which she regarded as rather foolish, "no better than the capitalist politicians who stand in high places and harangue about petty matters, while millions of people are underpaid, underfed, thrown out of work and dying." There are many ways to work for the cooperative commonwealth, she concluded, and "those who are on the workers' side of the battle are our Comrades . . . [and] can never cease to be our Comrades." [35]

Frank Bohn, a friend of Haywood's and member of both IWW and SPA, called for rapprochement. He argued that it was the SPA reformists who were the sectarian fanatics who cared "more for the success of some faction or clique within the organization or movement than for the success of the movement as a whole." But Bohn's arguments were aimed chiefly at Haywood and the Wobblies who seemed to be abandoning the party by the thousands, as the reformists had hoped. "For the time being forget Section 6," Bohn pleaded, "and the day will come when those who passed it, realizing their shame and disgrace, will vote to repeal it. . . . Wrong as [the reformists] were, their error is not one tenth as great as that of the member who deserts the standards under fire." [36]

But Bohn was among the last of the advocates of IWW-SPA collaboration. Haywood said little about the affair at first, wanly hoping for reconciliation. He continued to speak in favor of political action after the recall, but devoted most of his time to the IWW and none to the SPA. By the time of World War I, bitterness had displaced hope of reconciliation, and for the first time Haywood spoke in terms of rejecting all politics, several times defining the IWW in terms other than "socialism." Sometime between 1913 and 1918, he allowed his SPA membership to lapse.

Years later, Haywood spoke of the affair in detail for the first time and largely in terms of the reformists' betrayal of socialist principle. "The Communist Manifesto of Marx and Engels meant nothing to them. They cast aside its primary teachings." He also pointed out what less partisan observers independently noted, that Section 6 was something of a forerunner of the Criminal Syndicalism laws under which the IWW was later prosecuted into impotence. "The Criminal Syndicalism laws have been upheld by the United States Supreme Court," Haywood wrote, "and hundreds of men and women have been sent to the penitentiaries though not one of them had committed any offense except that of holding an opinion or being a member of the Industrial Workers of the World. . . . The many who have been persecuted can thank the traitors of the Socialist Party who adopted Article 2, Section 6 against the working class." [37]

Reflecting over a decade of simmering bitterness and written at a time when the SPA and the Communist Party were at loggerheads (with Haywood's sympathies with the latter), Haywood's point is somewhat overstated. What is clear, however, is that Article II, Section 6 marked a significant milestone in the decline of the IWW. The Industrial Workers of the World needed the Socialist Party. Despite the Wobblies' cheery sense of self-reliance, the union never acted in a vacuum. Sometimes willing, sometimes not, the SPA functioned as a buffer for the IWW. It was respectable—something the IWW was not—and in many parts of the country exerted sufficient power to be above both legal and extralegal harassment, an immunity which it could extend to the IWW.

The party was often generous in contributing to IWW strike funds; some claimed that the SPA spent more on the Lawrence strike than it did on the presidential campaign of the same year. And the party did "withhold the policeman's club" where the party controlled it; it was in SPA-governed Haledon, New Jersey, that the Wobblies rallied when they were prevented from assembling in Paterson. Wobbly success in Schenectady, New York (where the IWW claimed it fought the first "sit-down" strike) owed much to the cordiality of the SPA administration there, and the IWW prospered in Butte, Montana, under the mayoralty of Socialist Lewis Duncan. Thus it was a major blow when the Party effectively repudiated the IWW in 1912 and 1913. Followed shortly by the defeat at Paterson (which one prominent Wobbly, Patrick Quinlan, blamed on SPA disinterestedness), the IWW never recovered in the East.

The decline of the IWW was no unpleasant prospect to the SPA reformists, but another effect of Section 6 was not so welcome. The reformists had assumed that with the unsavory revolutionists out of the party the way was open to a glorious future as a major reform party. If they had any misgivings about rejecting the theoretical right of insurrection, those were more than compensated for by statements such as the *New York World*'s to the effect that the SPA could now "honestly appeal to public opinion as a party that recognizes the rules of orderly government and rejects the theory that the lawless shall gain power by intimidation and lawlessness." The *Metropolitan Magazine* congratulated the "thousands upon thousands of good citizens" within the party who could not tolerate the "Haywood element." Now that the SPA's true character was revealed, the magazine continued, the party would "immediately attract the real Progressives." [38]

But 1912 proved to be no harbinger of a glorious new era, but only the apogee of Socialist Party success. Hardly streaming to the SPA, progressives remained within their own parties. Moreover, it became painfully apparent that the SPA had needed the IWW as much as the union needed the party. The SPA had actually enjoyed its largest membership in May, 1912, when there were some 135,000 dues-paying members. Membership declined to 100,000 after Section 6 was adopted, a development the reformists anticipated as the welcome exodus of the "Haywood element." But the decline was not over. During the four months after Haywood's recall membership dropped precipitously to 80,000. A slow recovery followed, but it was already apparent that there was no "golden age" imminent; it had already come and gone.[39]

Reflecting the same trend, reverses in local elections in 1913 all but wiped out the victories of 1910, 1911, and 1912. Some of the most important cities previously won by the SPA returned to Republican, Democratic, or fusion control. In addition, official and unofficial socialist newspapers found themselves suddenly without their accustomed financial support. Within the few months before August, 1913, such seemingly well-established papers as the *Daily Socialist* (Chicago), the *Coming Nation,* and the *Cleveland Socialist* closed down their presses. The *Washington National Socialist* merged with the *Appeal to Reason.* In complete control of the party by 1916, the reformists accomplished Victor Berger's long-standing wish to nominate a reformist for President in the person of Journalist Allan Benson. Benson polled only 3 per cent of the total vote, proportionately half what Debs had won in 1912. After the election, the party's decline continued. The brief revival during and just after World War I was an aberration related to the party's stand against the war. It was a last gasp.[40]

The reformists had badly misinterpreted the source of the party's membership and votes before 1912. The recall of Haywood and repudiation of the IWW was based on the premise that progressive voters responding to the SPA's "immediate program" had given the party its victories between 1910 and 1912. In retrospect it appears that the SPA's support was of another sort altogether. With the notable exception of Milwaukee (where the large German population's old-country socialism made the city politically unique), the SPA flourished best between 1910 and 1913 in those areas where it was most militant and languished where the reformists framed party policy. It was in the revolutionist areas as well that the party suffered its worst losses beginning in 1913. The reformists might have paid closer attention to Haywood when he spoke of the many SPA members he recruited in Lawrence. The Socialist Party did especially well in areas where the IWW was active. In Paterson, where before the Wobbly strike the reformist New Jersey SPA had been able to muster only some 1,650 votes, the SPA mayoralty candidate after the silk weavers' strike received 5,155 votes, only 2,000 fewer than the victorious anti-socialist fusion candidate.[41]

Not that Wobblies themselves provided this increase; the union was never large enough to furnish more than a few thousand votes to the SPA. But the IWW did win considerable support to the Socialist Party which the reformists never recognized. They were overly impressed by the fact that Haywood and the IWW were inevitably and unqualifiedly condemned by newspaper editorialists, city governments, police, employers associations, campaigning politicians, and chambers of commerce. The reformists missed the more important fact that the IWW often rallied considerable public opinion to its side during its strikes and free-speech fights. IWW agitation indeed benefited the SPA, and when the party divorced itself from the union this considerable support went too.

Haywood did not appreciate the necessity of SPA-IWW cooperation in such explicit terms. His motives for supporting the alliance were to benefit the IWW. But inasmuch as he was the leading advocate and symbol of IWW-SPA cooperation, he was to some degree an ignored prophet of a possibly brighter future for both. Not that a militant Socialist Party of America allied to the IWW could have necessarily withstood the powerful conservative strain in American political behavior (or the stern reaction of World War I) and become a major political party. But it is apparent that the SPA faltered when it did in part because its tacticians adopted a diametrically incorrect policy, an irony in the sense that the reformists were political opportunists before they were anything else.

7

Bête Noire

The only factional fight which Haywood ever won took place within the IWW during 1913 and 1914. Division within the union amounted to a certain tension between the IWW's revolutionism and its practical unionism and, curiously, it drew along sectional lines. The Wobblies of the West came to represent the IWW's revolutionary commitment. Drifting from logging camps to construction sites to large-production farms, the western Wobblies worked and lived under conditions as wretched as any in the nation. Their misery on the job was exacerbated by their outcast status off it. Although they were essential to the development of the West, they were almost universally despised as the scum of society. It was an attitude which, among other things, provided their employers with a rationale for their exploitation.[1]

Not surprisingly, the response of the migrant workers was indelicate. The rhetoric of class warfare rang true to them, and they meant to put it literally into practice. The western Wobblies came the closest to the anarchistic image of the IWW which the newspapers painted. They provided most of the colorful legends which have earned the IWW its niche in American folklore, and it is to them that old-timers refer when they speak of the IWW's "matchless spirit." The spokesman for the westerners on the IWW's General Executive Board was Frank Little, a one-eyed half-breed who summed up their attitude with: "better to go out in a blaze of glory than to give in."[2]

That sort of talk disturbed Haywood and other eastern Wobblies like Joe Ettor and Ralph Chaplin. Haywood was a westerner by birth, of course, but he came from a different West than the migrant workers. His hard-rock miners were, first of all, rather sedentary. Unlike the migrant workers, they had families and jobs only remotely responsive to the seasons, and they worked for highly organized corporations headquartered in middling-to-large cities. Moreover, since leaving the mines Haywood had moved within the context of highly organized industry. His experiences as an IWW organizer dealt with workers in the oldest industry of all, textiles; one of the newest, rubber; and the biggest, steel. In a word, Haywood lived his entire life in the industrial age. Increasingly after 1913, he thought primarily in terms of forging an IWW like the old Western Federation of Miners, a union as highly organized and disciplined as the corporations it combatted.

Not that Haywood ever disowned his revolutionism. The tension between his administration of the IWW and the western Wobblies represented a difference of attitude rather than program. The westerners were fiercely individualistic men in a dispersed and fragmented mode of employment; Haywood and the easterners thought in terms of looming mills and factories employing thousands under one roof. The two factions clashed in 1913 and 1914, characteristically, on the question of the IWW's organization. The westerners called for the IWW to re-form as a loose alliance of nearly autonomous "guerrilla" forces which would adapt their tactics to local conditions. Haywood, on the contrary, conceived of a highly centralized union structure more in keeping with the IWW's original design. His attitude prevailed.

In 1914, when Haywood succeeded Vincent St. John as the IWW's secretary-treasurer, the union also abandoned the westerners' tactic of the free-speech fight, substituting for it the Agricultural Workers Organization. Instead of propagandizing the migrants while they wintered in the coastal towns, the AWO aimed at organizing them "on the job." Mobile "job delegates" followed the harvests, worked along with the other "stiffs," and signed up men in the fields. Haywood's prejudices about concentrating on "the point of production" were obvious in the reshuffle. And, ironically, the adaptation of industrial methods to pre-industrial conditions paid off handsomely. The AWO quickly evolved into the only established industrial union within the IWW and represented the largest single power bloc, holding 252 of 335 votes at the IWW's 1916 convention. The AWO was also responsible for boosting the IWW's annual income from $9,000 to $50,000 in one year.[3]

It was well for Haywood that he could claim partial credit for the success as the AWO became the center of decentralist spirit within the IWW. But the AWO did support Haywood while chafing under his centralism; he maintained his position more out of personal popularity than because of his ideological position. In addition, Haywood was having his other successes in the East. Involuntarily freed of his Socialist Party duties, Haywood threw himself wholeheartedly into organizational work after 1913. Between September, 1914, and August, 1916, for example, he played a major role in chartering 74 union locals in the northeastern states out of a national total of 116. In 1917 Haywood estimated that the IWW had 5,000 delegates organizing on the job—possibly an exaggeration, but conceivable in view of the union's membership of over 100,000.[4]

The IWW's newfound prosperity permitted Haywood to function much as he had with the Western Federation, alternating between the exhilaration of leading strikes and the routine of administering a large organization. Haywood is remembered chiefly as an exciting man of action, but he never found the role of bureaucrat uncongenial either. He moved the IWW's offices into a large headquarters with the pride of a small businessman, and seemed to revel in the addition of each new typist to the staff. He formalized the IWW's administrative procedures. Charles Ashleigh, an English-born Wobbly organizer, recalled that in Vincent St. John's IWW he was once dispatched on a mission to discipline an errant Local with a few verbal instructions and a Colt .45. "This couldn't have happened just that way a year or two later," Ashleigh commented of Haywood's administration, "There would have been a formal letter." By 1915 Haywood had so structured the IWW's procedures that he disciplined his friends Elizabeth Gurley Flynn and Carlo Tresca for decisions made in a Mesabi Range strike, decisions that earlier would have been grist for cordial argument. Offended, Flynn and Tresca quit the union.[5]

Haywood did not singlehandedly transform the IWW into a formalized "business union," of course. Bureaucratization was the almost inevitable result of the organization's modicum of success. As John Graham Brooks wrote presciently in 1913, "on the first approach of definite responsibility," the union's leaders "reflect, compare, and balance." They acted as the politician acted. In the thrill of the revolutionary moment, with thousands of strikers surrounding them, IWW speakers mouthed ominous and uncompromising slogans. "But, in the first assurance that the battle was to be won, compromise was a necessity. With as much shrewdness as haste, the strikers took to the ordinary bartering of practical men. As the theory passed into a situation that must be met, they met it in the spirit of a sensible trade union or an arbitration board—the spirit of a wholsesome opportunism." [6]

While the Haywood IWW was not necessarily becoming a "responsible" trade union in the worst sense of the word, it was settling into a stability which augured permanence on the American industrial scene. Whether Haywood would have become a conservative with his success, duplicating the history of the Congress of Industrial Organizations some twenty years later, or whether he would have turned the IWW into a viable radical alternative to the American Federation of Labor is a moot question, for factors beyond his control soon intervened with a vengeance.

It is the colossal irony of his career and the IWW's history, however, that the federal government crushed the union just as it showed signs of transcending its erratic past and digging in for a long, workaday battle. Or perhaps there is no irony at all. It may have been the government's very perception that the reorganized IWW did indeed present a threat to both AFL hegemony and the profits of industrial and agricultural employers that prompted its intervention. At any rate, it was World War I and the specter of worldwide revolution that provided the backdrop for the deed.

When Haywood spoke about revolution he said that it would be brought about by a general strike of the majority of the working class. The revolution would probably not be violent, he thought. To Haywood, the factories were the basis of society. Once they were paralyzed and lifeless, their owners would have no choice but to surrender them to those who did the work. With these ideas, Haywood did not seriously expect to see the revolution during his lifetime. It presupposed the organization of labor and, while prospering, the IWW was still tiny and the large AFL was committed to the established system. The general strike was many years in the future.

Thus, unlike revolutionists who have believed the cataclysm imminent and thus subjected themselves to prosecution by publicly exhorting the workers to take up arms, the question of literal class war—violent revolution—never arose as an important question with Haywood. He was no pacifist, of course. Haywood shunned violence as a tactic in industrial disputes, but only for reasons of expediency. He refused to apologize when workers did strike at their employers. He defended John and James McNamara when they confessed to bombing the *Los Angeles Times* Building in 1911, after most Socialists and trade unionists washed their hands of the pair. "I'm with the McNamaras and always will be," Haywood said, "You can't view the class struggle through the eyes of capitalist-made laws." The IWW newspaper, *Solidarity,* also expressed his views: "Must we weakly apologize for those of our kind who occasionally strike back under great provocation? The capitalist sowed the wind and reaped a little zephyr of a cyclone. . . . Let the blood be upon the heads of our masters." Haywood applied the same principle to the possibility of violence in the overthrow of capitalism. He hoped it could be avoided. But, if the actions of the ruling class necessitated retaliation in kind, the workers should not hesitate to take up arms to achieve their goals.[7]

National wars, however, were an altogether different matter. Haywood was a consummate internationalist. Unlike virtually every other American labor leader of his time (weirdly including some anarchists), Haywood condemned all immigration restriction with a curt, "We are the Industrial Workers *of the World.*" Apparently lacking any ethnic prejudices and reinforced by his rudimentary Marxism, Haywood condemned war based on national differences and interests. His personal experiences with the "state" confirmed Haywood's belief. These experiences had not been pleasant. The state had functioned in his life as the class enemy; it was inconceivable to him that wars between states could be anything other than capitalist family quarrels in which the workers had no interest. Certainly the workers should not shoulder arms to defend their oppressors. They must be wary of the patriotic drivel which bade them do so. Haywood-the-sloganeer subscribed wholeheartedly to the epigram about rich men's wars and poor men's fights.

Moreover, although the lesson would be far more vivid after 1917, Haywood had some understanding of the immediate consequences to unionists and radicals of a nation run amok on patriotism and militarism. The troops which destroyed several WFM strikes after 1900 were often units from the Spanish-American War. The politico's resort to patriotism to combat his domestic enemies is a theme of a later era than Haywood's, but even this was foreshadowed in the strikes Haywood helped fight in Lawrence and Paterson. The "back to work" movement launched by the New Jersey employers had been heralded by draping the city in red, white, and blue.

If Haywood envisioned patriotism as a delusion foisted on the working class in order to divide it, however, he never underestimated the power of the delusion. Shortly after the

United States declared war on Germany in 1917, John N. Beffel met Haywood in a Chicago bookstore popular with radicals. Haywood was leafing through a book on Australia:

> This is the first time in my life that I haven't felt confident about everything ahead. . . . The war may last years. It will give the flag wavers and the A.F. of L. a chance to throw rocks at the I.W.W. That'll be sport for Gompers. . . . But what sickens me most is the way this country has been dragged in. There'll have to be conscription. Not enough men will volunteer to break up a *Sängerfest*. After that, bloody horrors enough to satisfy all the stay-at-home patriots. And it will be the blood of the workers.[8]

But Haywood was not so perceptive of the war's larger implications. If erudite statesmen were befuddled by the rapidity with which European equilibrium disintegrated in the summer of 1914, a person like Haywood was flabbergasted. Despite two trips to Europe and acquaintance with revolutionaries from England, Ireland, and the Continent, Haywood knew very little of international affairs. "What is this war all about?" he asked his friend, Frank Bohn, when the war broke out. His world was the industrial factory in general and American industrial relations in particular. He was utterly unprepared for the event. "I was struck dumb," he wrote. "For weeks I could scarcely talk. I spent much time in the libraries, the chess club and Udell's little book store on North Clark Street in Chicago. I could not concentrate my mind on chess, but at least there was no conversation as I watched the game. I could not read, as my mind was fixed on the war." [9]

Haywood added that "I never felt any doubt about the United States becoming involved," but this was convenient hindsight. Like most Americans in 1914 and 1915, Haywood could not conceive of the United States going halfway around the world for a fight, and he spoke very little on the subject. He directed his own and the IWW's activities as if the world were not undergoing a major transformation. This was not difficult during 1914, 1915, and even 1916. If Americans were divided on the war, the preponderant opinion insisted that the country should have nothing to do with it. "I Didn't Raise My Boy To Be A Soldier" was a popular song, and President Woodrow Wilson ran for re-election with the slogan, "He Kept Us Out Of War." Perhaps unsavory socialists were the noisiest advocates of nonintervention, but this was one time that much of the nation agreed with them.

At the same time, the government of Woodrow Wilson, which had previously dedicated itself to reshaping domestic America, was preoccupied after 1914 with war-connected issues and neglected internal problems. Molders of public opinion such as newspapers and magazines naturally turned from the humdrum of everyday life for their copy to the more exciting doings in Flanders Fields and on the high seas. That, after all, was the real thing. Most of the violence even in Wobbly strikes had to be manufactured on the typewriter. As a result, the IWW faded somewhat from the notoriety it had known during 1912 and 1913. The Wobblies never quite left the front pages, especially in the farm belt, but the war was bigger news.

This relative obscurity proved a mixed blessing to the union. On the one hand, it provided an atmosphere conducive to the introspection Haywood's innovations required. In the long run, however, Haywood's unconcern with international developments proved costly to both himself and the IWW. The nation's mood toward the war changed radically during 1916 and 1917, almost unnoticed by the IWW. When Wilson asked Congress for a Declaration of War against Germany in April, 1917, the Wobblies were sadly unprepared for the new temper of the United States.

On September 5, 1917, the federal government simultaneously raided the IWW's central headquarters in Chicago and forty-eight other Wobbly halls across the nation, confiscating several tons of files and propaganda. Less than a month later the Justice Department indicted Haywood and over a hundred other Wobbly leaders for conspiring to impede the execution of the war. Other counts cited the IWW for conspiring to violate legitimate contracts; to incite draft-eligible men to refuse to register and inductees to desert; to cause military insubordination; and to defraud employers. Most of the indicted Wobblies, including Haywood, submitted readily to arrest and were imprisoned under miserable conditions in the antiquated Cook County Jail. Their five-month-long trial began on April 1, 1918, with 101 defendants in the dock. Kenesaw Mountain Landis was presiding judge; George F. Vanderveer of Seattle was the IWW's chief defense attorney; and Frank K. Nebeker, whose chief experience, symbolically, involved corporation law, was the principal prosecutor. The trial ended according to the government's program, with all defendants convicted and sentenced to prison terms varying from a few months to twenty years. After two other trials in Wichita and Sacramento, seventy more Wobblies were imprisoned.[10]

By the almost unanimous agreement of those who have studied the great IWW trial, it was a shabby affair at best and an indelible blot on American civil liberties at worst. The men were not tried for actions nor even for personal beliefs. They were tried and convicted for what the prosecution alleged were the beliefs of an organization to which they belonged. It requires almost a suspension of reason to understand the state of mind which World War I generated in the United States. Shortly after it ended, the editor of the *New York World* wrote of the home front, "Government conscripted public opinion as they conscripted men and money and materials. Having conscripted it, they dealt with it as they dealt with other raw recruits. They mobilized it. They put it in charge of drill sergeants. They goose-stepped it. They taught it to stand at attention and salute." [11]

World War I marked the first time that the United States government attempted to create a mass psychology to further its ends. Just how much of the wartime hysteria was a spontaneous mass phenomenon and how much was the result of government policy is impossible to say. Certainly the most ludicrous and lurid violations of individual rights took place at the grassroots. Schools prohibited the teaching of the German language; orchestras expunged Beethoven and Wagner from their repertoires; hamburger sandwiches became "Salisbury Steaks," and sauerkraut "Liberty Cabbage." Reluctant patriots were publicly humiliated into kneeling and kissing the Star-Spangled Banner, and suspected aliens and radicals were beaten, harried from their homes, tarred and feathered, and even murdered.[12]

The two most notorious incidents involving the IWW were the deportation of over a thousand striking miners from Bisbee, Arizona, on June 12, 1917, to the Hermanas Desert where they were left without food and water, and the murder of Frank Little in Butte, Montana. Little, whose leg had been broken in Bisbee, was directing a strike against the Anaconda Copper Company in Butte when at three in the morning on August 1, 1917, six men crashed into his hotel room, beat him, drove through the streets of the city with Little's body dragging behind the car, and hanged him from a railroad trestle outside the city. But the cases of Bisbee and Frank Little point up the fact that the wartime persecutions of the Wobblies and other radicals were not simply the rampage of barbaric mobs. Haywood twice telegraphed Woodrow Wilson in the Bisbee matter and was not given the courtesy of a reply. Wobblies were convinced that Little's murder had been engineered in the offices of Anaconda Copper at the least, and perhaps in governmental circles. Whether or not their suspicions were correct, the police expended little effort to find the perpetrators of the sordid deed.[13]

Indirectly, the state and federal governments condoned such outbreaks through their trumpeting of super-patriotism. The most effective of their tools was the Committee on Public Information, a propaganda agency devoted on the one hand to disseminating tales of "Hun atrocities" in Europe and, on the other, to hammering home the need for vigilance against internal enemies. A melange of ostensibly private agencies such as the National Security League, the American Defense Society, and the American Protective League carried out the same labor, converting "thousands of otherwise reasonable and sane Americans into super-patriots and self-styled spy-chasers." They too were tacitly encouraged and assisted by the government.

The government's basic legal devices for stifling the voices raised against the war were three, none of which was worded with juridical precision sufficient to pass a bar examination. The Espionage Act of 1917 provided penalties of $10,000 fine and twenty years' imprisonment for any person who conveyed "false reports or false statements" with the intent of interfering with the operation of American Armed Forces or of contributing to the success of America's enemies. The same penalties applied to anyone who attempted "to cause insubordination, disloyalty, mutiny, or refusal of duty" in the Armed Forces.[14]

The Sedition Act of 1918 provided the same penalties for persons who uttered, printed, wrote, or published "any disloyal, profane, scurrilous, or abusive language about the form of government of the United States, or the Constitution of the United States, or the uniform of the Army or Navy of the United States, or any language intended to . . . encourage resistance to the United States, or to promote the cause of its enemies." [15]

The third law, passed several months after the Sedition Act, excluded from immigration aliens who were Anarchists, believed in the violent overthrow of the government, or advocated the assassination of public officials. The law also provided deportation for any aliens already in the United States who fell into any of the three categories.[16]

It is not important that terms such as "scurrilous" and "abusive" were undefinable when applied to a wisecrack about something like a military uniform. The intention of the acts was not so much to enforce loyalty or respect for the uniform (federal authority never intervened when returning Negro soldiers' or Wobbly Wesley Everest's uniforms were shown disrespect to the point that they were lynched in them), as it was to provide a pretext for crushing radicalism in the

United States. As the third wartime act indicated, antiradicalism went hand in hand with nativism. On the upsurge during the decade before the war, nativism fairly exploded during the conflict and provided the men in Washington with the tools to translate their antiradicalism into action.[17]

The Wobblies were, of course, neither pro-German nor dominated by aliens. The largest proportion of foreign-born in any mass arrest of IWW members was about 50 per cent, and the union's leaders were native Americans almost to the man. But propaganda such as the absurd canard that "I.W.W." stood for "Imperial Wilhelm's Warriors" caught the popular imagination and won support for the government's campaign to crush the union. The hysteria which underpinned the government's destruction of the IWW was not necessarily the panicked reaction of a people who had lost faith in their own ideals. The government which led them was no rock-ribbed nineteenth-century lackey of avaricious employers. If it had been, there might have been a great deal more liberal outcry on behalf of the Wobblies.

The persecutors of the IWW were progressives who smiled on "responsible" trade unionists and frowned on irresponsible businessmen. Woodrow Wilson still occupies a hallowed grotto in the liberal garden of saints. George Creel, who headed the shrill Committee on Public Information, could tolerate Bill Haywood in a time of no crisis as late as 1915. The Congress which wrote the Espionage and Sedition Acts was elected with Wilson in 1916. The coiner of "Imperial Wilhelm's Warriors" was a Wilsonian Democrat. The Secretary of Labor, William Wilson, who reluctantly acquiesced in the government's policies of suppression and deportation, was a member of the American Federation of Labor. The wartime campaign against dissent, in short, was a "progressive" program.

The Wobblies thought that the AFL was behind the campaign to eliminate them. "That'll be sport for Gompers," Haywood noted laconically of the imminent prosecutions. Whether or not the AFL had a guiding hand in the policy,

Gompers and the Federation's other leaders did nothing to stem what was at least in part an anti-labor policy, and the Federation capitalized grandly from its collaboration with the Wilson government. If the IWW was harried during the war for the very reason that it was presenting a viable radical alternative to the AFL, and there is thus no irony in the fact that it was crushed at the most vital point in its career, it remains ironical that even by the government's impeachable criteria neither Haywood nor the IWW could have been found guilty in a fair trial.

In neither Haywood's writings and speeches nor in the IWW's official policies had anything been done or said which was intended to interfere with the success of the American Expeditionary Force nor, certainly, to aid Imperial Germany. Hardly insubordinate, disloyal, or mutinous, thousands of Wobblies enlisted in the service—not, to be sure, with IWW approval, but neither with any sanction not also practiced by the AFL. Only one of the eligible defendants at the Chicago Trial had refused to register for the draft.

Haywood was especially sensitive on an issue he knew could send him straight to jail. "It is not for me, a man who could not be drafted for war," he said, "to tell others that they should go to war, or tell them they should not go to war." To the head of the IWW's Construction Workers Union, Haywood wrote shortly after the United States' declaration, "no official stand has been taken on the question of registration, believing that the individual member was the best judge of how to act upon this question." A month before, he had written to Frank Little that "I am at a loss as to definite steps to be taken against the war." On the question of registration he took none.[18]

Although many were deported, alien members of the IWW did not really violate the act of October, 1918, by virtue of their membership in the union. The IWW was neither anarchistic, an advocate of the violent overthrow of the government, nor an organization which approved the assassination of public officials. Nor, of course, did the IWW, regardless of its advocacy, represent a threat to the war effort. According to the Secretary of Labor, in fact, the Wobblies were involved in only three of 521 strikes during the crucial period.

The final irony of the affair was that not only was the IWW not the leading anti-war organization in the United States, but it did not go on record against the war to the extent of the unprosecuted Socialist Party or the La Follette Progressives. The union took a remarkably passive position on the question, and even accommodated itself to the hysterical patriotism of the era. In his autobiography, Haywood placed himself in the adamantly anti-war faction of the IWW. But this was a retroactive concession to the anti-war heritage of the Communists he later joined. During the first months of the war and during the trial itself, Haywood led the dominant group in the union which felt that the IWW should maintain a gingerly hands-off policy on the question. Haywood opposed anything more than a curt rhetorical gesture condemning American entrance, and hoped that this inaction would win immunity from prosecution. It was, once again, a matter of expediency.[19]

Haywood opposed turning the IWW into an anti-war organization. He argued that the IWW was a labor union first and foremost: its arena was the factory and its game was industrial conflict. To divert the members' attention to opposing the war was to make the same error the western Wobblies had made in the free speech fights and Haywood had made with the Paterson Pageant: trying to turn a union into something it was not. "Keep a cool head; do not talk," Haywood wrote to Frank Little. "A good many feel as you do but the world war is of small importance compared to the great class war." He dispatched the same admonition to a group of Wobblies in Detroit. "Keep cool and confine our agitation to job control. . . . Now is the time for cool heads, sane judgement and earnest work. There is no need of going on record for or against any movement that arises from other sources." [20]

Haywood led the IWW into compliance with the letter of the capitalist-made laws of which he once professed only contempt. He defied only American society's most extreme directive—that he think like it and support the war. This, of course, he would not do; he was still a dissenter. But Haywood did not think it worth scuttling a union for the sake of an internationalism already discredited by most of the socialists of Europe. His attitude was ultimately fatalistic. The war was unfortunate, tragic, and utterly wrong. But it had begun, the United States had joined it, and there was nothing that the Industrial Workers of the World could do about that. Better to concentrate on organization, so that when the bloodletting was ended the union would emerge stronger than ever.[21]

Haywood did not merely keep the IWW within the letter of the law, he accommodated to the hysteria of the home front almost to the point of compromising its revolutionary aspects. One Wobbly wrote to the Chicago Office demanding that the General Executive Board make good its prewar threat of a general strike. Haywood replied evasively that "of course, it is impossible for this office . . . to take action on your individual initiative. However, I have placed your communication on file for future reference." The reduction of a revolutionary manifesto to the tenor of an interoffice memorandum was hardly the Big Bill Haywood pictured in the sensationalist press. In 1917, when President Wilson appointed a commission to investigate the IWW, Haywood responded with unlikely grace for the "evil genius" prosecutor Nebeker later described —he invited Wilson's investigator to examine the IWW's files. But the government preferred to make a raid, in which light even account books would look sinister.[22]

Haywood suspended sabotage propaganda shortly after the United States entered the war. Inasmuch as none of it advocated violent sabotage of the sort vaguely condemned in the wartime acts, the action was clearly designed to appeal not to the law but to public opinion and to attempt to rob enemies of the IWW of an opportunity to distort its principles.

Haywood effected various accommodating editorial changes in other Wobbly literature, such as "The Little Red Songbook." He deleted songs which might be misconstrued or which might be "Offensive" from the wartime editions. For example, John F. Kendrick's "Christians at War," a parody of "Onward Christian Soldiers":

> Onward Christian Soldiers! Duty's way is plain;
> Slay your Christian neighbors, or by them be slain.
> Pulpiteers are spouting effervescent swill,
> God above is calling you to rob and rape and kill.
> All your acts are sanctified by the Lamb on high;
> If you love the Holy Ghost, go murder, pray and die. . . .[23]

Several interesting changes appeared in Vincent St. John's pamphlet history of the IWW. The statement, "the question of 'right' and 'wrong' does not concern us" was dropped completely. The phrase, "an armed truce" between the classes became "only a truce." " 'Sabotage' is used to force the employers to concede the demands of the workers" was shaved down to a propitiatory "a more favorable time is awaited to force the employers . . . ," and so on. When the government issued warrants for the arrest of the leading Wobblies and some urged resistance or flight, Haywood urged that all submit peacefully.[24]

Whatever Haywood's actions indicate of the path he might have taken if the government had not interrupted his career, they also show that he did not comprehend the lengths to which the government was willing to go in order to put the IWW out of action. He knew that the IWW was not guilty of the counts lodged against it, and he realized that the government's motives in prosecuting the union had little to do with its public allegation that the Wobblies were handicapping the war effort. But Haywood never realized that the atmosphere in the nation both during and after the war made rational judgment of his case impossible. "Ten thousand crimes!" he snorted in reference to the first indictments, "If they can make the American people or any fair-minded jury believe that, I don't see how they'll do it." His friend, Ralph Chaplin, wrote that "we were convinced that acquittal was certain—if we could only manage to get our side of the case to the public."

But the mood of the people was being shaped not by the prosecution's lack of facts but by sensations such as that glowing on a cinema marquee outside the Cook County Jail: "The menace of the I.W.W." and "The Red Viper." A credulous public accepted spectacles such as that of former governor of Arizona Thomas Campbell's arrival in Chicago with "a suitcase full of proofs that the I.W.W. was paid by Germany." Campbell waited noisily around Chicago for several weeks waiting for his turn to testify and then announced that the suitcase had been stolen by a Wobbly disguised as a Pullman porter. Haywood's accommodation to the war was quite futile. He proved that his roots were in the healthiest of American traditions at the very time he was branded a foreign agent and the nation was flaunting its own seamier side. But moral victory proved to be little consolation.[25]

The Great IWW Trial thrust Haywood from the routine of the central office into a grassroots camaraderie he had not known since his days as a miner in Nevada and Idaho. The Wobblies indicted at Chicago comprised a remarkable cross-section of the IWW of legend. They came from all over the country, represented a dozen occupations and a score of ethnic groups, and had known among them enough exciting experiences to fill a shelf of potboilers. George Andreytchine was known for his taciturn but colorful defiance of class enemies and would soon become the only American member of the Comintern. Richard Brazier was one of many Wobbly poets, as was Ralph Chaplin; both later became chroniclers of the Wobbly past. James T. "Red" Doran was a leading Wobbly organizer in the Pacific Northwest who gave lectures on economics worthy of a good university. Benjamin Fletcher was a Negro organizer who had been instrumental in organizing the Wobbly strongholds among black timber workers in Louisiana and dockworkers in Philadelphia.[26]

John Reed, recently returned from Russia and reporting the trial for the newly founded *Liberator,* doubted "if ever in history there has been a sight just like" them, lounging in the front rows of the court in varying degrees of attention. Arturo

Giovannitti, not under indictment, wrote, "Wobblies as far as the eye could see. Why, it did not look like a trial at all, it looked like a convention." They awed their guards at the Cook County Jail where, except for a few who were overcome by the ordeal or were shipped out to other jails, they maintained a morale and solidarity such as the old prison had never seen.[27]

"What's your religion?" the guards asked each one as they were registered. "The Industrial Workers of the World," some replied. "That's no religion," the guards answered. "Well, that's the only religion I've got."

"Who's your best friend?" One Wobbly replied: "Bill Haywood." "He can't do you any good, he's in here with you." "That's all right, he's my best friend." [28]

Once a week the prisoners held an "entertainment," complete with hand-lettered programmes announcing "calisthenics" by William Tanner, a Finnish miner, "anecdotes" by James Rowan or some other Wobbly, and similar fare. Hywood's specialties were "fables" of his own device. One was called "The Girl Who Was Seven Feet Tall" and another, "The Monkey Strike in California." The latter described how, after Japanese labor failed to solve the problems of the fruit growers, they decided that it would be even more profitable to import chimpanzees and train them for the job. But when the animals were turned loose for the harvest, "instead of doing as they had been taught—to bring the fruit down and put it in a box, the mischievous little rascals would dart about, selecting the choicest fruit, take a bite or two, throw the rest away, and go after more." An attempt to muzzle the chimpanzees likewise failed, and the growers appealed to the governor "who regretfully replied that as the offenders were not men, they were not amenable to the law. If they were I.W.W.'s, he could have them imprisoned and perhaps have the leaders shot, but over monkeys he had no jurisdiction.

"The Society for the Prevention of Cruelty to Animals, who had never interested itself on behalf of the I.W.W. or the Japanese, learning that the monkeys were being neglected, threatened to prosecute the fruitgrowers if the little animals were not properly taken care of." The growers then attempted to retrain the monkeys to harvest cotton, but the chimpanzees discovered a fine game in throwing tufts into the air and "in some peculiar manner the monkeys on other plantations learned of the fun, and their pranks caused the same disastrous result." In a conclusion wryly topical to the Wobblies, the chimpanzees were deported.[29]

The writing Wobblies worked their wit into a penciled newspaper, "The Can-Opener," datelined, "Cook County Can, Chicago." The November 15, 1917, issue was headlined:

> WUXTRA!! I.W.W. PLOT
> JAIL DELIVERY NIPPED IN THE BUD
> BELIEVED TO BE NATIONWIDE CONSPIRACY
>
> What is believed to be a nation-wide plot was uncovered when a bean was found in the cell of A. Wobbly, alleged I.W.W. It is darkly hinted that the cook is involved for allowing said bean while dishing up soup.
>
> Another I.W.W. was found wearing a pair of 39¢ suspenders and "can" officials believed they intended to cooperate and make sling shots of said galluses and shoot beans at the jail screws and thus effect a wholesale jail delivery.[30]

The high spirits carried over into Leavenworth Penitentiary, to which the Wobblies were transferred after conviction. But, as weeks dragged into months, enthusiasm flagged. The Wobblies thought of themselves as political prisoners who, "when the war was over and sanity had returned, would be released by pardons or amnesty." But that was not to be the case.[31]

The unimprisoned part of the IWW, meanwhile, was completely transformed. From the viable industrial union into which it had been developing, it was reorganized into little more than a defense committee to raise funds and agitate for the release of its imprisoned leaders. Much of the effective labor was carried out by Elizabeth Gurley Flynn and Joseph Ettor who, although they had left the union in 1916, came to Chicago to be indicted and, when they were not, devoted themselves to defense. Most of the national leaders were released on bail, pending appeal, during the summer of 1919. Haywood's bail, ostensibly $30,000, very possibly cost more. It was raised by his friend of the days on the *International Socialist Review,* Mary Marcy, and by William Bross Lloyd, the son of Henry Demarest Lloyd and a flamboyant and wealthy Communist who sometimes drove his expensive car about Chicago with a red flag flying from the back seat.

Haywood's activities were ceaseless. With Ralph Chaplin, who was released shortly after himself, Haywood assumed effective leadership of the defense movement, appealing for funds and setting out on a lecture tour. He narrowly escaped arrest on several occasions and was finally brought back into court during the Palmer Raids, when he again surrendered voluntarily. In the meantime, the U.S. Court of Appeals denied Attorney Vanderveer's plea for a new trial and the IWW's last chance went to the Supreme Court.

The IWW would re-emerge during the twenties, but in quite different form from what it had been before the war. Despite a deceptively large membership early in the decade—perhaps as many as a quarter of a million at one time—the postwar IWW lacked the organizational cohesiveness it had known locally in such towns as Lawrence, and the widespread effectiveness it had exercised through the Agricultural Workers Organization immediately before the great trials. In part this was due to the appearance of the Communist Party in the United States which, in the long run, attracted a great many of the IWW's members. But the government prosecutions also had their effect. They robbed the organization of 170 of its most effective leaders for almost two years in all cases, and longer in most. Similar state and local actions and vigilante harassments dispersed the membership and destroyed the IWW's local organizations. Moreover, the IWW lost its identity as a union in the effort to free its imprisoned members and never fully recovered it when the pressure eased in 1921.

When he was sentenced to twenty years in prison, Ralph Chaplin told the court that he was proud to have climbed high enough for the lightning to strike him. Indeed, it seems that nothing less than the federal government's ultimate effort could have crushed a group of men possessed of a spirit the nation has rarely known. Four years after they were sentenced, seventy Wobbly prisoners still languished at Leavenworth. The government's guilty conscience prompted an offer of commutations to various individuals but only a handful accepted, the rest retorting, "any individual application for clemency, pardon, or 'individual' amnesty only offers an opportunity to our oppressors to pretend that there was some element of justice and fairness entering into the circumstances of our alleged trial and should be spurned." [32]

It was a sentiment worthy to climax the career of Big Bill Haywood, but he was not there to voice it.

8

Communist

When the news of the Bolshevik Revolution reached the Wobbly cell block of the "Cook County Can" in November, 1917, the response was raucous singing and cheering that continued late into the night. Few of the men knew exactly what they were cheering about. Russia had been of interest to them only as little more than an example of the lengths to which oppression could go. The March Revolution had seemed to change nothing but the names of the oppressors, although the IWW, through its Russian members, aided some exiles in returning to Russia. The victory of authentic revolutionaries was entirely unexpected, and the bright contrast to the IWW's own plight at the moment launched the giddiness. From then on, the news from Russia was a topic of conversation second only to IWW affairs. When Haywood was released on bail during the spring of 1918 he hosted John Reed in Chicago and heard Reed's famous account of the "ten days that shook the world." Haywood later read Reed's book in Leavenworth.[1]

The October Revolution shook the entire American Left. Radicals who had devoted their lives to a revolution that never came and contented themselves with minor successes quite within the social structure could not help but be fascinated by the phenomenal victories of a group which had seemed, a few years before, as insignificant as themselves. They inevitably deferred at least briefly to their successful comrades, and some looked forward to a unified and omnipotent revolutionary movement. But the emergence of Communism in the

United States was to splinter rather than unite the American radical movement.

The Socialist Party after 1913 had enjoyed few of the victories its leaders anticipated. Before the outbreak of war the party first declined and then stood still, maintaining its influence in Milwaukee but losing the gains of 1910–1912 almost everywhere else. When the United States entered the war, some party leaders supported the allies and left the party. John Spargo, Robert Hunter, and Algie M. Simons—three who had played a crucial part in ousting Haywood in 1913—all lined up behind Wilson's government. Even William English Walling—a former supporter of the IWW, devotee of the SPAs left wing, and scourge of Simons, Hunter, and Spargo—moved rapidly and seemingly comfortably under the umbrella of Wilsonian liberalism.

The party itself, however, declared ringingly against the United States entrance and Victor Berger, Morris Hillquit, and Debs stayed with it. Berger was twice denied his seat in the House of Representatives due to his stand, and Debs made his last race for the presidency in 1920 from Atlanta Penitentiary. But the party, unlike the IWW, was not prosecuted by the government. In fact, while it brought adversity, the war also revived the SPA; party candidates won, or nearly won, more important offices on the basis of their opposition to the war than they had for four previous years.[2]

Limited success in elections, however, was nullified by the effects of the Bolshevik Revolution within the party. The remnants of the revolutionist wing, concentrated in the foreign-language sections of the party, were transfixed by the Revolution and convinced that similar success was imminent in the United States. And, as ever, they were hostile to the reformists' lack of militance. By the fall of 1918, behind the leadership of John Reed, Louis Fraina, and James Larkin (all formerly friendly to the Wobblies), the revolutionists organized to win control of the party. They were well disciplined, published their own newspapers and pamphlets, and attacked what they saw as the party leadership's coolness toward the Bolsheviks.

They were so successful in enrolling SPA locals in their cause that an alarmed National Executive Committee, meeting in Chicago in May, 1919, expelled seven foreign-language federations including over 30,000 of the party's 100,000 members. Unlike in 1913, when Haywood's partisans shrugged off his purge from the NEC, the revolutionists remaining in the party determined to capture it. They called a conference of the left-wing elements to meet in Chicago concurrently with the Emergency Convention of the Socialist Party.[3]

In the meantime, some of the expelled socialists organized a Communist Party and announced that their first convention would meet in Chicago at the same time as the Socialists. The ensuing spectacle showed how far toward dissolution the SPA had gone. The SPA convention met in the assembly room of a machinist's hall while the left wing of the party caucused in a billiard room a floor below. When the revolutionists attempted to take their seats as delegates they were ejected. Although about half of the leftists later won their seats, they soon discovered that they did not have a majority of the convention. They bolted, briefly considered an alliance with the Communist Party, and ended up organizing their own "real Socialist party," the Communist Labor Party. The SPA was still the strongest of the radical parties, but the split took its toll on it as the years passed.[4]

For a short time the entire IWW responded favorably to the Bolshevik Revolution. Wobbly publications briefly substituted "industrial communism" for "industrial democracy" on their mastheads, and during the General Strike at Seattle in 1919 the IWW collaborated in the establishment of a workers, soldiers, and sailors council on the model of the Russian soviets. But, like the SPA, the IWW soon split. The eastern centralist wing rallied enthusiastically behind the Bolsheviks and stayed with them. The westerners, however, soon grew suspicious of soviet centralization of power and patent lack of democracy. For awhile, the pro-soviet Haywood wing held its own; the General Executive Board declared for the Third International in 1919. But the wartime prosecutions had chiefly affected the centralists who held the most conspicuous positions of power and, after 1919, the western wing gained ascendancy. A different General Executive Board in 1920 was cooler toward the Comintern and refused to send a delegate to its Second Congress in July. When Wobbly George Hardy returned from Moscow and recommended that the union affiliate with the newly established Red International of Labor Unions (Profintern), the General Executive Board overruled him and suggested a policy of watchful waiting. A confused referendum appeared to support the Board's position.[5]

George Williams represented the IWW at the Profintern's meeting in July, 1921, where Haywood urged him to bring the IWW into the movement. But the Communists declared for a policy of "boring from within" the conservative unions at that congress, a policy which the IWW had unequivocally condemned for fifteen years. When Williams returned to the United States he wrote a scathing attack on the Bolsheviks to which the General Executive Board affixed its imprimatur; the two movements parted ways. A few Communist sympathizers agitated within the IWW until 1924, when the anti-Bolshevik decentralizers came out decisively on top. As from the SPA, the Communists won many of the IWW's best leaders as well as a substantial chunk of the union's membership. The IWW declined steadily until by 1928 its membership stood at a low of under 10,000.[6]

Haywood played no part in the founding of the two Communist groups and very little in the activities within the IWW. He was in the Cook County Jail when the news of the October Revolution reached the United States. Out on bail the following spring, he was still preoccupied by the trial. It lasted from April 1, 1918, to the end of August. From Chicago Haywood was taken to Leavenworth where he was imprisoned until July 28, 1919, when he was released pending appeal. For the next eighteen months he toured the country speaking on behalf of the IWW and those Wobbies still in jail. His health declined drastically. He suffered recurrent diabetic attacks (insulin was still in the future), and his eyesight had failed sufficiently at Leavenworth so that he was removed from his bookkeeper's job in the prison store.

Like other radicals, Haywood was intensely and uncritically interested in the events in the Soviet Union, and was privileged to have a firsthand report from John Reed. He did not share in the suspicions of many Wobblies who felt "a little hurt"—according to Harrison George—"that the IWW's recipe for revolution, the general strike, lost its monopoly of prominence amid the thunder of the guns." Haywood belonged to the industrial unionist group which, with a little imagination, could see in the workers' soviets which had effected the revolution an equivalent of the IWW's program of building the new society within the shell of the old through industrial unions of all the workers.[7] "Here is what we have been dreaming about," he called to Ralph Chaplin as they sat in IWW headquarters early in 1918. "Here is the I.W.W. all feathered out!" Haywood hoped to contact Lenin with a plan he had devised to organize Soviet production along IWW lines, "the IWW chart in operation!" The reports of steady success from Russia contrasted sharply with Wobbly reverses. "The Russian Revolution is the greatest event in our lives. . . . It represents all that we have been dreaming of and fighting for all our lives. It is the dawn of freedom and industrial democracy. If we can't trust Lenin, we can't trust anybody," said the man who a year before had trusted confidently that no jury would convict the IWW of the charges against it.

"Does that mean you have made your choice?" Ralph Chaplin asked him.

"It means . . . that there is only one choice to make," Haywood replied. "The world revolution is bigger than the I.W.W."[8]

The choice to which both men referred was not merely a matter of advocacy. Sometime during 1920 the Bolsheviks offered Haywood, Chaplin, and George Andreytchine the opportunity to come to Moscow. Andreytchine would join the staff of the International. Chaplin would put his pen to work for the revolution. Haywood would help develop a mining region in the Urals while agitating for the revolution in the United States and advising Lenin on the organization of the Red International of Labor Unions.[9] Anti-Communist Wobblies later insisted that Lenin knew he must eliminate the IWW if he were to control American radicalism, and that he thought to cripple the union by wooing and detaining its foremost leader. The truth is less sinister. The Soviets still thought in terms of imminent world revolution in 1919, and reasoned that Haywood would be more valuable agitating from abroad (as the leading Bolsheviks had done) than he would be rotting in Leavenworth. Their estimation of Haywood's prestige among the American working class as a whole was as erroneous as their expectations of world revolution.

Another Soviet mistake concerned Haywood's capacity as an organizer of industry. The Soviet leaders were unstinting admirers of American technology. Lenin advocated importing films teaching "Taylorism," and Stalin early called for the combination of "the wide outlook of the Russian revolutionist" and "American practicality in work." This almost stereotypical vision of all Americans as hard-nosed practical wizards was reinforced by the services rendered the Kerensky government by American engineers under John F. Stevens, who helped put the Russian railroad system into efficient operation, and men like the American geneticist, H. J. Muller, who helped found Soviet scientific research. Haywood was known as a miner as well as a revolutionary leader. As an American, it was thought, he could not but be invaluable to the impending Kuzbas project to develop Russia with international radical aid.[10]

Ralph Chaplin never seriously considered the trip to Moscow, and George Andreytchine determined to accept from the first. For Haywood, however, the Soviet invitation represented an agonizing dilemma. He sorely wanted to see a revolution. But he was out on bail through the generosity of William Bross Lloyd and Mary Marcy, both good friends who stood to lose a great deal of money if he defected. His Soviet contacts reassured him that the International would make good these losses.[11]

A more trying problem was the fact that it had been Haywood, more than any other Wobbly, who in 1917 quashed the movement to evade arrest and urged all IWW members under indictment to surrender and fight their battle through the courts. Could he now desert the fellow workers who had reluctantly followed him then and had since been sentenced to long prison terms? Wobbly "solidarity" would not hear of such a thing; Haywood must go to prison with the rest. In his autobiography, Haywood implied that his objections on this account were overcome when he heard a report that President Harding had told Socialist Congressman Meyer London that all imprisoned members of the IWW would be pardoned except Haywood. Elizabeth Gurley Flynn recounted a somewhat different version—that Haywood felt that if he were eliminated from the scene the others would more readily be pardoned.[12]

While conceivably true, both tales have the ring of rationalization. Haywood did abandon the Wobblies because he was convinced that "big work," bigger than the IWW, awaited him in Moscow. Moreover, as he was constantly reminded, his health was poor and made worse by the conditions of the Cook County Jail and his relentless work on behalf of the IWW Defense Committee. Prison, friends told him truthfully enough, would mean a death sentence. There was something evidently wrong with him as early as the trial. Richard Brazier wrote, "he did not have the old fire. He talked in low tones, and occasionally had to be asked to speak a little louder. It is my belief that Big Bill was even then afflicted with the disease that eventually proved fatal." [13]

At any rate, when in October, 1920, the Supreme Court upheld the IWW's conviction and ordered all those out on bail to report to Leavenworth early the next year, Haywood and nine other Wobblies were not among them. Haywood dropped from sight in early March, 1921, shortly after speaking at the socialist Rand School and visiting old friends in New York. With the inevitable false passport, he boarded the *Oscar II*, Henry Ford's "peace ship" just a few years before. Hidden in the steerage until the ship cleared the piers, Haywood came up on deck as the *Oscar* passed the Statue of Liberty. "Saluting the old hag with her uplifted torch, I said: 'Good-by you've had your back turned on me too long. I am now going to the land of freedom.' " [14]

Rumors of Haywood's flight, soon confirmed by his arrival in Latvia, were shrugged off indifferently by a nation engaged in an orgy of deportations. But the news exploded like a bomb on the IWW. A Wobbly defense attorney branded the flight "the act of a coward," and Elizabeth Gurley Flynn acknowledged that the union was "pretty sore" about it. The friend of a Wobbly convicted at Sacramento wrote that those at Leavenworth did not "think much of Haywood for deserting them. I think that the I.W.W. is too good for Haywood. What do you at San Quentin think of Him?" A delegate to the IWW's 1921 convention claimed that Haywood had fled to escape responsibility for a large shortage of funds in the Defense Committee treasury. Haywood was no longer the leader of the Wobblies as either an official or a symbol.[15]

Haywood's party made its way to Riga and then, in boxcars and with a military escort, to the Russian border. At the frontier there was a welcoming party which burst into cheers and song. It was an exhilarating experience. Toward Moscow, "the train moved along like a red flame. Red bunting, red banners, and red kerchiefs were flying to the breeze." Aware of the anger vented on him at home, Haywood wrote shortly after arriving in the Soviet Union that "I shall return to America when I have finished the work assigned to me by the International Council of Trade and Industrial Unions [the Red International of Labor Unions] and when the interests of the workers demand my return."

But the Wobblies, who thought Haywood's assignments should be made by the IWW and that he should be in the United States, were already trying to forget him. His intimates remained remarkably loyal, a testimony of his personal friendship. Ralph Chaplin, near the outer fringe of the political right by 1947, could bring himself to write nothing bad of him to the end of his life. Richard Brazier, a Wobbly into the

1960's, who sat in prison while Haywood fled, refused to blame Haywood for his betrayal. The IWW's denunciation of the Soviets in 1921 courteously neglected to mention Haywood's name although he had acquiesced in the policies they condemned.[16]

The promise to compensate Haywood's bondsmen was never honored. John Reed was said to have been bringing money for this purpose when he sickened and was arrested in Finland, then returning to Moscow to die. If so, there were no further attempts, and the loss of the large bail did not endear the Communists to the IWW. Richard Brazier maintained that the Soviets did not even pay Haywood's fare; that monies for a round-trip ticket and a six-month stay in Russia were raised by a group of women who sympathized with Big Bill.[17]

Emma Goldman and Alexander Berkman, deported from the United States on the *SS Buford* and already disillusioned with Soviet Communism by mid-1921, were surprised to find Haywood joining them in Moscow. "Could he have jumped bail," they wondered. Berkman immediately believed he had. The anarchist gave Haywood short shrift because of the latter's refusal to collaborate with him in 1914. Emma Goldman was not so quick to judge, but she spoke with Haywood shortly after his arrival and he confessed that he had indeed "run away."

"The prison was not the deciding factor," Haywood told her. "It was Russia, Russia which fulfilled what we had dreamed about and propagated all our lives, I as well as you. Russia, the home of the liberated proletariat, was calling me." Haywood reassured Emma Goldman that he had left his comrades only because "the Revolution was more important and its ends justified all means." His bail would be paid, he argued, and he hoped that his old friend would "understand his motives and not think him a shirker."

The revolutionist did indeed believe he had arrived home and, for a time at least, continued to think that the Soviet Union vindicated Wobbly methods. "I feel as if I'd always been there," he told Max Eastman. "You remember I used to say that all we needed was fifty thousand real IWW's, and then about a million members to back them up? Well, isn't that a similar idea? At least I always realized that the essential thing was to have an organization of *those who know*." Haywood had an interview with Lenin and asked him "if the industries of the Soviet Republic are run and administered by the workers?" Lenin replied, "Yes, Comrade Haywood, that is Communism." [18]

The available facts of Haywood's years in the Soviet Union are as few and even more obscure than the facts of the Steunenberg affair. During his first months in Russia Haywood was one of dozens of radical celebrities who spoke at rallies, brought moral support to the Bolsheviks, and urged their own countrymen to do what the Russians had done. But he soon plunged into the work of building a society which had been promised him. On November 22, 1921, with S. J. Rutgers, Dutch-American Radical, Haywood signed an agreement with Lenin by which they and several thousand Americans would rebuild and expand an old industrial complex in the northern Ural Mountains. The Americans were to recruit some 6,000 skilled workers in the United States and to receive half of any increase they realized in production. Haywood initially supervised the Nadjedinski Iron Works, but shortly transferred to a coal mining complex at Kemerov in the Kuznetsk Basin, another part of the Americans' Kuzbas Autonomous Colony.

It was as close to Haywood's dream of a worker-administered industry as he ever came. Most of the labor was American, much of it made up of renegade Wobblies like himself. Their task was exciting, "an experiment," as Walter Duranty called it, "in which American red proletarians were to help restore Russia's industries in the Urals." Duranty also called the project "unlucky" and, indeed, many of the Americans were quickly disillusioned. Living conditions were primitive in all respects and many of the workers soon departed in disgust for Moscow or the United States. Haywood's opinion of the venture was tinged with bitterness. "Too many soapbox orators," he grumbled, "Most of these guys would sooner talk than work." [19]

But in the long run, the contribution of the Kuzbas Colony was a valuable one. Despite the conditions the industry was restored, and today the coal mines which Haywood supervised still feed the huge Kuznetsk Steek Works. How much of this was Haywood's personal accomplishment is difficult to say. He did not stay in the region full time for very long, but was constantly commuting to Moscow for one or another Congress or commemoration. Although the original two-year contract with the Americans was renewed until 1927, Haywood became a resident of Moscow long before. Failing health probably accounted for the move, but it was also true that the old agitator was no success as a technocrat. "Here was the revolution, mighty, irrevocable, making the nations tremble," wrote John N. Beffel. "But the time had come for engineers and technicians, and Bill was neither. He did not fit in." [20]

After he left the Kuznetsk Basin, Haywood aided in the formation and administration of International Labor Defense, a nonpartisan organization which worked for the release and relief of some 106 union men imprisoned in the United States, including scores of Wobblies, two obscure Anarchists in Rhode Island, a group of AFL coal miners in West Virginia, and two organizers in Maine. The ILD had no luck in freeing the men, but performed small services through its special Christmas Fund for the prisoners' families, and sent $5 a month spending money to each of the 106. Haywood "was deeply concerned about the persecution of workers in America," the Trotskyite Jim Cannon remembered. "He wanted to have something done for the almost forgotten men lying in jail all over the country." Cannon discussed the ILD extensively with Haywood on a visit to Moscow. "When we completed the plans," he continued, "and when I promised him that I would come back to America and see to it that the plans did not remain on paper; that we would really go to work in earnest and come to the aid of the men in prisons—the old lion's eyes—his one eye, rather—flashed with the old fire. He said, "I wish I could go back to give a hand in that job. . . . Up to the end of his life he continued to be an active participant in the work of the ILD by correspondence." It was Haywood's penance for his desertion.[21]

As the excitement of revolution gave way to the routine of constructing a society, exiled agitators proved to be little more value than incompetent technocrats. Haywood continued to attend the annual conferences of the Profintern, sitting prominently on the platform, but he had little influence in its deliberations. Only at the Third Congress of the Comintern, which met shortly before the Profintern in 1921 and set the pattern for the latter meeting, did Haywood even speak up. Gregory Zinoviev, the Chairman of the International, had all but directed the IWW to liquidate itself and "get into the old trade unions in order to revolutionize them."

At the Eighteenth Session, Haywood dissented, stating that, "in general, it is absolutely impossible to carry on any work inside the Federation, so reactionary is it." Haywood quoted Samuel Gompers as saying that American workers should not aid the Bolsheviks, and challenged Leon Trotsky's insistence on the liquidation of dual labor organizations like the IWW. "Such an attempt would be absolutely unsuccessful," Haywood continued. "Capitalism with its press and third degree tried to kill our movement, but met with no success, simply because the Industrial Workers of the World is a revolutionary organization, and although numerically small, it is a product of and necessarily created by the particular conditions of the American workers movement."

Haywood made his plea on the basis of the IWWs dogged adherence to the doctrine of class struggle, and he attempted to convince the doughty Russians of the similarities between Bolsheviks and Wobblies which had helped to bring him to Russia. It was no use. Eight non-Russians attacked Haywood and the IWW while only one, identified only as Comrade Fiur, supported him. The Chairman of the Session, Gennari of Italy, declared the list of speakers exhausted at that point and announced that "the final word on the report would be given by Comrade Zinoviev." The question which affected the core of the IWW's very existence was given no more time than speeches celebrating the sixty-fifth birthday of Clara Zetkin at the preceding session. After a brief huddle with Lenin and Trotsky, even Haywood capitulated, voted for Zinoviev's report, and dispatched an exhortation to the IWW urging the union to follow Communist policy: "They are carrying out the original aims and purposes of the IWW." He had served his purpose, and Haywood became little more than platform bunting.[22]

For most of his years in Russia, Haywood lived in the Hotel Lux near the center of Moscow, a once-plush residence set aside by the Bolsheviks for visiting foreign Communists and showcase radical exiles. He remained one of the required sights for foreigners on the Grand Tour of the new society, especially Americans, and enjoyed his long talks with American friends. He attempted to learn the Russian language but had little success, and sought out the company of the city's English-speaking residents. "Bill's position is a bit tragic," Charles Ashleigh wrote, "or was when I was there. There was nothing for him to do in Russia, and time was heavy on his hands." Haywood was friendly with Walter Duranty of the *New York Times,* who found Haywood "easier to talk to" than the Communists. On occasion Haywood would walk the quarter-mile from the Lux to Duranty's small apartment in which the reporter had installed an open English fireplace, a favorite rendezvous of foreigners in Moscow during the long winters. But most of the time, as Ashleigh wrote, there was nothing to do. Haywood found some diversion in the writing of his autobiography during his last several years, and shortly before his death married a Russian woman who held a minor government position. He held minor posts himself and received a small pension.[23]

Haywood's ultimate judgment of the Soviet experiment is a matter of considerable disagreement. Walter Duranty pointed out at the time that Haywood played the role of "monument" for the Soviets. He was the warrior for a classless society forced to live far from his home by the oppressions of the capitalist system. A typical Soviet obituary described him as "one of the pioneers of the revolutionary proletarian movement" who, though a "pure-blooded American," renounced the chauvinistic and "presumptious assertion that the United Staes appears to be the most democratic country." "In the revolutionary struggle with capitalism," Haywood "gave all his strength to his last breath." [24]

Haywood was also abused as a symbol by those who damned the Soviets. From anti-Soviets of the extreme political Right like Benjamin Gitlow and Ralph Chaplin to "true-blue" revolutionary Wobblies like Richard Brazier, Haywood is compositely pictured as a great man to the end, deluded into fleeing to Soviet tyranny and, once there, kept as truly imprisoned as if he had surrendered to the authorities at Leavenworth in 1921. Until his death Haywood wrote regularly to Ralph Chaplin. His letters, Chaplin wrote, "although cordial, did not ring altogether true. . . . They didn't sound like Bill somehow. . . . Bill's letters impressed me as having been written with someone breathing down his neck." Never enthusiastic about the Bolsheviks, Chaplin soured completely on the Soviet experiment long before Haywood's death. But he remained personally loyal to his friend and would not believe that Bill Haywood could be permanently taken in by a movement Chaplin personally found revolting.[25]

Benjamin Gitlow's lamentations for Haywood seem less sincere. A socialist politician who passed through the Communist movement to become an "informer" of the most unreliable variety, Gitlow was merely an acquaintance of Haywood's before the world war, but posed in retrospect as an intimate privy to Haywood's most profound confidences. Gitlow used the symbol quite as cynically as the Soviets did. He pictured the pre-Communist phase of American radicalism as something of a golden age of idealists who would, no doubt, have been Red-baiting super-patriots in the 1940s. "Haywood loathed the Soviet system," Gitlow wrote, "for he was essentially an individualist who cherished liberty and freedom of action. The dictatorship of the proletariat denied both to the individual. He realized that he had run away from one prison into another, one from which he could not flee, the prison this time being a vast country in which the human lives of millions counted for nothing." [26]

"Look to America for freedom and hope," Gitlow has Haywood say as the exile lay on his deathbed: "Haywood looked out of his one eye intently as if he were trying to see eternity. Clasping my outstretched hand, his own trembling, he said in a low, tremulous voice, 'It's goodbye this time. Good luck and remember me to America.' " [27]

Old Wobblies and other radical friends such as Emma Goldman did not remember Haywood so much as a symbol as a tragic figure. Emma Goldman had been truly close to Haywood, and recalled the days in New York when her apartment at 210 East Thirteenth Street was Haywood's retreat from both the picket line and Greenwich Village. "Frequently he spent his free evenings at our place," she wrote. "There he could read and rest to his heart's content, or drink coffee 'black as the night, strong as the revolutionary ideal, sweet as love.' " In Russia, to which she had been deported and to which Haywood voluntarily fled, she saw him as "a pathetic harlequin, . . . so rooted in his native soil and its traditions, so alien to Russia, ignorant of her language and her people."

She was disturbed by Haywood's weak explanation of why he had violated Wobbly solidarity, but was finally disgusted with him only when Haywood refused to buck the Soviet leadership and support Goldman's and Berkman's attempts to stop the persecutions of the Russian Anarchists. Haywood sat on the platform when the two presented their petition and did not even nod to them when they passed. "Having gone back on his comrades in distress, it was not surprising that he should also deny his former friends," Goldman wrote. "Sasha had been right; there was no need to worry about Bill's future. He could see no more with his good eye than with his blind one and would 'fit in.' I felt no anger; I was only unspeakably sad." Emma Goldman also predicted Haywood's future in the Soviet Union: Haywood "would be cast on the refuse pile, like so many before him, after he had served the propaganda purposes of Moscow." [28]

Richard Brazier, who knew Haywood well only during the wartime period, reflects the same pathos in his recollections. Brazier remained fiercely loyal to the Wobbly ideal as well as to the IWW, and viewed Haywood's Russian years from that perspective. Brazier believed that Haywood intended to attend the Comintern and Profintern Congresses in 1921, make a brief lecture and sightseeing tour of the country, "and then return home to face the music" but was either deluded or forced into remaining. "I know that Haywood's ashes are now buried in the Kremlin's walls," he wrote later, "and he is immortalized as a dedicated Commie, but one half of his ashes came back here and are buried close to Joe Hill's ashes. I have never believed—nor will I believe—that he was anything but a dedicated Wobbly who died a sick, broken and disillusioned man by his Russian experiences. He expected to find a genuine proletarian revolution, and found one captured by politicians and intellectuals. He became just a show-piece for the Communists to exhibit on occasion." [29]

Haywood certainly died lonely and disillusioned in the Soviet Union. But this was hardly due to an anti-Communism which many cite but none demonstrate. Haywood would dearly have liked to return home, but never to a prison and certainly not because he looked to America "for freedom and hope." Haywood could not have been disillusioned with Communism for he was never a Communist. He never understood the ideology of the Soviets and their concern for theory vexed him. "The trouble with us old Wobbies," he told Walter Duranty, "is that we all know how to sock scabs and mine guards and policemen or make tough fighting speeches to a crowd of strikers but we aren't so long on this *ideological* stuff as the Russians."

Duranty suggested that whereas the Wobbies were trying to destroy, the Soviets were trying to build. "There's something in that," Haywood replied, "but it goes far deeper. These Russians attach the hell of a lot to *ideological* theory, and mark my words, if they're not careful they'll come to blows about it one of these days. Don't you know that most of them would sooner talk than work, or even eat." [30]

Bolshevism had appealed to Haywood because it had gotten something done. It was as if the Bolsheviks had accomplished the ultimate strike. When Haywood explained to Max Eastman why he supported the Communists he skipped over their expropriation of property almost as if it were incidental. The aspect of the Revolution which most appealed to Haywood was education for children. "And, by God, for that one thing alone I'd favor a revolution in this country." Second, Haywood noted relief from labor to women eight weeks before and eight weeks following a confinement. "In this country [the United States] we do it for thoroughbred horses and pedigreed cattle," Haywood noted. He came to the transfer of land to peasants and skipped over it lightly although he conceded, "of course that is a more fundamental thing." With such an attitude toward the Revolution, Haywood could not be soured by Soviet anti-democracy but only by the failure of the Communists to sustain their tangible benefits to the Russian masses.[31]

Haywood's unhappiness in the Soviet Union was due first to homesickness; second, to the fact that he simply had nothing to do; and third, to his personal obscurity. As Elizabeth Flynn wrote embarrassingly but probably accurately, Haywood "longed for the land of baseball and burlesque, big steaks and cigars, cowboys and rodeos, strikes and picket lines, to see the Mississippi River and the Rocky Mountains, the America which was his home." She added that he belonged in America, "in its militant struggles against capitalism" but "was not well enough to start a new life in a young country." She neglected to add that, after a year or two, the Soviets had no new life for him.

When the International abandoned its hopes for imminent world revolution in 1921, Haywood's value as a liaison man with the American movement quickly dissipated. Big Bill had traditionally stood for policies such as dual unionism which the Comintern rejected and, moreover, the old warhorse had little influence on an increasingly new American left. The Wobblies were in rapid decline, strongly anti-Communist, and not likely to listen to one who had abandoned them. The moderate Socialist Party was also weakening fast, had never been friendly to Haywood, and had found a successor to Debs in Norman Thomas. The Communist Party was producing its own leaders, many of them old Wobblies like William Z. Foster, Earl Browder, and James Cannon, all of them younger than Haywood and sufficiently loyal to the Russian Communists directly that a "front man" like Haywood was quite unnecessary. The man who had rarely begun a day without an impossible schedule of things to do vegetated in inactivity. The stormy petrel of a dozen "causes" chafed in the obscurity of a lonely retirement. *Outlook* magazine was close to the truth when it observed in an obituary that Haywood's disillusion in Russia was largely due to the fact that he was a nonentity.[32]

The tragedy of Haywood's years in the Soviet Union is the cynical use made of his person by Soviet propagandists and reactionary anti-Communists like Benjamin Gitlow. His final years were certainly anticlimactic.

In April, 1928, Haywood went to a Kremlin Hospital for treatment of his diabetes. On May 16 he suffered a stroke which paralyzed one side of his body. On the following day he seemed improved, talked with his wife, and discussed politics with several friends. The next day Haywood ate a large meal and died in his sleep at the age of fifty-nine. His body was taken in a red hearse to the front yard of the Club House of Political Prisoners, socially Moscow's *ne plus ultra*. A thousand foreign exiles and visitors paid homage. There were few flowers; Haywood had requested that money for them go instead to Lenin's Homeless Children's Fund.[33]

On May 19 Haywood was cremated in the municipal crematorium, formerly the Donskaya Monastery, "a strange semi-fortified enclosure with walls and battlements on the outskirts of Moscow." The editions which brought the news to the United States featured stories on a Coolidge veto of a pay raise for postal employees, trouble between Japanese and Chinese in Manchuria, and the early closing of the stock exchange to "ease strain on workers." [34]

9

Frustration of a Radical

William Dudley Haywood's practical accomplishments were neither considerable nor permanent. He helped to win a better life for thousands of hard-rock miners, but his part in their battle was passing and intangible. The miners' self-reliance, militance, and diligence were deeply ingrained in them; their union was strong and established before Haywood became a molding force in it, and long survived him. The Wobblies, more dependent on Haywood, were less lucky. Their demise as an effective group was not Haywood's fault. His policies, in fact, were infusing the IWW with a promising stability when the Socialist Party's rebuff and the federal government's repression started the union toward oblivion.

No institution stands as Haywood's monument. No gleaming aluminum and glass "labor temple" is named for him, and his uncomely face has never adorned a postage stamp. His legacy is historical and symbolic. He exemplified for the world the doughtiness of the western miner. He stood up for wretched immigrant workers when the organized labor movement scorned them. He gave the nation an unnoticed lesson in personal freedom from racial bigotry in an age when racism ruled labor union, university, and White House. And Haywood was willing, in all but the last instance, to risk the penalties of being a dissenter in a country which is at the same time the most libertarian of lands and the meanest scourge of dissent.

Haywood's enduring image as the epitome of the American

dissenter is almost entirely the government's doing, for he was by no means the type for the role. Personally, Haywood was a conventional sort. Acquaintances invariably commented either on the force and power of his presence or his extreme sensitivity to misery and misfortune, but none noted originality or nonconformism. Haywood contributed nothing novel to the dialogue of his day on the nature of society and society's Marxism with which he claimed to abide. Haywood's vision was the short one. He was the day-to-day, hard-nosed, practical, pragmatic American. Romanticizers of Big Bill overlooked the fact that he was quite the bureaucrat, comfortable and content in the routine of administering an organization and, until he tried his hand at building a revolutionary industry, not at all bad at the job. He also knew how to run an effective strike and "sock scabs," as he put it. He must be remembered as, in his day, the leading exponent of unionism for the unskilled, the industrial union structure, mass picketing, and a dozen devices of maintaining striker morale which it took the Congress of Industrial Relations to employ to fruition during the 1930's.

Haywood had a wide romantic streak too. His radicalism derived as much from a nostalgia for a pre-industrial arcadia as from a revulsion to capitalism itself. He clung tenaciously to a faith in the inherent wisdom of "the masses" despite their refusal to embrace what Haywood believed was the answer to their problems. He was given to forays into a fantastic future, and romanticism occasionally distracted him from his typical prudence into making fatal tactical errors. But Haywood only rarely lost touch with the harsh realities of his profession. He was no impulsively striking social guerrilla. He spurned the revolutionary who struck with no hope of success, the rebel who craved symbolic martyrdom, and the nihilist who reacted indiscriminately to society's mores.

Haywood was both cautious and expedient, a disciple of the possible. He was a coward to many of his associates, but he did not want the revolution less for all his prudence. He simply saw no sense in acts which could have no tangible and constructive result. Far from impulsive, Haywood was generally slow to commit himself and deliberate in accommodating to actual conditions. He cultivated the role of union regular until he rose to the top of the Western Federation of Miners. He committed himself fully to the Industrial Workers of the World relatively late in the union's short career. He attempted to salvage his position in the Socialist Party by bearing silently the most spurious attacks. He cajoled the IWW into attempting to ride out a war he and the union despised by adjusting to it. He frequently trusted to the legal procedures which he condemned as devices of the class enemy. He toed the line again in the Soviet Union when he found himself in a subordinate position.

To Haywood, the survival of the *movement* was most important. To bend seemed wiser than to risk years of work by acting fanatically on abstract principle. Nor was he selfless or mindless of person and position. Those who gilded him as a hero felt betrayed in 1921 when Haywood humanly chose exile rather than prison.

Bill Haywood was not the leading radical of his day. Daniel DeLeon was far more brilliant. Victor Berger was infinitely more successful. Debs was certainly the more attractive and heroic individual. But Haywood was an important figure, for his career illustrated not only his own frustrations but the frustrations of American radicals in the industrial age. Haywood was vexed and perplexed by the seemingly inexplicable failure of the working class to recognize their exploited position in society and their necessarily inexorable conflict with their masters. He never despised the workers for their social lethargy; he blamed it on oppression, opportunistic socialist politicians, labor fakirs, or others of that like. Educated in an industry where class conflict was literal and clear-cut, he never grasped the flexibility of his generation's capitalists, which permitted them not only to survive but to checkmate his own and subsequent anticapitalist movements.

Haywood's failure was also the failure of American radicalism in that it was his misfortune to suffer from the sectarianism which has plagued the American left since Karl Marx introduced the virus to the United States by shipping the First International out of Michael Bakunin's reach to New York and Hoboken. Haywood found himself the usually unwilling collaborator of a militant faction throughout his life. Worse for him, but immaterial to the movement as a whole, his faction was usually the losing one.

He was ousted from the Western Federation when Charles Moyer found him too fiery for Moyer's future plans. Haywood saw, as the result of the squabble, the virtual secession of a large union from the revolutionary movement. He was the center of a dispute in the Socialist Party when one faction virtually excommunicated another and, in the process, turned the first spadeful for the party's grave. He successfully maintained his predominance in the relatively catholic Industrial Workers but sowed an ill-feeling which later rebounded, not only on his own head but on the IWW's last chance for survival as a viable labor organization. And, though he did not participate during his two decades in the forefront of American radicalism Haywood witnessed the interminable backbiting between Socialist Laborites and Socialists, two destructive splits in the IWW, and the founding of two Communist parties within months of one another, both presumably to accomplish the classless society. From exile he watched the IWW, SPA, SLP, CP, CLP, and CPA waste their energies in damning one another. Mercifully for him, Haywood died before the worldwide repercussions of the Stalin-Trotsky dispute were fully felt, although the faction-weary old radical anticipated that too.

American radicals, much more than their European counterparts, have proved incapable of presenting a popular front to their common enemy, despite their less ideological dispositions and their weaknesses which make the infighting so ludicrous. Haywood, with a moral basis to his radicalism and a practical approach to his revolutionism, disliked and could never understand this penchant for factionalism. Revolutionaries should act, he thought. It was absurd to scramble for the social spoils before the established society had even begun to totter.

Finally, Haywood knew too well the governmental and informal repression that met every leftist radical movement in the United States which began to show genuine vitality. He knew it with the WFM when every force at the government's disposal was arrayed against the miners. He knew it with the IWW at Lawrence, Paterson, and the Mesabi Range. He felt the ultimate hammer-blow in the World War I trials when he was confronted with the cruel choice of personal martyrdom or betrayal of comrades. With its healthiest of national traditions, the United States has by no means vindicated its democracy of the criticism that it is a mob easily led into a destruction of liberty. American capitalism is indeed flexible. The system has been capable of adjustments necessary for the survival of even its most obsolete aspects. But, when criticism threatens to tell, it can react monstrously against its critics. Haywood suffered for his flight to Moscow in his American disgrace, his Russian obscurity, his loneliness, inactivity, and feeling of social worthlessness. But the ultimate ignominy for his flight falls on his native land. Haywood's betrayal of comrades looks less grievous next to a nation's betrayal of its avowed principles.

Bibliographical Note

A list of all the sources consulted in writing this book would unnecessarily duplicate the footnotes. This brief note mentions only the most important and readily available sources relevant to Bill Haywood's career. There are, unfortunately, no "Haywood Papers." Rumors of small collections in private hands are heard from time to time, but investigation has led to nothing. Various other manuscript sources provide some Haywood material, including the IWW Collection in the Labor History Archives of Wayne State University; the Labadie Collection of the University of Michigan Library; the Socialist Party of America Collection in the Duke University Library; the Algie M. Simons, Morris Hillquit, Elizabeth Gurley Flynn, William English Walling, and Daniel DeLeon papers at the State Historical Society of Wisconsin; the Tamiment Institute of New York City; and the Ralph Chaplin Collection of the University of Washington.

The *Miners Magazine* is a valuable periodical source for Haywood's writings as are the *International Socialist Review* and the *New Review*. Other Socialist, Wobbly, and anarchist journals of the day—of which there are a spate—are also helpful.

There is no full-length biography of Haywood. William J. Ghent wrote a short but accurate account of his life for the *Dictionary of American Biography,* Volume VIII, 468, and Carl Hein contributed a good essay on Haywood to Harvey Goldberg's *American Radicals* (New York: 1957). T. K. Gladkov's *Zhizn Bolshovo Billa* (Profizdat, 1960) represents the only Soviet biographical research on Haywood, but it has not been translated into English and is difficult to secure in the United States even in its Russian edition. A less important Soviet account is B. Reinshteyn's note in the *Bol'shaia Sovietskaia*

Entsiklopediia (first edition, Volume XIV, 1929). There is, of course, *Bill Haywood's Book* (New York: 1928). The book suffers from the flaws of autobiographies in general. Haywood inflates his role in some events, deflates it in others less happy, entirely omits mention of actions he later regretted, and inevitably projects later ideas into earlier situations. On the whole, however, the book compares well with other autobiographies with a purpose to serve.

Several writers have maintained that Haywood did not even write the book, that it was, in Stewart Holbrook's phrase, "an alleged autobiography . . . largely ghostwritten by a Communist hack to meet the current party line." Late in his life, Ralph Chaplin told an interviewer that he was offered the job of writing the book and, when he refused, it was done by Louise Bryant, John Reed's wife. Vernon Jensen is the curtest of all: "In *Bill Haywood's Book,* which of course was not written by Haywood, he is made to say. . . ." Curtness is understandable for there is no evidence for the allegation. To the three, Haywood's end as a Communist was at best inglorious. Just as Haywood's American devotees could never accept the reality of his flight, they could not accept the validity of a book which concludes with Haywood agog in the presence of V. I. Lenin. Haywood ends up there surely enough but, interestingly, the book does not lead inexorably to his interview with Lenin by any means. It is not the climax of the story.

Curiously also, for a book they so perfunctorily discredited, both Holbrook and Jensen make use of *Bill Haywood's Book* as their sole source in other sections of their works. They did not err in doing so. It cannot be said with certainty just what the nature of Haywood's role was in writing the book: whether he sat down with pen and paper, dictated it to Louise Bryant or a secretary, or told his story to a ghostwriter who drafted the actual manuscript. The latter is unlikely, for the writing is in Haywood's style. And the book is surely not fabrication. Haywood wrote to friends in the United States about his project, and the internal evidence of picayune details corroborated elsewhere point to his authorship. It is possible—even likely—that the book was edited before leaving Moscow, or in the New York offices of International Publishers. But the book remains the first source for the researcher on the subject. It *is* "Bill Haywood's Book."

A better-founded story relates that Haywood also wrote of his Soviet experiences. (An editor's note in the book claims that he died with this intention unfulfilled.) Whether or not those who write of a secret "Russian diary" would have been rewarded with the documentation of the anti-Communism they impute to him is another matter. At any rate, Haywood's final seven years remain disappointingly obscure.

The best book on the Western Federation of Miners is Vernon Jensen's *Heritage of Conflict* (Ithaca: 1950). The Steunenberg Case is the subject of a novel, Stewart Holbrook's *Rocky Mountain Revolution* (New York: 1956), which is based on Harry Orchard's confession and finds Haywood guilty. The case is also discussed in virtually every labor history of the period. The best case for a "frame-up" is in Philip S. Foner's *The Industrial Workers of the World* (New York: 1966). David H. Grover's *Debaters and Dynamiters* (Corvallis: 1964) is concerned chiefly with the workings of public opinion in regard to the case.

Of Haywood's personal life, the chief sources are the memoirs of friends, although there is also a wealth of contemporary journalism on the subject. Emma Goldman's *Living My Life* (New York: 1931) tells of Haywood in New York City and later in the Soviet Union with that remarkable woman's honesty and perception. Mabel Dodge Luhan's *Movers and Shakers* (New York: 1936) contains some glimpses of Haywood's life in her circle. Elizabeth Gurley Flynn's *I Speak My Own Piece* (New York: 1955) provides information about Haywood's activities on the picket line. Ralph Chaplin, *Wobbly* (Chicago: 1948), written when its author had swung to the extreme right of the political spectrum, is quite unbiased in its accounts of Haywood and the IWW during the 1910's.

The classic history of the IWW is Paul F. Brissenden's *The IWW: A Study of American Syndicalism* (New York: 1919). Somewhat outdated in its methodology and by the emergence of new sources, Brissenden's book is notable for its scholarly tone in an age when the IWW was the center of a great deal of hysterical nonsense. It has been displaced as the major informational source on the IWW by Philip S. Foner's book, a detailed and basically accurate work. The reader interested in the IWW, however, would be best advised to consult first Patrick Renshaw, *The Wobblies: The Story of Syndicalism in America* (London: 1967) which, while it perpetuates some misconceptions on the subject, is the best short work. An IWW publication, *The IWW: Its First Fifty Years* (Chicago: 1955) by Fred Thompson, is necessarily brief on the period before World

War I but is a valuable account. Joyce Kornbluh's *Rebel Voices* (Ann Arbor: 1964) is a fine anthology of Wobbly writings, which were both considerable and eloquent. Robert L. Tyler, *Rebels of the Woods* (Eugene: 1967) is an excellent recently published narrative of the IWW in the Pacific Northwest.

The best single volume on the Socialist Party is David A. Shannon's *Socialist Party of America* (New York: 1955). On the period encompassing Haywood's career the best account is Ira Kipnis, *The American Socialist Movement* (New York: 1952). Ray Ginger, *The Bending Cross: A Biography of Eugene Victor Debs* (New Brunswick: 1949) is a study of a subject inseparable from Socialist Party history.

The best study of socialism on a local level is Henry F. Bedford, *Socialism and the Workers in Massachusetts* (Amherst: 1966). A comprehensive survey of American socialism is represented by Donald Drew Egbert and Stow Persons, *Socialism and American Life*, 2 vols. (Princeton: 1952). Indispensable for the background of the story is Howard H. Quint, *The Forging of American Socialism* (Columbia, S.C.: 1953).

An interesting recent interpretation of the socialists, which also discusses the origins of American communism, is James Weinstein, *The Decline of Socialism in America* (New York: 1967). Theodore Draper's, *Roots of American Communism* (New York: 1957) traces the same events in somewhat more detail.

The best analysis of the World War I trials is William Preston, Jr., *Aliens and Dissenters* (Cambridge: 1963). H. C. Peterson and Gilbert Fite, *Opponents of War* (Madison: 1955), provides a factual backdrop of the events. Robert K. Murray, *Great Red Scare* (Minneapolis: 1955), remains the standard study of the postwar hysteria.

Notes to Chapters

Chapter 1: Worker

1. George Wharton James, *Utah: Land of Blossoming Valleys* (Boston: 1922), pp. 310–11; William D. Haywood, *Bill Haywood's Book: The Autobiography of William D. Haywood* (New York: 1928), pp. 10–13; Dale L. Morgan, "Changing Face of Salt Lake City," *Utah Historical Quarterly,* XXVII (July, 1959), 216; Leonard J. Arrington, *Great Basin Kingdom: Economic History of the Latter Day Saints* (Lincoln: 1966).

2. *Salt Lake City Directory for 1869,* quoted in Daughters of Utah Pioneers, *Tales of a Triumphant People* (Salt Lake City: 1947), p. 303.

3. *A Compendium of the Ninth Census,* June 1, 1870 (Washington: 1872), pp. 128, 242, 349; William Mulder, "Salt Lake City in 1880: A Census Profile," *Utah Historical Quarterly,* XXIV (July, 1956), 233–36; Morgan, "Changing Face," 227–28; *Bill Haywood's Book,* pp. 9, 13, 14, 18; Leonard J. Arrington, "Banking Enterprises in Utah: 1847–1880," *Business History Review* (1955), 312–34.

4. *Bill Haywood's Book,* pp. 7–8.

5. *Ibid.,* pp. 8, 10.

6. Walter R. Crane, *Gold and Silver* (New York: 1908), pp. 106–107; 107; Leonard J. Arrington, "Abundance from the Earth," *Utah Historical Quarterly, XXXI* (Summer, 1963), 208.

7. *Bill Haywood's Book,* pp. 10–12; Diary of Maggie Tolman Porter, quoted in Tooele City Daughters of Utah Pioneers, *History of Tooele County* (Salt Lake City: 1961), pp. 377, 379.

8. *Bill Haywood's Book,* p. 17.

9. Mulder, "Census Profile," 236; *Bill Haywood's Book,* pp. 12, 14–17.

10. Morgan, "Changing Face," 227–28; *Bill Haywood's Book,* p. 10.

11. Dale L. Morgan, *The Humboldt: Highroad of the West* (New York: 1943), pp. 4–5; *Bill Haywood's Book,* p. 21; *Reproduction of Thompson and West's History of Nevada: 1881* (Berkeley: 1958), pp. 443–44, 451, 459–60.

12. *Bill Haywood's Book,* pp. 23, 24, 26, 29–31, 248.

13. *Ibid.,* p. 28. Prof. William Hutchinson of Chico State College helped me to corroborate this obscure incident.

14. *Ibid.,* pp. 10–15, 19, 23–26.

15. *Ibid.,* pp. 30, 33–37, 190; *History of Nevada: 1881,* p. 444.

16. *Bill Haywood's Book,* pp. 39, 45–46.

17. *Ibid.,* pp. 41, 42, 51–53.

18. Crane, *Gold and Silver,* p. 343.

19. Charles Howard Shinn, *Mining Camps: A Study in American Frontier Government* (New York: 1884), (New York: 1965), p. 2.

20. *Ibid.,* p. 110.

21. D. Bacon, quoted in *ibid.,* p. 173. The same old miner, an editor of the *Boise City Republican* during the 1880's, observed that different systems adopted in the newer mine fields such as Idaho and Montana which permitted exclusivist claims of up to twenty acres "produced bitter fruit. The smaller plots of the California miners were much better for the community. All were contented, and none were hopelessly poor."

22. *Ibid.,* p. 110; *Congressional Globe,* June 19, 1866.

23. *Ibid.,* pp. 29, 116; *Bill Haywood's Book,* p. 53. It is also notable that theft of ore or "high-grading"—surreptitiously removing very valuable ores from the mine at the end of a day's shift—became almost an established custom among the industrialized miners.

24. For a history of railroad expansion in the mining states, see Crane, *Gold and Silver,* pp. 136–43; *History of Tooele County,* p. 380; Vernon Jensen, *Heritage of Conflict: Labor Relations in the Nonferrous Metals Industry up to 1930* (Ithaca: 1950), pp. 19–23; Glenn Chesney Quiett, *Pay Dirt: A Panorama of American Gold Rushes* (New York: 1936).

25. W. Turrentine Jackson, "British Impact on the Utah Mining Industry," *Utah Historical Quarterly,* XXI (Fall, 1963), 349.

26. Shinn, *Mining Camps,* p. 6.

27. *Bill Haywood's Book,* pp. 97–98.

28. *Miners Magazine* (February, 1900), 7; *History of Nevada: 1881,* pp. 447, 451.

29. *Bill Haywood's Book,* pp. 32, 49; Frank A. Crampton, *Deep Enough: A Working Stiff in the Western Mine Camps* (Denver: 1956), Preface, unnumbered page.

30. E. Lord, *Comstock Mining and Mines* (Washington: Department of the Interior, United States Geological Survey: 1883), Monographs IV, 182.

31. *Mines and Minerals,* XXV, 1–3, quoted in Crane, *Gold and Silver,* p. 441 (emphasis in original); Crampton, *Deep Enough,* p. 102.

32. *The Nation* (May 30, 1928), 601; *Bill Haywood's Book,* p. 208.

33. Shinn, *Mining Camps,* p. 290.

34. Quoted in *Bill Haywood's Book,* pp. 52, 208.

Chapter 2: Unionist

1. William D. Haywood, *Bill Haywood's Book: The Autobiography of William D. Haywood* (New York: 1928), pp. 61–62, 64; Elizabeth Gurley Flynn, *Debs, Haywood, Rutherberg* (New York: 1939), p. 22.

2. *Bill Haywood's Book,* pp. 70, 79; William J. Ghent, "William D. Haywood," *Dictionary of American Biography,* VIII, 468.

3. *Bill Haywood's Book,* pp. 79, 80, 82–84.

4. *Ibid.,* pp. 89–91; *Dictionary of American Biography,* VIII, 468.

5. For an astute discussion of the origins of western radicalism, see Melvyn Dubofsky, "The Origins of Western Working Class Radicalism, 1890–1905," *Labor History,* VII (Spring, 1966), 131–54.

6. *Bill Haywood's Book,* p. 1; *Final Report and Testimony Submitted to Congress by the Commission on Industrial Relations* (64th Congress, 1st Session, Senate Document 415) (Washington, 1916), XI, 10569; see Timothy L. Smith, "New Approaches to the History of Immigration in Twentieth Century America," *American Historical Review,* LXXI (July, 1966), 1265–79.

7. John Graham Brooks, *American Syndicalism* (New York: 1913), prefatory note; Ralph Chaplin, *Wobbly: The Rough and Tumble Story of an American Radical* (Chicago: 1947), pp. 139, 347; Covington Hall, *Battle Hymns of Toil* (Oklahoma City: n.d.); Hall, "Labor Struggles in the Deep South," Typescript, Labor History Archives, Wayne State University.

8. *Bill Haywood's Book,* p. 62; for a history of the early miners' unions, see, Vernon Jensen, *Heritage of Conflict: Labor Relations in the Nonferrous Metals Industry up to 1930,* pp. 11–18; Melvyn Dubofsky, "The Leadville Strike of 1886–1897: An Appraisal," *Mid-America* (April, 1966); *Butte Daily Miner,* January 1, 1886; *Western Federation of Miners, Proceedings of the 15th Annual Convention, 1907,* p. 162; *Bill Haywood's Book,* p. 86; Stewart Holbrook, *Rocky Mountain Revolution* (New York: 1956), p. 2.

9. *Bill Haywood's Book,* pp. 62–64.

10. Jensen, *Heritage of Conflict,* pp. 59–60; *American Federation of Labor, Proceedings of the Convention of 1896,* pp. 62–63. Reproduced in *Coeur d'Alene Labor Troubles* (56th Congress, 1st Session, Senate Document 142).

11. *Pueblo Courier,* June 3, 1898.

12. *Bill Haywood's Book,* pp. 65, 69.

13. "Minute Books," Silver City, Idaho Miners Union Local 62, Bancroft Library, University of California.

14. Jensen, *Heritage of Conflict,* pp. 72–74.

15. Melvyn Dubofsky, "James H. Hawley and the Origins of the Haywood Case," *Pacific Northwest Quarterly* (January, 1967), pp. 23–32. *Bill Haywood's Book,* p. 80; Jensen, *Heritage of Conflict,* pp. 74–75; *Coeur d'Alene Labor Troubles* (56th Congress, 1st Session, House Document 1999), pp. 31–32.

16. *Bill Haywood's Book,* p. 81; Jensen, *Heritage of Conflict,* p. 76; *Idaho Tribune,* May 3, 1899, reproduced in *Coeur d'Alene Mining Troubles* (56th Congress, 1st Session, Senate Document 24), IV, 30; *Miners Magazine* (June, 1900), 14–15.

17. See, for example, Holbrook, *Rocky Mountain Revolution,* p. 64; *Bill Haywood's Book,* p. 81.

18. *Ibid.,* p. 82.

19. Dubofsky, "Working Class Radicalism," 154.

20. *Bill Haywood's Book,* p. 94; *In Re Eight Hour Bill, 21 Colorado 29,* 91895; Jensen, *Heritage of Conflict,* pp. 97, 101–104.

21. *Bill Haywood's Book,* p. 95. While the WFM tacitly supported Eugene V. Debs for President in 1900, the word was passed by implication that a vote for Bryan was preferable to a vote for McKinley. Compare, the *Miners Magazine* wrote, the "insignificant McKinley with the strongly individualized Bryan; the loud-mouthed blowhard Roosevelt with the dignified Stevenson." (November, 1900), 3–4. The 1900 convention also supported several congressmen from the major parties and called for the defeat of Frank Steunenberg of Idaho, a backhanded endorsement of his Republican opponent. (June, 1900), 19.

22. *Industrial Workers of the World, Proceedings of the First Annual Convention, 1905,* p. 144.

23. *Miners Magazine* (August 27, 1903), 4; Jensen, *Heritage of Conflict,* p. 107.

24. *Bill Haywood's Book,* p. 96.

25. *Ibid.,* p. 65.

26. See, for example, the mine owners' *Labor Disturbances in Colorado.*

27. However, Executive Committee approval was required in order for the local to receive financial support. Western Federation of Miners, *Proceedings of the Conventions of 1893,* pp. 7–8; *1906,* pp. 270–71; *1907,* p. 935. *Pueblo Courier,* May 19, 1899; Philip S. Foner, *Policies and Practices of the A.F. of L.: 1900–1909* (New York: 1964), p. 403; see also Jensen, *Heritage of Conflict,* pp. 70–71.

28. *Bill Haywood's Book,* p. 97.

29. Foner, *Policies and Practices,* p. 401.

30. Jensen, *Heritage of Conflict,* p. 58.

31. *Bill Haywood's Book,* p. 127; Jensen, *Heritage of Conflict,* p. 38; *ibid.,* p. 38; *Annual Cripple Creek Directory, 1905,* quoted in Sprague, *Money Mountain,* p. 300; Quiett, *Pay Dirt,* p. 302.

32. *Ibid.,* p. 296; Harry J. Newton, *Yellow Gold of Cripple Creek* (Denver: 1928).

33. Jensen, *Heritage of Conflict,* pp. 53, 119; *Bill Haywood's Book,* p. 118; Morris Friedman, *The Pinkerton Labor Spy* (New York: n.d.), pp. 30–37; Jensen, *Heritage of Conflict,* p. 119; *Miners Magazine* (April, 1903), 2.

34. Quiett, *Pay Dirt,* p. 302; *Bill Haywood's Book,* p. 128. The Easterner's misrepresentation of Cripple Creek as a roaring town of "Rocky Mountain toughs" had early origins. See, for example, William James, *Pragmatism,* originally published in 1907 (Cleveland: 1955), pp. 22–23.

35. Jensen, *Heritage of Conflict,* pp. 120–21; *Miners Magazine* (April, 1903), 5.

36. *Bill Haywood's Book,* p. 118; Jensen, *Heritage of Conflict,* pp. 121–22.

37. *Ibid.,* p. 129.

38. *Bill Haywood's Book,* pp. 140, 138; Jensen, *Heritage of Conflict,* pp. 130–31, 133; *Miners Magazine* (October 8, 29, 1903), 6, 7.

39. *Bill Haywood's Book,* p. 146.

40. *Ibid.,* pp. 165–66.

41. *Ibid.,* p. 129.

42. *Ibid.,* pp. 141, 159–60; Jensen, *Heritage of Conflict,* pp. 144–45.

43. *Bill Haywood's Book,* pp. 145–46, 161–62.

44. *Weekly People,* September 4, 1915; Western Federation of Miners, *Proceedings of the 16th Annual Convention* (Report of President Moyer), pp. 17–18.

45. Accounts are several: Philip S. Foner, *The Industrial Workers of the World: 1905–1917* (New York: 1965); Paul F. Brissenden, *The I.W.W.: A History of American Syndicalism* (New York: 1919); Patrick Renshaw, *The Wobblies: The Story of Syndicalism in America* (London: 1967).

46. Joyce Kornbluh, *Rebel Voices: An I.W.W. Anthology* (Ann Arbor: 1964), pp. 7–9; Foner, *The I.W.W.,* pp. 17–19.

47. *Bill Haywood's Book,* p. 184.

48. *Ibid.,* p. 187.

Chapter 3: Undesirable Citizen

1. Luke Grant, "The Idaho Murder Trial," *Outlook* (April 6, 1907), 805.

2. Harry Orchard, "Confession and Autobiography," *McClure's Magazine* (November, 1906), 122.

3. William D. Haywood, *Bill Haywood's Book: The Autobiography of William D. Haywood* (New York: 1928), pp. 191, 193.

4. *Ibid.*, p. 193; *Outlook* (April 6, 1907); Abe C. Ravitz and James N. Primm, *The Haywood Case* (San Francisco: 1960), p. 13.

5. Melvyn Dubofsky, "James H. Hawley and the Origins of the Haywood Case," *Pacific Northwest Quarterly* (January, 1967), 23–32.

6. Arthur Weinberg, ed., *Attorney for the Damned* (New York: 1957), p. 449.

7. *Ibid.*, pp. 451, 465–66.

8. *Ibid.*, pp. 460, 484, 497–98.

9. *Ibid.*, pp. 486–87.

10. *Appeal to Reason,* January 11, 1908; Weinberg, *Attorney for the Damned,* p. 488.

11. This subject is discussed in detail in Stephen Scheinberg, "The Haywood Trial: Theodore Roosevelt's Undesirable Citizens," *Idaho Yesterdays,* IV (Fall, 1960).

12. *Miners Magazine,* January, 1901; Ravitz and Primm, *The Haywood Case,* p. 24.

13. His angels might have paid handsomely for his friendship. The *Miners Magazine* (January, 1900) asked how the penniless Steunenberg of 1898 was able in 1900 to muster $4,000 to secure the Democratic gubernatorial nomination. Furthermore, the magazine stated, "on a salary of $3,000 a year, he was able to spend $4,000 to control the Democratic convention and, in addition to this, in less than two years he has bought several thousand sheep and holds bank stock and other valuable property. . . . How this villain has risen in four years from the editor of a weekly paper on the Snake River desert to a wealthy sheep owner, mine owner, and stockholder!" See Ravitz and Primm, *The Haywood Case,* p. 24.

14. Boise *Capital News,* December 26, 1907; *Miners Magazine,* January 4, and January 11, 1906.

15. Samuel P. Orth, *The Armies of Labor* (New Haven: 1921); Vernon Jensen, *Heritage of Conflict* (Ithaca: 1950); Richard O. Boyer and Herbert M. Morais, *Labor's Untold Story* (New York: 1955), pp. 116–20; Thomas R. Brooks, *Toil and Trouble: A History of American Labor* (New York: 1965), pp. 116–17. Dr. Merle Wells, historian of the Idaho State Historical Society, who knows the sources of the case as well as anyone, still regards the question of Haywood's complicity as unresolved. Ravitz and Primm, *The Haywood Case,* p. 1.

16. Jensen, *Heritage of Conflict,* p. 201.

17. Some other variations later emerged. Judge Hilton and Edmund Richardson, confidants of the WFM leadership, were reported to have felt that Haywood might have been implicated while Moyer and Pettibone definitely were not. (Jensen, *Heritage of Conflict,* pp. 204, 216.) These implications must be viewed in light of the fact that after the Boise Trial Haywood and Moyer had a bitter falling out and were ever after hostile

toward one another. Both Richardson and Hilton, as well as the sources of their alleged implications, were Moyer's partisans within the WFM. Haywood very vaguely hints in his autobiography that Moyer might have been involved in the bombing with an eye toward eliminating Haywood. He related a "subterfuge" used by Moyer to get away from Denver. "It was not long after this," Haywood continued, "that the startling news was in the papers that ex-governor Steunenberg of Idaho had been killed by a bomb at his home in Caldwell." But the reference is vague and Haywood does not pursue it. (*Bill Haywood's Book,* p. 191.)

18. This appears as Chapter 2 of Vol. IV of Philip S. Foner's *History of the Labor Movement of the United States: The Industrial Workers of the World* (New York: 1965). While I do not agree with all of Foner's conclusions, I have benefited greatly from his account in the following analysis. A more detailed scrutiny of Foner's argument appears in Joseph R. Conlin, "The Haywood Case: An Enduring Riddle," *Pacific Northwest Quarterly* (January, 1968), 23–32.

19. Foner is incorrect in calling the reports "hitherto unpublished." Large extracts were published in 1960 in Ravitz and Primm, *The Haywood Case,* pp. 66–117. (Foner, *The I.W.W.,* p. 41.)

20. Ravitz and Primm, *The Haywood Case,* p. 67.

21. *Pinkerton Reports,* January 22, 1906; Ravitz and Primm, *The Haywood Case,* p. 70; Foner, *The I.W.W.,* pp. 41–42.

22. *Pinkerton Reports,* January 22, 1906; Ravitz and Primm, *The Haywood Case,* p. 71.

23. *Pinkerton Reports,* January 25, 1906; Ravitz and Primm, *The Haywood Case,* pp. 75–76; Foner, *The I.W.W.,* pp. 42–43.

24. *Pinkerton Reports,* January 25, 1906; Ravitz and Primm, *The Haywood Case,* p. 78; Foner, *The I.W.W.,* p. 43; *McClure's Magazine* (July through November, 1907).

25. Foner, *The I.W.W.,* p. 44.

26. In a footnote (*The I.W.W.,* p. 45), Foner makes the entirely warranted criticism of David Grover, *Debaters and Dynamiters* (Corvallis: 1964), p. 63, that Grover devotes only one sentence to McParland's interviews with Orchard.

27. James Hawley discusses Adams' confession from the point of view of the prosecution in "Steve Adams' Confession and the State's Case Against Bill Haywood," *Idaho Yesterdays,* VII (Winter, 1963–1964); see also *Industrial Union Bulletin,* March 9, 1907; Foner, *The I.W.W.,* pp. 49–50.

28. Harry Orchard, "Confession and Autobiography."

29. Orchard remained a devoted adherent of the church until his death in prison at the age of 88 in 1954. *Life Magazine* (March 13, 1950), p. 116; *Pinkerton Reports,* January 22, 1906; Ravitz and Primm, *The Haywood Case,* p. 72.

30. *Pinkerton Reports,* January 25, 1906; Ravitz and Primm, *The Haywood Case,* pp. 74, 81.

31. *Pinkerton Reports,* January 25, 1906; Ravitz and Primm, *The Haywood Case,* pp. 79, 81, 90.

32. James McParland, letter to Frank Gooding, February 9, 1906; Ravitz and Primm, *The Haywood Case,* pp. 98–99; Foner, *The I.W.W.,* p. 50.

33. *Idaho Daily Statesman,* June 30, 1907; *Life Magazine* (March 13, 1950), 116; Stewart Holbrook, *Rocky Mountain Revolution* (New York: 1956), p. 14.

34. John N. Beffel, "Four Radicals," *American Mercury,* XXV (April, 1932), 443.

35. Weinberg, *Attorney for the Damned,* pp. 443–87.

36. *Pinkerton Reports,* March 16, 1907; Foner, *The I.W.W.,* p. 46.

37. See, for example, Henry David, *History of the Haymarket Affair* (New York: 1963); Philip S. Foner, *The Case of Joe Hill* (New York: 1965); Felix Frankfurter, *The Case of Sacco and Vanzetti* (Boston: 1927).

38. For a discussion of this phenomenon see Foner, *The I.W.W.,* pp. 51–55; Grover, *Debaters and Dynamiters;* Brooks, *Toil and Trouble,* pp. 116–17.

39. *Pinkerton Reports,* February 16, 1906; Foner, *The I.W.W.,* pp. 47–48.

40. *Bill Haywood's Book,* p. 194; Weinberg, *Attorney for the Damned,* p. 412; Scheinberg, "The Haywood Trial."

41. Dubofsky, "James H. Hawley," 23–30.

42. James H. Hawley, letter to William Puckett, June 19, 1899 and July 2, 1899, Hawley Papers, quoted in Dubofsky, "James H. Hawley," 31.

43. *Bill Haywood's Book,* p. 197.

44. *Ibid.,* pp. 198, 200, 205.

45. *Ibid.,* p. 216.

46. *Ibid.,* p. 217.

Chapter 4: The Eminent Man

1. Arthur W. Thompson, "The Reception of Russian Revolutionary Leaders in America: 1904–1906," *American Quarterly,* XVIII (Fall, 1966), 470.

2. Philip S. Foner, *The Industrial Workers of the World: 1905–1917* (New York: 1965), pp. 51–55; William D. Haywood, *Bill Haywood's Book: The Autobiography of William D. Haywood* (New York: 1928), p. 220.

3. *Ibid.,* p. 94.

4. *First Convention of the Industrial Workers of the World: Proceedings,* p. 580.

5. *Bill Haywood's Book,* p. 217; Clarence Darrow, *The Story of My Life* (New York: 1932), p. 155.

6. *Bill Haywood's Book,* pp. 229–30; Adolph Germer Manuscripts, State Historical Society of Wisconsin.

7. *Western Federation of Miners, Fifteenth Annual Convention* (1906), pp. 582, 586.

8. *Bill Haywood's Book,* p. 224.

9. *Ibid.,* p. 90.

10. *Ibid.,* p. 23; The Adolph Germer Manuscripts, while fragmentary, tell the story of the unsuccessful attempts to unite the WFM and the United Mine Workers during 1906 and 1907.

11. *Bill Haywood's Book,* pp. 220–26, 229.

12. *Ibid.,* p. 228.

13. *Ibid.,* p. 223; "Haywood in Europe," *International Socialist Review,* XI (November, 1910), 288.

14. *Bill Haywood's Book,* p. 213.

15. *New York Call,* May 12, 1915.

16. *Final Report and Testimony Submitted to Congress by the Commission on Industrial Relations* (64th Congress, 1st Session, Senate Document 415) (Washington: 1916), XI, 10583. Testimony of May 12, 1915; *Int. Soc. Rev.,* XI (April, 1911), 648.

17. *New Review, I* (May, 1913), 505.

18. Carl Van Vechten, *Peter Whiffle,* p. 20.

19. Mabel Dodge Luhan, *Intimate Memories,* III (New York: 1936), 90; Van Vechten, *Peter Whiffle,* pp. 125–26, 137; Daniel Aaron, *Writers on the Left* (New York: 1961), p. 11.

20. Van Vechten, *Peter Whiffle,* pp. 135–36. This is from a novel, but enough of the account is corroborated elsewhere to authenticate it. Christopher Lasch, in *The New Radicalism in America, 1889–1963* (New York: 1965), adds a fascinating new dimension to the radical inclination of Mabel Dodge Luhan, *Intimate Memories,* III, 104–40.

21. Mabel Dodge Luhan, *Intimate Memories,* III, 90.

22. *Ibid.,* III, 59.

23. *Ibid.,* III.

24. John Collier, letter to Mabel Dodge, December 31, 1913, in *ibid.,* III, 145–46.

25. *Ibid.,* III, 147–49.

26. *Final Report of the Industrial Relations Commission,* XI, 10540–569; II, 1456. St. John's response as reported by the record was unqualified.

27. *Final Report of the I.R.C.,* V, 4936–50; V, 4240–41.

28. *Ibid.,* XI, 10569–71, 10574.

29. *Ibid.,* XI, 10574–75.

30. Graham Adams, *Age of Industrial Violence* (New York: 1966), p. 63.

31. *Final Report of the I.R.C.*, XI, 10576.

32. *Ibid.*, XI, 10576.

33. *Ibid.*, XI, 10577.

34. *Ibid.*, XI, 10577–78.

35. *Ibid.*, XI, 10578–79.

36. *Ibid.*, XI, 10580.

37. *Ibid.*, XI, 10582

38. *Ibid.*, XI, 10583.

39. *Ibid.*, XI, 10584.

40. *Ibid.*, XI, 10592.

41. *Ibid.*, XI, 10592, 10595–99.

42. *Colliers,* LII (October 18, 1913), 6; *Final Report of the I.R.C.*, XI, 10574; Elizabeth Gurley Flynn, *Debs, Haywood, Rutherberg* (New York: 1939), p. 27.

43. *Bill Haywood's Book,* pp. 232–33; Ramsay MacDonald, *Syndicalism* (London: 1913), pp. 36–37. Haywood wrote in his autobiography that when he arrived in the Soviet Union in 1921 Lenin reminded him that they had met at Copenhagen.

44. MacDonald, *Syndicalism,* pp. 36–37; *Bill Haywood's Book,* pp. 234–36, 272–74; on the subject of Haywood's tour of England I have benefited from the information proffered by Mr. Patrick Renshaw of Oxford. Letter in the author's possession, July 18, 1966.

45. W. J. Ghent, *Dictionary of American Biography,* VIII, 468; Andre Tridon, "Haywood," *New Review,* I (May, 1913), 502.

46. *New Review,* I (May, 1913), 502; Emma Goldman, *Living My Life,* II (New York: 1931), 537.

47. Quoted in Luhan, *Intimate Memories,* III, 186; Van Vechten, *Peter Whiffle,* p. 136; G. D. H. Dole, *The World of Labour* (London: 1915), p. 147; Elizabeth Gurley Flynn, "Personal Recollections of the Industrial Workers of the World," Speech at Northern Illinois University, November 8, 1962, tape recording at the Labor History Archives, Wayne State University.

48. *New Review,* I (May, 1913), 504.

49. Ralph Chaplin, *Wobbly: The Rough and Tumble Story of an American Radical* (Chicago: 1947), pp. 289–90.

50. *Ibid.*, p. 102.

51. *Dictionary of American Biography,* VIII, 468; see, for example, "An Appeal for Industrial Solidarity," *Int. Soc. Rev.*, XIV (March, 1914), 544–46.

52. *Bill Haywood's Book,* p. 94; Haywood's contributions to the *Miners Magazine* appear regularly between 1900 and 1906.

53. *Int. Soc. Rev.*, XII (December, 1911), 345.

54. "Shots for the Workshop," in *ibid.*, XI (April, 1911); "Blanket Stiff Philosophy," in *ibid.*, XII (December, 1911), 370.

55. Van Vechten, *Peter Whiffle,* p. 134; *Final Report of the I.R.C.,* XI, 10574.

56. *Bill Haywood's Book,* p. 269; "Haywood's Battle in Paterson, *Literary Digest,* XLVI (1913), 1043–44.

57. *Int. Soc. Rev.,* XI (May, 1911), 680–84.

58. *Bill Haywood's Book,* p. 260; Haywood, "With the Copper Miners of Michigan," *Int. Soc. Rev.,* XI (August, 1910), 65.

59. *Bill Haywood's Book,* p. 171.

60. *Ibid.,* p. 226.

61. *Ibid.,* p. 265.

62. Joseph R. Conlin, "Wobblies and Syndicalists," *Studies on the Left,* VI (March–April, 1966).

63. Covington Hall, "Labor Struggles in the Deep South," Personal Narrative, photostatic copy of typescript in Labor History Archives, Wayne State University, p. 156; Goldman, *Living My Life,* II, 537, 904.

64. *The Survey,* XXVII (March 30, 1912), 205; "Program of the Paterson Pageant," June 7, 1913, Labadie Collection, University of Michigan.

65. *The World's Work,* XXVI (1913), 417.

Chapter 5: Wobbly

1. Max Hayes, "World of Labor," *International Socialist Review,* VII (February, 1907), 502; quoted in Elizabeth Gurley Flynn, *I Speak My Own Piece: The Autobiography of the Rebel Girl* (New York: 1955), p. 161; Industrial Workers of the World, *Proceedings of the First Annual Convention, 1905,* pp. 584–86.

2. William D. Haywood, *Bill Haywood's Book: The Autobiography of William D. Haywood* (New York: 1928), pp. 189, 202.

3. This, of course, is a necessarily brief account of the proceedings. The actions of the 1906 conclave are available at the Labadie Collection of the University of Michigan Library. They are also discussed in Paul F. Brissenden, *The I.W.W.: A History of American Syndicalism* (New York: 1919) and Philip S. Foner, *The I.W.W.: 1905–1917* (New York: 1965), pp. 74–79. Both accounts overemphasize ideology as the key to the struggle and play down the power-struggle aspect. An account which attempts to remedy this point of view is in Joseph R. Conlin, "The Wobblies: A Study of the Industrial Workers of the World Before World War I," unpublished Ph. D. dissertation, University of Wisconsin, 1966, pp. 110–26.

4. These meager assets were later disposed of by the Socialist Party when Sherman gave up hope of recapturing the IWW's membership; Max Hayes, "World of Labor," *Int. Soc. Rev.,* VII (February, 1907), 502.

5. Covington Hall, "Labor Struggles in the Deep South," typescript in Labor History Archives, Wayne State University, p. 230.

6. Conlin, "The Wobblies," pp. 126–39. Other accounts which again overemphasize ideological fine points can be found in Brissenden, *The I.W.W.* and Foner, *The I.W.W.*, pp. 103–13. The original preamble may be found in the *Proceedings* of the IWW's First Convention, or in virtually any other Wobbly publication before 1908. A more convenient source is Kornbluh, *Rebel Voices,* pp. 12–13.

7. "The Industrial Workers of the World," IWW pamphlet (1908?), IWW Collection, State Historical Society of Wisconsin.

8. Joseph R. Conlin, "Wobblies and Syndicalists," *Studies on the Left,* VI (March–April, 1966); overwhelmed at the 1908 convention, the DeLeonites bolted the IWW, maintaining weakly that they had "expelled the anarchists." On that premise they established their own IWW with headquarters in Detroit. The Detroit IWW (as opposed to St. John's "Chicago IWW") retained the original preamble, published a few newspapers, and organized several locals. For the most part, the union had no success. Much of its energy was expended in attacking the "Chicago Anarchists." By 1914, after DeLeon's death, the masquerade was obviously over; the Detroit group renamed itself the Workers International Industrial Union. The membership of the WIIU never exceeded 10,000 and, with no known mourners, gave up the ghost in 1925. See Walter Galenson, *Rival Unionism in the United States* (New York: 1940), p. 8; Leon Wolman, *Ebb and Flow in Trade Unionism* (New York: 1936), pp. 190–91.

9. *Bill Haywood's Book,* p. 222.

10. Andre Tridon, *The New Unionism* (New York: 1914), p. 188; Louis Adamic, *Dynamite: The Story of Class Violence in America* (New York: 1931), p. 160; Foner, *The I.W.W.*, p. 98.

11. *Bill Haywood's Book,* p. 225; in *The 42nd Parallel,* John Dos Passos is incorrect in considering Haywood as primarily a Wobbly at the time, although his error is shared by many historians.

12. *Bill Haywood's Book,* pp. 17–19.

13. *Ibid.*, pp. 241–42; Covington Hall, letter to Allen A. Holland, Jr., n.d., Labadie Collection; Hall, "Labor Struggles," 73.

14. Daniel DeLeon, August 3, 1907, letter to William D. Haywood, *Daniel DeLeon, The Man and His Work: A Symposium* (New York: 1920), p. 59.

15. *Bill Haywood's Book,* p. 222.

16. See Conlin, "The Wobblies," pp. 150–85 and Foner, The *I.W.W.*, pp. 172–213.

17. Carlton Parker, *The Casual Laborer and Other Essays* (New York: 1920), pp. 17, 78–80; Nels Anderson, *The Hobo: The Sociology of the Homeless Man* (Chicago: 1923, 1961), p. 234.

18. *Songs to Fan the Flames of Discontent* ("The Little Red Songbook"), (Chicago: 1964), p. 38; Elizabeth Gurley Flynn, "The Free Speech Fight at Spokane," *Int. Soc. Rev.*, X (December, 1909), 484.

19. See, for example, Barrie Stavis, "Joe Hill/Poet Organizer," *Folk Music* (June–August, 1964), 40; Fred Thompson, *The I.W.W.: Its First Fifty Years* (Chicago: 1955), p. 49.

20. Thompson, *The I.W.W.*, p. 49; Flynn, *I Speak My Own Piece*, pp. 94, 97; Fred D. Heslewood, "Barbarous Spokane," *Int. Soc. Rev.*, X (February, 1910), 712.

21. Heslewood, "Barbarous Spokane," 706; Ed Delaney and M. T. Rice, *The Bloodstained Trail: A History of Militant Labor in the United States* (Seattle: 1927), p. 54; *The Industrial Worker*, December 8, 1910; Kornbluh, *Rebel Voices*, p. 107; "News and Views," *Int. Soc. Rev.*, X (April, 1910), 948.

22. Flynn, "Free Speech Fight," 484; Thompson, *The I.W.W.*, p. 49.

23. Flynn, *I Speak My Own Piece*, p. 95; Delaney and Rice, *Bloodstained Trail*, p. 53.

24. Paul Kellog, "The McKee's Rocks Strike," *The Survey* (August 7, 1909), 656–65; Foner, *The I.W.W.*, pp. 282–95; Conlin, "The Wobblies," pp. 204–10.

25. *The Nation*, September 6, 1909.

26. United States Government, Thirteenth Census, 1910; G. D. H. Cole, *The World of Labour* (London: 1915), p. 145; *The Survey*, XXVII (February 17, 1912); 1772; Thompson, *The I.W.W.*, p. 55; Mary Heaton Vorse, "The Trouble At Lawrence," *Harper's Weekly* (March 16, 1912).

27. Justus Ebert, *Trial of a New Society* (Cleveland: 1913), pp. 12–13.

28. Fred Beal, *Proletarian Journey: New England, Gastonia, Moscow* (New York: 1937), pp. 55–56; *Report on the Strike of Textile Workers at Lawrence, Massachusetts* (62d Congress, 2nd Session, Senate Document 870), 1912, p. 72; *The Survey*, XXVII (February 3, 1912), 1695–96.

29. Vorse, "Lawrence," *Harper's; Report on the Strike of Textile Workers*, p. 158; Elizabeth Shapleigh, "Occupational Diseases in the Textile Industry," *New York Call*, December 29, 1912.

30. Beal, *Proletarian Journey*, p. 38.

31. *Report on the Strike of Textile Workers*, p. 40.

32. *Final Report and Testimony of the Commission on Industrial Relations* (Washington: 1916), III, 1550; John N. Beffel, "Biographical Sketch of Joseph J. Ettor," typescript dated February 25, 1948, Labor History Archives, Wayne State University: *Harper's Weekly*, March 16, 1912.

33. *Bill Haywood's Book*, p. 252; Beal, *Proletarian Journey*, p. 49.

34. See *Solidarity*, February 24, 1910.

35. *Philadelphia Women's Committee Report to the House Committee on Rules*, quoted in Ralph Chaplin, *Wobbly: The Rough and Tumble*

Story of an American Radical (Chicago: 1947), p. 136; *The Survey,* XXVII (March 2, 1912), 1822; Ebert, *Trial of a New Society,* p. 76.

36. Vermont State AFL, "Open Letter," September 4, 1912, in Steelinck Collection, Labor History Archives; Adamic, *Dynamite,* p. 171; Ebert, *Trial of a New Society,* p. 88; Confederazione Generale del Lavoro, *Consiglio Direttivo,* 16 ottobre 1912; *Comitato Esecutivo,* 16 diciembre 1912 in *La Confederazione Generale del Lavoro negli Atti, nei Congressi 1906–1926* (Milan: 1962), 162–63.

37. Ebert, *Trial of a New Society,* p. 30; Delaney and Rice, *Blood-stained Trail,* pp. 69–70; "Fear," IWW pamphlet (Chicago: n.d.), IWW Collection, State Historical Society of Wisconsin; Cole, *World of Labour,* p. 151.

38. "Report to the Industrial Relations Commission" (anonymous), typescript, Economic Division, National Archives, Washington.

39. *The Survey,* XXX (April 19, 1913), 81.

40. Mary Brown Sumner, "Broad Silk Weavers of Paterson," *The Survey,* XXVII (March 16, 1912), 1933; "Strike of Jersey Silk Workers," *The Survey,* XXX (April 19, 1913), 81.

41. Patrick Quinlan, "The Paterson Strike and After," *New Review,* II (January, 1914), 28; *Final Report of the Industrial Relations Commission,* III, 2457 (Testimony of Adolph Lessig).

42. John Fitch, "The I.W.W.: An Outlaw Organization," *The Survey,* XXX (June 7, 1913), 81.

43. *New York Times,* February 26, 1913.

44. Gregory Mason, "Industrial War in Paterson," *Outlook,* CIV (June 7, 1913), 297.

45. *Bill Haywood's Book,* pp. 262–63.

46. *Ibid.,* p. 263.

47. Quoted in *New York Times,* June 8, 1913.

48. Mabel Dodge Luhan, *Intimate Memories,* III (New York: 1936), 205.

49. Quoted in *The Survey,* XXX (June 28, 1913), 428; *New York Times,* June 8, 1913.

50. Elizabeth Gurley Flynn, "The Truth About Paterson," Speech delivered at the New York Civic Club Forum, January 31, 1914, typescript by Agnes Inglis, Labadie Collection; *Bill Haywood's Book,* p. 272.

51. Flynn, "The Truth About Paterson."

52. *New York Times,* July 21, 1913: Quinlan, "The Paterson Strike," 30–31.

53. Haywood, "Testimony Before the Industrial Relations Commission," IWW pamphlet (Chicago: 1913), pp. 50, 67–69.

54. *Bill Haywood's Book,* pp. 247–53.

55. *Ibid.,* p. 272.

56. *Ibid.,* pp. 256, 265, 267; Emma Goldman, *Living My Life,* II (New York: 1931), 524, 642, 902.

Chapter 6: Socialist

1. Ira Kipnis, *The American Socialist Movement* (New York: 1952), p. 192; William D. Haywood, *Bill Haywood's Book: The Autobiography of William D. Haywood* (New York: 1928) p. 202; *Social Democratic Herald,* August 11, 1906; Charles Sprague Smith, March 18, 1908, letter to Morris Hillquit, Hillquit Papers, State Historical Society of Wisconsin.

2. The standard works for the early history of the Socialist Party are Kipnis, *American Socialist Movement;* David A. Shannon, *The Socialist Party of America* (New York: 1955) ; and Ray Ginger, *The Bending Cross: A Biography of Eugene Victor Debs* (New Brunswick: 1949) ; Howard H. Quint, *The Forging of American Socialism: Origins of the Modern Movement* (Columbia, S.C.: 1953).

3. Philip S. Foner, *Jack London: American Rebel* (New York: 1947), p. 96.

4. William English Walling, "Industrial or Revolutionary Unionism," *New Review,* I (January 11, 1913), 49; "What is the Matter With the Socialist Party?" *International Socialist Review,* X (November, 1909), 451; Frank Bohn, "The Ballot," *Int. Soc. Rev.,* X (June, 1910), 1120.

5. Louis Duchez, "The Strikes in Pennsylvania," *Int. Soc. Rev.,* X (September, 1909), 203.

6. Bohn, "The Ballot," 1120; Haywood and Bohn, "Industrial Unionism," *Int. Soc. Rev.,* XII (December, 1911), 368; Walling, "Industrial or Revolutionary Unionism," 49.

7. *American Labor Union Journal,* December, 1904; Mary B. Sumner, *The Survey,* XXIX (February 1, 1913), 630.

8. Sumner, "Parting of the Ways," 630; Haywood, "Socialism the Hope of the Workers," *Int. Soc. Rev.,* XII (February, 1912), 462.

9. Haywood, "Letters to Members of the SPA On Accepting Post in the General Executive Committee," *Int. Soc. Rev.,* XII (December, 1911), 375; Sumner, "Parting of the Ways," 626; William E. Walling, *Socialism As It Is: A Survey of the Worldwide Revolutionary Movement* (New York: 1912), 372–73; *The Survey,* XXVII (March 16, 1912), 1944.

10. See, for example, *Solidarity,* June 8, 1912.

11. "Proceedings of the Socialist Convention," *Int. Soc. Rev.,* VIII (June, 1908), 727, 729.

12. "Brief Biographies of Socialists," typescript, Information Department File, SPA Collection, Duke University Library.

13. "The Mistake in Belgium," *Social Democratic Herald,* June 14, 1902; *Die Wahrheit,* March 18, 1905; "Who is Afraid of the Social Democratic Victory in Milwaukee?" *Social Democratic Herald,* March 24, 1906; *Milwaukee Journal,* February 17, 1906.

14. "The First Socialist Congressman," *New Review,* I (March 8, 1913), 290.

15. Haywood, "Socialism the Hope of the Workers," 462; M. B. Butler, letter to *Int. Soc. Rev.,* XI (November, 1910), 315; see also, Ralph Chaplin, *Wobbly: The Rough and Tumble Story of an American Radical* (Chicago: 1947), p. 83; Frank Bohn, "Is the IWW to Grow?" *Int. Soc. Rev.,* XII (July, 1911), 42–44; Leslie H. Marcy and Frederick Sumner Boyd, "One Big Union Wins," *Int. Soc. Rev.,* XII (April, 1912), 200–201; *Bill Haywood's Book,* pp. 249–50.

16. The first quoted statement was made at a lecture in Peoples House, Christiania, Norway. "Haywood in Europe," *Int. Soc. Rev.,* XI (November, 1910), 288; *Solidarity,* December 24, 1910; Elizabeth Gurley Flynn, *I Speak My Own Piece: The Autobiography of the Rebel Girl* (New York: 1955), p. 63.

17. *Socialist Party of America: Proceedings of the National Convention,* 1912, p. 100; *Bill Haywood's Book,* p. 246; Walling, *Socialism As It Is,* p. 373; Haywood, "Solidarity in Prison," *Int. Soc. Rev.,* X (June, 1910), 1065.

18. Victor Berger and E. H. Thomas, *The Voice and Pen of Victor Berger* (Milwaukee: n.d.), p. 699.

19. Algie M. Simons, "The Chicago Conference for Industrial Unions," *Int. Soc. Rev.,* V (February, 1905), 498–99.

20. Algie M. Simons, "Circular Letter," November 19, 1909. Either the original or an early copy of this letter, as well as various other items of correspondence on the subject, are in the SPA Collection, Duke University. In addition, the William English Walling Papers at the State Historical Society of Wisconsin contain considerable correspondence on the subject. See also, *Int. Soc. Rev.,* X (January, 1910), 595.

21. All references to Walling's "Circular Letter," dated November 26, 1909, are taken from a copy made by John Spargo for the National Executive Committee, SPA Collection.

22. Walling, letter to Fred Warren, February 26, 1910, Walling Papers.

23. Adolph Germer Papers, State Historical Society of Wisconsin; John Spargo, letter to Algie M. Simons, November 29, 1909, SPA Collection; Arthur Bullard, letter to Algie M. Simons, January 26, 1910, SPA Papers.

24. "Annual Report of the Secretary of the Socialist Party," January 1 to December 31, 1911, *Socialist Party Monthly Bulletin,* January, 1912; "National Office File," SPA Collection.

25. "National Office File," SPA Collection.

26. Charles Sprague Smith, letter to Morris Hillquit, May 18, 1908, Hillquit Papers, State Historical Society of Wisconsin; Walter Weyl, letter to Morris Hillquit, November 4, 1908, Hillquit Papers; Robert Hunter, "The Socialist Party and the Present Campaign," *American Review of Reviews,* XXXVIII (September, 1908), 297–98.

27. Elizabeth Gurley Flynn, "Sabotage," IWW pamphlet (Chicago: n.d.), p. 5.

28. Andre Tridon, *The New Unionism* (New York: 1912), pp. 43, 50.

29. John Spargo, *Syndicalism, Industrial Unionism, and Socialism* (New York: 1913), p. 42.

30. Tridon, *New Unionism,* pp. 49–50.

31. Elizabeth Gurley Flynn, "The Truth About Paterson," Speech Delivered at the New York Civic Club Forum, January 31, 1914, Typescript by Agnes Inglis, Labadie Collection, University of Michigan Library; Emile Pouget, *Sabotage* (Translated by Arturo Giovannitti) (Chicago: 1913; *Socialist Party of America: Proceedings of the National Convention, 1912,* p. 132.

32. *S.P.A., Proceedings, 1912,* p. 132; "Danger Ahead!" *New Review,* I (August, 1913), 675.

33. C. E. Reeves, letter to Carl D. Thompson, December 9, 1913, "National Office Collection," SPA Collection.

34. *Socialist Party Monthly Bulletin,* March–April, 1912; Kipnis, *American Socialist Movement,* pp. 389–90.

35. Sumner, "Parting of the Ways," 627; "Helen Keller Speaks to Her Comrades," Undated clippings from the *National Socialist,* SPA Collection. A conservative reply from Carl D. Thompson emphasized the significance of tactics, "the *way* we take" to Socialism, an essentially evasive answer in that Thompson believed public ownership of utilities to be socialism. "Controversies in the Socialist Party: An Open Letter to Helen Keller," February 22, 1913, typescript in SPA Collection.

36. Quoted in *The Agitator,* August 15, 1911; Frank Bohn, "The State of the Party," *Int. Soc. Rev.,* XIV (October, 1913), 240.

37. *Bill Haywood's Book,* p. 259.

38. Quoted in *The Survey,* XXIX (March 29, 1913), 909; Quoted in "Danger Ahead!" *New Review,* I (August, 1913), 676.

39. "National Office File," SPA Collection; *The Party Builder,* June 28, 1913.

40. See Shannon, *The Socialist Party of America;* Kipnis, *American Socialist Movement;* "Danger Ahead!" 674.

41. For a detailed discussion of this topic, see Joseph R. Conlin, "The IWW and the Socialist Party," *Science and Society,* XXXI (Winter, 1967), 22–36; Patrick Quinlan, "The Paterson Strike and After," *New Review,* II (January, 1914), 31–33; "Glorious Paterson," *Int. Soc. Rev.,* XIV (December, 1913), 355–57.

Chapter 7: Bête Noire

1. Carlton Parker, *The Casual Laborer* (New York: 1920); Nels Anderson, *The Hobo: The Sociology of the Homeless Man* (Chicago: 1923, 1961).

2. Ralph Chaplin, *Wobbly: The Rough and Tumble Story of an American Radical* (Chicago: 1947), p. 209.

3. *Industrial Workers of the World: Proceedings of the 1916 Convention,* pp. 106–107.

4. *I.W.W.: 1916 Proceedings,* "Report of the Secretary-Treasurer," pp. 5–11; Donald M. Barnes, "The Ideology of the Industrial Workers of the World, 1905–1921," unpublished Ph.D. dissertation, University of Washington, 1962, p. 41.

5. Patrick Renshaw, *The Wobblies: The Story of Syndicalism in America* (London: 1967), pp. 171–72, 179.

6. John Graham Brooks, *American Syndicalism: The I.W.W.* (New York: 1913), pp. 217–218.

7. *Los Angeles Examiner,* December 5, 1912; *Solidarity,* January 4, 1912.

8. John N. Beffel, "Four Radicals," *American Mercury,* XXV (April, 1932), 442.

9. Renshaw, *The Wobblies,* p. 206; William D. Haywood, *Bill Haywood's Book: The Autobiography of William D. Haywood* (New York: 1928), pp. 280–81.

10. Philip Taft, "The Federal Trials of the I.W.W.," *Labor History,* III (Winter, 1962), 61.

11. Frank Cobb, "The Press and Public Opinion," *New Republic,* XXI (December 31, 1919), 144.

12. Accounts of patriotic excesses can be found in virtually every history of the period.

13. *Bill Haywood's Book,* p. 300.

14. Robert K. Murray, *Red Scare: A Study in National Hysteria* (Minneapolis: 1955), p. 12; *Statutes at Large,* XL, 219; William Preston Jr., *Aliens and Dissenters* (Cambridge: 1963).

15. *Statutes at Large,* XL, 553.

16. *Ibid.,* XL, 1012; Murray, *Red Scare,* pp. 13–14.

17. Preston, *Aliens and Dissenters,* pp. 203, *passim.*

18. *United States* v. *William D. Haywood* et al., IV, 12, 611; Haywood, letter to Thomas Buckley, June 7, 1917; letter to Frank Little, May 6, 1917, quoted in Renshaw, *The Wobblies,* p. 227.

19. *Ibid.,* p. 228.

20. Haywood, letter to Frank Little, May 6, 1917; letter to James Rowan, April 5, 1917, quoted in Renshaw, *The Wobblies,* p. 226.

21. See, *ibid.,* p. 217.

22. Taft, "The Federal Trials of the I.W.W.," 59; Renshaw, *The Wobblies,* p. 220.

23. "Evidence and Cross-Examination of William D. Haywood," General Defense Committee pamphlet (Chicago: n.d.), p. 97; "Songs to Fan the Flames of Discontent," 31st Ed. (Chicago: 1964).

24. Vincent St. John, *The I.W.W.: Its History, Structure, and Methods* (New Castle, Pa., and Chicago: several editions), pp. 17–18. The idea of this comparison was conceived by Donald M. Barnes, "The Ideology of the I.W.W," 82.

25. *Chicago Daily News,* October 2, 1917; Chaplin, *Wobbly,* pp. 231, 237–38, 285; John Reed and Art Young, "The Social Revolution in Court," *Liberator,* I (September, 1918), 24.

26. A list of the IWW convicts appears in an appendix to *Bill Haywood's Book,* pp. 366–68.

27. Arturo Giovannitti, "Selecting a Perfect Jury," *Liberator,* I (July, 1918), 8.

28. *Bill Haywood's Book,* p. 304.

29. *Ibid.,* pp. 306–307.

30. The original copy of this number of "The Can-Opener" is in the Labadie Collection of the University of Michigan Library.

31. Richard Brazier, "The Mass I.W.W. Trial of 1918: A Retrospect," *Labor History,* VII (Spring, 1966), 192.

32. American Civil Liberties Union, "The Truth About the I.W.W." (New York: 1922), p. 34.

Chapter 8: Communist

1. Ralph Chaplin, *Wobbly: The Rough and Tumble Story of an American Radical* (Chicago: 1947), p. 235; William D. Haywood, *Bill Haywood's Book: The Autobiography of William D. Haywood* (New York: 1928) p. 308.

2. William English Walling Papers, State Historical Society of Wisconsin; James Weinstein, "Anti-War Sentiment and the Socialist Party, 1917–1918," *Political Science Quarterly,* LXXIV (June, 1959), 215–39; Weinstein expands on these ideas in *The Decline of Socialism in America* (New York: 1967).

3. David A. Shannon, *The American Socialist Party* (New York: 1955), p. 128.

4. Theodore Draper, *The Roots of American Communism* (New York: 1957); Shannon, *American Socialist Party,* pp. 126–49.

5. Robert Freidheim, *The Seattle General Strike* (Washington: 1964).

6. *One Big Union Monthly,* January, 1921, p. 51; Patrick Renshaw, *The Wobblies: The Story of Syndicalism in America* (London: 1967), pp. 246–49; *The First Congress of the Red Trade Union International at Moscow, 1921: A Report of the Proceedings by George Williams, Delegate from the I.W.W.* (Chicago: n.d.).

7. Harrison George, "The Can-Opener," *Liberator* (January, 1924), 16.

8. Chaplin, *Wobbly,* pp. 282, 298.

9. *Ibid.,* p. 302.

10. *Partiya o Kino* (Moscow: 1938); Julian Towser, *Political Power in the USSR 1917–1941* (Oxford, 1948), p. 396; Frederick C. Barghoorn, *Soviet Image of the United States* (New York: 1950), pp. 28–29, 34; Andrew J. Steiger, *American Engineers in the Soviet Union* (New York: 1944), p. 4.

11. Chaplin, *Wobbly,* p. 302; John N. Beffel, "Four Radicals," *American Mercury,* XXV (April, 1932), 444.

12. *Defense News Bulletin,* December 1, 1917; *Bill Haywood's Book,* p. 359; Elizabeth Gurley Flynn, *Debs, Haywood, Ruthenberg* (New York: 1939), p. 28.

13. Beffel, "Four Radicals," 444; Richard Brazier, "The Mass I.W.W. Trial of 1918: A Retrospect," *Labor History,* VII (Spring, 1966), 188.

14. *Bill Haywood's Book,* p. 361.

15. Patrick Renshaw, *The Wobblies: The Story of Syndicalism in America* (London: 1967), p. 241; Fanny Bixby Spencer, letter to Nicolaas Steelinck, November 11, 1921, Steelinck Collection, Wayne State University.

16. *Bill Haywood's Book,* p. 362; *New York Times,* April 30, 1921; *First Congress of the R.T.U.I." A Report by George Williams.*

17. Brazier, "The Mass I.W.W. Trial," 189.

18. Emma Goldman, *Living My Life,* II (New York: 1931), 902–903; *Bill Haywood's Book,* p. 362.

19. *New York Herald Tribune,* May 19, 1928; *New York Times,* May 20, 27, 1928. Also see Raymond H. Anderson, "Americans Played Role in Early Economic Development of the Soviet Union," *New York Times,* November 1, 1967.

20. Beffel, "Four Radicals," 444; Flynn, *Debs, Haywood, Ruthenberg,* p. 28.

21. James Cannon, letter to Theodore Draper, February 10, 1959, quoted in Cannon, *The First Ten Years of American Communism: Report of a Participant* (New York: 1962), pp. 162–63.

22. Beffel, "Four Radicals," 444; Max Eastman, "Bill Haywood, Communist: An Interview," *Liberator,* IV (April, 1921), 13; *Theses and Resolutions Adopted at the Third World Congress of the Communist International, June 22–July 12, 1921* (New York: n.d.), p. 139; *Third Congress of the Communist International: Report of Meetings Held at Moscow, June 22nd–July 12th, 1921* (London: n.d.), pp. 141–48.

23. Walter Duranty, *I Write As I Please* (New York: 1935), pp. 167–68; Charles Ashleigh, letter to Ralph Chaplin, January 22, 1924, Chaplin Collection, Washington State Historical Society; Duranty, *I Write As I Please,* pp. 167–68, 170.

24. Y. Vilenkyin, "Vilyam Kheyvud," *Krasnyi Internatsional Profoyuzov* (Moscow: 1928) p. 629.

25. Chaplin, *Wobbly,* p. 234.

26. Benjamin Gitlow, *The Whole of Their Lives* (New York: 1948), p. 50.

27. *Ibid.,* p. 51.

28. Goldman, *Living My Life,* II, 489–90, 904, 909, 915.

29. Richard Brazier, "The Great I.W.W. Trial of 1918 in Retrospect," typescript in Labor History Archives, Wayne State University, pp. 15–16; Brazier, letter to Joseph R. Conlin, May 18, 1966, in the author's possession.

30. Duranty, *I Write As I Please,* pp. 169–70; *New York Times,* May 20, 1928.

31. Eastman, "Bill Haywood, Communist," 13–14.

32. *Outlook* (May 30, 1928), 121; Flynn, *Debs, Haywood, Ruthenberg,* p. 28.

33. *New York Times,* May 19, 20, 1928; *New York Herald Tribune,* May 19, 1928; W. J. Ghent, "William D. Haywood," *Dictionary of American Biography,* VIII, 468.

34. *New York Times,* May 19, 1928.

Index